"Stashower weaves fact with such related story lines as the lurid newspaper coverage, inept police work and, most provocatively, Edgar Allan Poe's fictionalized 'Marie Rogêt' exposé of the case. . . . Intrigue is revived with each new break in the case."
—*USA Today*

"Stashower's book conjures a writer in search of inspiration and a girl whose beauty and gruesome death would be immortalized in Poe's 'The Mystery of Marie Rogêt.'" —*New York Daily News*

"Daniel Stashower's *The Beautiful Cigar Girl* not only establishes itself as the book on the Mary Rogers case, but offers an enormously important look into how Americans think about murder, as well as a unique portrait of our most undervalued literary genius, Edgar Allan Poe. Books like this are an increasing rarity, and should be snapped up by all audiences."
—Caleb Carr, author of *The Alienist*

"Writing simultaneously as a novelist, biographer, historian, and sleuth, Daniel Stashower unfolds a suspenseful detective story inside a detective story inside a detective story."
—Kenneth Silverman, author of
Edgar A. Poe: Mournful and Never-Ending Remembrance

"Daniel Stashower masterfully re-creates 1840s New York and the murder that captivated the city. If you loved *The Devil in the White City*, you'll love *The Beautiful Cigar Girl*. It's an impressive work of history with all the drive and passion of a finely tuned novel."
—Harlan Coben, author of *Promise Me*

"*The Beautiful Cigar Girl* is a beautiful melding of literary research, biography, and creativity. Seldom has Poe himself emerged so sympathetically as the tortured, alcoholic, brilliant, and enigmatic man he was. After reading this fascinating book, no one will be able to read 'The Mystery of Marie Rogêt' again without acknowledging the haunting ghosts brought forth by Stashower."
—Stuart M. Kaminsky, Mystery Writers of America
Grand Master and author of *Always Say Goodbye*

"Stashower makes the past so vivid you feel as if you must have been there and walked these streets yourself."
—Anne Perry, author of *We Shall Not Sleep*

"An informative, swift-moving account . . . Stashower knows murder, and he knows the craft of biography. . . . [He] brings to this current, complex task both considerable intelligence and wide-ranging research." —*Kirkus Reviews* (starred review)

"Readers who enjoyed Erik Larson's *The Devil in the White City* will like mystery novelist and biographer Stashower's work here. . . . Well researched and accessible, here is a gripping story that is hard to put down; literary buffs in particular will enjoy this wonderful back story to the creation of Poe's sequel to 'The Murders in the Rue Morgue.' " —*Library Journal*

"Absorbing . . . Poe's genius and literary legacy are hauntingly drawn." —*Publishers Weekly*

"Stashower's well-paced, thoroughly researched blend of historical narrative and detective novel is imaginative and ably captures the boisterous sprawl of nineteenth-century New York, the activities of its numerous cutthroat newssheets and the sad lives of both Rogers and Poe." —*BookPage*

"[An] intriguing story, one that sheds considerable light on the snares of a big city for a young woman." —*Booklist*

Praise for
Teller of Tales: The Life of Arthur Conan Doyle

"Mystery writer Stashower pieces together clues from his subject's iconoclastic life to create a gripping, sympathetic bio that proves that Doyle was anything but elementary." —*Entertainment Weekly*

"Marked with a nice mixture of affection . . . and the detachment to be expected from the winner of the Raymond Chandler Fulbright Fellowship in Detective and Crime Fiction Writing." —*The Washington Post Book World*

continued . . .

THE BEAUTIFUL CIGAR GIRL

MARY ROGERS, EDGAR ALLAN POE,

AND

THE INVENTION OF MURDER

DANIEL STASHOWER

BERKLEY BOOKS, NEW YORK

THE BERKLEY PUBLISHING GROUP
Published by the Penguin Group
Penguin Group (USA) Inc.
375 Hudson Street, New York, New York 10014, USA
Penguin Group (Canada), 90 Eglinton Avenue East, Suite 700, Toronto, Ontario M4P 2Y3, Canada
(a division of Pearson Penguin Canada Inc.)
Penguin Books Ltd., 80 Strand, London WC2R 0RL, England
Penguin Group Ireland, 25 St. Stephen's Green, Dublin 2, Ireland (a division of Penguin Books Ltd.)
Penguin Group (Australia), 250 Camberwell Road, Camberwell, Victoria 3124, Australia
(a division of Pearson Australia Group Pty. Ltd.)
Penguin Books India Pvt. Ltd., 11 Community Centre, Panchsheel Park, New Dehli—110 017, India
Penguin Group (NZ), 67 Apollo Drive, Rosedale, North Shore 0632, New Zealand
(a division of Pearson New Zealand Ltd.)
Penguin Books (South Africa) (Pty.) Ltd., 24 Sturdee Avenue, Rosebank, Johannesburg 2196,
South Africa

Penguin Books Ltd., Registered Offices: 80 Strand, London WC2R 0RL, England

PRINTING HISTORY
Dutton hardcover edition / October 2006
Berkley trade paperback edition / December 2007

Berkley trade paperback ISBN: 978-0-425-21782-5

The Library of Congress has cataloged the Dutton hardcover edition as follows:

Stashower, Daniel.
The beautiful cigar girl : Edgar Allan Poe, Mary Rogers, and the invention of murder /
by Daniel Stashower.
p.   cm.
ISBN 0-525-94981-X

1. Poe, Edgar Allan, 1809–1849. Mystery of Marie Roget—Sources.   2. Detective and
mystery stories, American—History and criticism.   3. Rogers, Mary, 1820–1841.
4. Murder—New York (State)—New York—History—19th century.   I. Title.
PS2618.M83S73   2006
823'.3—dc22   2006019335

PRINTED IN THE UNITED STATES OF AMERICA

10   9   8   7   6   5   4   3   2   1

The publisher does not have any control over and does not assume any responsibility for author or third-
party websites or their content.

Most Berkley Books are available at special quantity discounts for bulk purchases for sales promotions,
premiums, fund-raising, or educational use. Special books, or book excerpts, can also be created to fit
specific needs.

For details, write: Special Markets, The Berkley Publishing Group, 375 Hudson Street, New York,
New York 10014.

For Miss Corbett.
We'll always have Breezewood.

CONTENTS

Descent into the Maelstrom

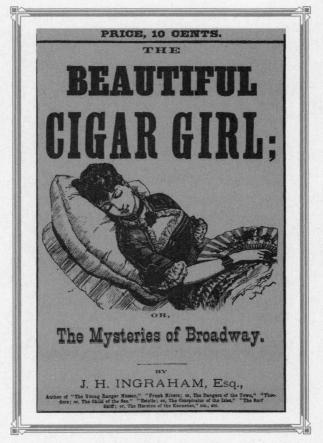

"Oh, Maria! Would to God you had reflected ere you had taken this step!" The cover of a novel published in 1844, based on the Mary Rogers case.

Courtesy of the author

IN JUNE OF 1842, Edgar Allan Poe took up his pen to broach a delicate subject with an old friend. "Have I offended you by any of my evil deeds?" he asked. "If so, how? Time was when you could spare a few minutes occasionally for communion with a friend."

Poe's correspondent, a magazine editor by the name of Joseph Evans Snodgrass, would have known only too well what was coming next. Once again, Poe would launch a tirade against the latest publisher or literary rival to have wronged him. This done, Poe would admit to finding himself in a state of "pecuniary embarrassment," with no work and few prospects, and would ask his old friend to offer some "very trifling aid" in the form of a loan.

Poe's latest letter, Snodgrass noted with relief, marked a departure from the usual pattern. "I have a proposition to make," he wrote. "You may remember a tale of mine published about a year ago . . . entitled the 'Murders in the Rue Morgue.' Its *theme* was the exercise of ingenuity in detecting a murderer. I am just now putting the concluding touch to a similar article, which I shall entitle 'The Mystery of Marie Rogêt—a Sequel to "The Murders in the Rue Morgue."' The story is based upon that of the real murder of Mary Cecilia Rogers, which created so vast an excitement, some months ago, in New-York."

Snodgrass needed no reminders of that vast excitement. Mary Rogers, who was widely known as "the beautiful cigar girl," had been a figure of note on the streets of New York City. From her post behind the cigar counter of John Anderson's Tobacco Emporium on lower Broadway, Mary Rogers had cast her spell over half the men in the city. Her famous "dark smile" was said to be as potent as cupid's arrow. Admirers from all walks of life, from the Bowery to City Hall, came to bask in her presence. Some offered up poems to her beauty. Others spoke in carrying voices of their business triumphs, sometimes patting their wallets and casting sidelong glances in her direction. All the while the cigar girl stood prettily behind the counter, eyes cast downward, pretending not to hear. Sometimes she would flutter her fingers to her mouth, as if shocked by a coarse phrase, but the eyes were cool and knowing.

It was feared by some that Anderson's impressionable young employee would come to grief in such rough company. The New York *Morning Herald* expressed an earnest desire that "something should be done instantly to remedy the great evil consequent upon very beautiful girls being placed in cigar and confectionery stores. Designing rich rascals drop into these places, buy cigars and sugar plums, gossip with the girl and ultimately affect her ruin."

These fears proved tragically prophetic. In July of 1841 Mary Rogers was found brutally murdered, sparking a massive public outcry and setting the stage for one of the most harrowing public dramas of the nineteenth century, driving one man to suicide, another to madness, and a third to public disgrace and humiliation. The death of the cigar girl, wrote one New Yorker, marked the "terrible moment when the city lost its innocence."

For good or ill, the crime also became a catalyst for sweeping change. The city's unregulated and disjointed police force proved unable to mount an effective investigation, prompting an ambitious slate of social and political reforms, even as the prurient details of the murder gave fuel to a furious newspaper circulation war, pushing American journalism into previously unimagined realms of sensationalism. The wily James Gordon Bennett of the New York *Herald* seized on the case as a "grim cautionary tale," giving himself a pretext to linger over the more lurid aspects of the case, and sparking a ferocious debate over the limits of journalistic propriety. "We cannot have the blood of murdered innocents served up to us at breakfast," declared one outraged reader. "Have the gentlemen of the press no shame?" The plea for restraint went unheard; the drama of Mary Rogers would be one of the earliest and most significant murder cases to play out in the pages of the American press, laying the groundwork for every "crime of the century" to follow, from Lizzie Borden's murders in 1892 to the murder of Stanford White in 1906, through the present day.

From the first, however, false leads and misconceptions dogged the case. In the days following the discovery of the body, it was widely assumed that Mary Rogers had fallen prey to one of the notorious "gangs of New York," such as the Plug-Uglies or the Hudson Dusters, who ran riot through the streets, apparently reveling in the complete absence of any effective police authority. "Must we yield our streets to these villains?" railed the New York *Tribune*. "Can we not call upon our elected officials to bring law upon the lawless?" The newspapers were eager to create a martyr. "In one emphatic word," declared the *Herald*, "New York is disgraced and dishonored in the eyes of the civilized world, unless one great, one big, one strong moral movement be made to reform and reinvigorate the administration of criminal justice, and to protect the lives and property of its inhabitants from public violence and public robbery. Who will make the first move in this truly great moral reform?"

As the public's indignation grew, Mary Rogers achieved the dubious distinction of becoming a bankable commodity. Within two weeks of the murder, a daguerreotypist had procured an engraving and struck a huge number of copies, said to be a "correct likeness" of the dead woman. "A peddler might sell a great number by taking them to Hoboken," he declared in an advertisement for his wares, "where so many people are visiting the spot daily." Pamphleteers also got into the act; a lurid account entitled *The Dark Deed* sold for six cents and recounted "several attempts of courtship and seduction brought about by her manifold charms." A potboiler novel called *The Beautiful Cigar Girl* would soon follow.

One year later, however, the crime remained unsolved, leaving lives ruined and reputations shattered. As public interest began to wane, Edgar Allan Poe saw a unique opportunity. His plan, as he told his friend Snodgrass, was to take up the case in a manner that had never been attempted, or even imagined. Through the lens of fiction, he would study the facts of the case, expose the weaknesses and false assumptions of the official inquiry, and offer his own conclusions as to what had occurred—even pointing a finger at the likely villain. In short, Poe suggested, he would lay out a solution that could well force the New York police to reopen their investigation.

It was an astonishing gambit. At the time of the murder, Poe had been enjoying a rare interlude of prosperity as an editor of *Graham's Lady's and Gentleman's Magazine*, an illustrated monthly journal. He had followed the details of the Mary Rogers case with great care, and is even said to have been a patron of Anderson's Tobacco Emporium, where the cigar girl had worked. Poe's tenure at *Graham's* marked a brief period of calm in an otherwise turbulent career. In spite of his obvious gifts as a poet and short story writer, Poe had a constant struggle to cobble together a living and was often reduced to begging for loans from sympathetic friends such as

Snodgrass. Whatever small reputation he enjoyed rested chiefly on his work as a literary critic, a field in which he displayed great sensitivity and insight, but also a ruthlessness that earned him many enemies. Much of Poe's greatest work had already been written at the time of the cigar girl's death, but fame and creative freedom continued to elude him. "I have not only labored solely for the benefit of others (receiving for myself a miserable pittance)," he wrote, "but have been forced to model my thoughts at the will of men whose imbecility was evident to all but themselves."

"The Mystery of Marie Rogêt," he hoped, would change all that. Poe's groundbreaking story "The Murders in the Rue Morgue," which introduced the amateur detective C. Auguste Dupin, had appeared in *Graham's* in April 1841, about two months before the Mary Rogers murder. Poe presented Dupin as a reclusive, brilliant figure, shuttered away in his dimly lit chamber, venturing out only at night to prowl the streets of Paris and enjoy the "infinity of mental excitement" afforded by his powers of observation. The story anticipated virtually every convention of what would become the modern mystery story—the brooding, eccentric sleuth; the comparatively dense sidekick; the wrongfully accused suspect; the unlikely villain; the false clue; and—perhaps above all—the impossible, locked-room crime. Today the story stands as a literary milestone—the genesis of the entire crime fiction genre—but its original publication drew only scant notice. By the following year Poe had left *Graham's* and his fortunes had taken a precipitous downward turn. Casting about for an idea he could sell, Poe decided to apply Dupin's powers of "ratiocination," or deductive reasoning, to a real-life puzzle, transforming the murder of Mary Rogers into "The Mystery of Marie Rogêt."

Seldom have a writer and his subject been better suited to one another. Poe's entire life had been shadowed by the deaths of the women who were closest to him, beginning with his own mother, who died of tuberculosis when her son was not yet three years old. As Poe sat down to write "The Mystery of Marie Rogêt," his own wife, Virginia, had entered the early stages of the same disease, beginning a long and agonizing decline. For Poe, these losses were not only the tragedy of his life but also the wellspring of his art, unleashing the seemingly limitless tide of melancholy from which he brought forth his most memorable heroines—Helen, Lenore, Madeline Usher, Annabel Lee, and countless others.

"The death . . . of a beautiful woman," Poe once wrote, "is, unquestionably, the most poetical topic in the world." In the saga of Mary Rogers, Poe appeared to have found a young woman culled from one of his own works. The victim was not only young and beautiful, but an aura of melancholy and injustice hung over the crime. Poe's ambitions for the story were enormous: "I have handled my design in a manner altogether novel in literature," he told Joseph Snodgrass. "I have imagined a series of nearly exact *coincidences* occurring in Paris. A young *grisette* [working-class girl], one Marie Rogêt, has been murdered under precisely similar circumstances with Mary Rogers. Thus, under pretence of showing how Dupin unravelled the mystery of Marie's assassination, I, in reality, enter into a very long and rigorous analysis of the New York tragedy. No point is omitted. I examine, each by each, the opinions and arguments of the press upon the subject, and show that this subject has been, hitherto, *unapproached*. In fact, I believe not only that I have demonstrated the fallacy of the general idea—that the girl was the victim of a gang of ruffians—but have *indicated the assassin* in a manner that will give renewed impetus to investigation."

Poe's confident tone could not conceal the desperation of his circumstances. Having set a price of forty dollars for his story, he ended his letter on a plaintive note: "Will you write me upon this point?—by return mail, if possible." As it happened, Snodgrass showed no interest in "Marie Rogêt," and the story went instead to a magazine called the *Ladies' Companion*, a publication Poe had previously derided for its "ill-taste and humbuggery." Even so, Poe had reason to feel hopeful about the prospects for "Marie Rogêt." He had given close scrutiny to the many twists and turns of the Mary Rogers saga, and constructed a solution that seemed both gripping and plausible. Even more intriguing was the manner in which Dupin, Poe's fictional detective, had reached his conclusions—"sitting steadily in his accustomed armchair," trusting solely to the power of ratiocination. "I feel convinced," Poe said, "that the article will excite attention."

Due to the unusual length of "Marie Rogêt," the editor of the *Ladies' Companion* chose to publish the story in three sections over the course of three monthly issues. Poe may have hoped that spacing the installments out in this manner would help to heighten the suspense, and spark the public's interest in Dupin's unraveling of the case in the final pages. But the first two installments of "Marie Rogêt" had already appeared when new and disturbing evidence surfaced in the case of Mary Rogers's murder, and the investigation that had been dormant for several months broke open once again.

The third and final installment of "Marie Rogêt," containing Poe's carefully reasoned elucidation of the case, was only days away from publication. With a solution to the real-life mystery now appearing close at hand, and with his deadline looming, Poe took a desperate gamble. His efforts to save his story and his reputation were both brilliant and wildly audacious, and form an emblematic chapter of his life. By the time he finished he had not only recaptured the story but bent it to his will.

Henry James once offered a blunt and telling remark when comparing Poe to the French poet Charles Baudelaire: "Poe was much the greater charlatan of the two," James observed, "as well as the greater genius." Both aspects of Poe's character, the genius and the charlatan, came into play as he grappled with "Marie Rogêt." At times, Poe veered from one to the other within the space of a single sentence, with extraordinary flashes of inspiration set off by an equal measure of guile. The result was a unique form of alchemy, transforming fact into fiction and back again. For Poe, Mary Rogers marked the point at which life and art converged. At a time when his own life was collapsing, her story offered a form of solace, a chance to emulate his famous detective and find order in chaos. In the process, he rewrote history—his own as well as that of the cigar girl—and found poetry in the heart of a murder.

PART ONE

Her Dark Smile

THE CIGAR GIRL.

"You would be exposed to the gaze of every creature . . ."
—*Sunday Morning Atlas* (New York)
September 13, 1840
Courtesy of American Antiquarian Society

The annals of crime are gorged with mysteries. The red band of murder has set its mark on many of its pages, but left no other sign of its identity. Of all the episodes enshrouded in this somber incompleteness, there is none more tantalizing than the case of Mary Cecilia Rogers.

—The New York *Police Gazette*, 1881

The true genius shudders at incompleteness—and usually prefers silence to saying something which is not everything it should be.

—Edgar Allan Poe

I

A Gallant Gay Lothario

FROM THE FRONT STOOP of the Rogers boardinghouse at 126 Nassau Street, one could see a great deal of New York City. At the time Nassau Street had been dubbed "the city's brain" for its many newspaper and publishing offices, "pulsating ever with the beating of a printing engine," though there were still some in the neighborhood who recalled a quieter era when the cobblestone street was known simply as "the road that runs by the pie-woman's."

To the north, only a few hundred yards away, stood the imposing bulk of City Hall, faced in Massachusetts marble and topped with an ornate dome that later proved to be highly flammable. At the rear of the building, the gleaming marble gave way to Newark brownstone, reflecting a shortage of funds during construction, and a belief, at the time of its completion in 1812, that the city was unlikely to grow much beyond Chambers Street.

Across the southern tip of City Hall Park stood the Astor House Hotel, a Greek Revival structure said to be the "grandest mass" in town. When the hotel opened in 1836, entrepreneur John Jacob Astor had been roundly criticized for putting his hotel in such a remote location. Astor's pioneering spirit soon paid off as the neighborhood flourished, and the hotel rapidly became the most fashionable address in the nation. Chief among its luxuries was running water, pumped by steam and available to each of its 309 rooms, even those on the fifth floor. At the palatial restaurant on the ground level, hotel guests and local businessmen could choose from some thirty menu selections each day, ranging from oyster pie and honeyed gammon to roast wild duck and game pudding.

A few blocks north, on land that had once been a freshwater pond, stretched the warren of narrow, muddy streets known as Five Points, notorious as the world's worst slum. At its heart, amid a scattering of slaughterhouses, glue factories, and turpentine distilleries, stood a dilapidated tenement called the Old Brewery, the most densely occupied building in the city, where hundreds of immigrants and wage laborers lived in conditions of unrelieved squalor. Five stories tall, the brewery also featured a "Murderer's Alley," where the city's "blackest hearts" were known to gather. "It is a region of wickedness, filth and woe," wrote the Reverend Matthew Hale Smith. "Lodging-houses are under ground, foul and slimy, without ventilation, and often without windows, and overrun with rats and every species of vermin. Bunks filled with decayed rags make the beds. . . . Rooms are rented from two to ten dollars a month, into which no human being would put a dog. Children are born in sorrow, and raised in reeking vice and bestiality, that no heathen degradation can exceed. The degraded women who tramp the streets in the viler parts of the city, who fill the low dance houses and drinking-saloons, graduate in this vile locality."

For those who preferred more wholesome entertainments, P. T. Barnum's American Museum—around the corner from the Rogers boardinghouse—formed the center of a growing entertainment district. Visitors thrilled to such star attractions as the "Swedish Nightingale" Jenny Lind, the "tiny and terrific" General Tom Thumb, and the exotic "Wondrous Mermaid from Feejee." For the admission price of twenty-five cents, visitors could also see jugglers and ventriloquists, bearded ladies and rubber men, fire-walkers, sword-swallowers, and dozens of other "varied entertainments of the most dazzling sort." Barnum had seized on a location on Broadway at Ann Street—convenient to both good and bad neighborhoods—in the hope that "high and low alike" would pass beneath his brightly striped awnings. "Mr. Barnum's rule has been to give all who patronize him the worth of their money," declared the New York *Sun*, "without being particular as to the means by which he attracts the crowd to his exhibitions. While these special features may not be all that the public expect, every visitor gets the worth of his money ten times in the immense amount of amusement that cannot be secured anywhere else."

John Anderson's cigar store at 319 Broadway also benefited from canny promotion and a prime location, north of City Hall at Pearl Street. A statue of Sir Walter Raleigh beckoned to passersby, while gold lettering above the door listed the various items on offer, including "seegars, fine cut & confections." Anderson made a particular specialty of fine cut, or chewing tobacco, in the days when using a cuspidor, rather than the floor, was considered a mark of breeding. When General Winfield Scott visited the store and praised Anderson's tobacco as a "great solace" to the fighting man, Anderson hit on the idea of packaging individual chaws in bright foil wrappers. "Anderson's Solace Tobacco" stayed fresh and slipped easily into the pocket, making it ideal for use by soldiers in the Mexican-American War or by gold miners in California. The inspiration would bring Anderson a fortune.

A man of tremendous energy and ambition, Anderson saw the tobacco business as a path to better things, possibly even a career in politics. Born in 1812, Anderson began his working life as a laborer in a wool-pulling plant, and later apprenticed as a bricklayer to a master mason who noted the young man's promise and helped secure his start in the cigar business. Within a few months Anderson was becoming one of the city's leading merchants, and even his competitors marked him as a man of promise.

Thanks to its convenient location, Anderson's emporium soon came to serve an informal "back parlor" function, where patrons from the nearby newspaper and government offices mingled on a footing that could be either social or professional, as the occasion required. Powerful newspaper editors such as Horace Greeley and William Cullen Bryant were regular customers, along with the great jurist and judge James Kent and James K. Paulding, the secretary of the navy. New York's literati also brought their custom to Anderson's, many of them drifting over from the nearby Shakespeare Tavern, at the corner of Nassau and Fulton, which had long been a second home to the city's poets and writers. Both Washington Irving and James Fenimore Cooper were frequent customers, and it is often said that the twenty-eight-year-old Edgar Allan Poe, who came to New York from Richmond in 1837, occasionally dropped in to rub elbows with the luminaries.

To Anderson's chagrin the store also proved popular with less desirable elements, notably the rough "young sports" who pursued women and games of chance with equal vigor. Anderson worried that lower-class patrons would muddy his political chances. Occasionally he could be heard making disparaging remarks about the "soaplocks and rowdies" cluttering up his shop. This drew a sharp rebuke from a newspaper called the *Whip*, whose editor wondered if "a certain biped of segar notoriety had not better be a little careful how he utters his imprecations against consumers of that commodity, lest he feel the force of the Whip."

In his early days as a tobacconist, Anderson could ill afford to give offense. Facing stiff competition from longer-established shopkeepers, the young entrepreneur struggled to gain his footing, and cast about for a means of setting Anderson's Tobacco Emporium apart from its rivals. The solution arrived in the form of an "ethereal and hypnotically pleasing" young woman named Mary Cecilia Rogers, who would soon be famous throughout the city as "the Beautiful Seegar Girl."

Born in 1820, Mary Rogers came to New York from Connecticut as a teenager, following her father's death in a steamship explosion. With money provided by an older brother, Mary and her mother would eventually open a boardinghouse off lower Broadway at 126 Nassau Street, within walking distance of the tobacco emporium.

By her sixteenth birthday, Mary was widely judged to be a great beauty, with one admirer offering a poem to her womanly figure, raven tresses, and "dark smile." One suitor, who lived for a time at the Rogers boardinghouse, described her as "amiable and pleasing, and rather fascinating in her manners."

Mary's attractions were such that in 1838 she came to the attention of John Anderson. Enthralled, he hired her at a generous wage to work behind his cigar counter, where it was thought that her raven tresses and fascinating manners would encourage the male patrons to linger. The hiring of attractive shopgirls, though very much the custom in Europe at the time, was still judged to be somewhat unseemly in America. It was feared that the rough manners of some of the patrons might have a "coarsening" effect on an impressionable young woman. Mary was permitted by her mother, Phoebe Rogers, to accept the position only after securing a promise from Anderson that Mary would never be left alone in the shop, and that she would be escorted home each evening.

Anderson's interest could not have been entirely altruistic. From the moment Mary took up her post at the cigar counter, her presence drew throngs of admirers and helped to insure the success of the fledgling business. "At least some of those who frequent Mr. Anderson's shop," noted one customer, "have no other object in mind than to preen and squawk before the young lady." One newspaper likened the effect to that of "a brilliant luminary, to catch the butterflies that love to flutter around so attractive a center." Anderson's emporium, which had been in business less than two years, now outpaced its competitors and established its enviable reputation as a literary salon. Along with Washington Irving and James Fenimore Cooper, the shop also drew a number of aspiring poets, at least one of whom was inspired to celebrate the beautiful cigar girl in verse:

> She's picked for her beauty from many a belle,
> And placed near the window, Havanas to sell
> For well her employer's aware that her face is
> An advertisement certain to empty his cases.

> Alas! That necessity ever should force
> A female to such an unwomanly course;
> To make her a magnet to draw in the spooney
> The coxcomb and puppy, for sake of their money.

> But still, 'tis our duty in every sphere
> That Providence places us, meekly to bear;
> And in none upon earth can our honor be stained
> If our own self-respect is with firmness maintained.

> List not to the flatterer's vows!—they're a joke!
> Like the weed he is smoking, they'll all end in smoke;
> Reflect on the danger that hems in thy station,
> And come out unsullied, exposed to temptation.

Newspapermen, too, proved remarkably susceptible to Mary's fascinations. As word of "the comely seegar vendor" began to appear in the social notes of various publications, Mary achieved a curious form of celebrity, becoming perhaps the first woman in New York to be famous for being talked about. "It is a most curious thing," one newsman noted drily. "Her notoriety is unencumbered by position or achievement."

It is not clear how John Anderson came to meet his celebrated employee, but his interest in her welfare clearly extended beyond the workplace. According to city records, Mary and her mother, Phoebe, settled themselves in Anderson's house on Duane Street when they arrived in New York in 1837, though this arrangement lasted only a few months. The following year, when Anderson bought a new house on White Street, Mary and her mother removed themselves to the home of Mrs. Hayes, one of Phoebe Rogers's sisters, on Pitt Street. Even so, the fact that the two women initially chose Anderson's household over that of a blood relation would seem to indicate something more than a chance circumstance. It has been suggested that Mary and her mother earned their keep by performing domestic duties for the young bachelor, and that perhaps Anderson developed romantic feelings for the beautiful young girl under his protection. Whatever the case, by the time they departed from Anderson's house Mary had begun working behind the counter of the cigar store, and the tobacco merchant would continue to serve as a friend and protector long afterward.

Many of the young men who vied for Mary's attentions would describe her as carrying herself in a manner that was pleasant but somewhat aloof. At times, recalled one admirer, a shadow would pass across her "beauteous features," as if she were "troubled by a great secret." Though such recollections are likely fanciful, and colored by the knowledge of what became of her, Mary would have had good cause for occasional flashes of melancholy. Though not yet out of her teens, her life to that point had been fraught with upheavals and tragedy.

Mary and her mother came to New York from Connecticut during the banking panic of 1837, a period in which many along the eastern seaboard had fallen on hard times as a result of crop failures and collapsing markets, forcing a mass exodus from the region. By May of that year the crisis had hit New York, touching off a disastrous run on the city's banks. "The volcano has burst and overwhelmed New York," wrote Philip Hone, a former mayor of New York best remembered as a diarist. "I was there . . . and witnessed the madness of the people. Women were nearly pressed to death, and the stoutest men could scarcely sustain themselves, but they held on, as with a death's grip, upon the evidences of their claims, and exhausted as they were with the pressure, they had strength to cry 'Pay! Pay!'" As the crisis deepened, New York, along with much of the rest of the country, faced an economic downturn that would last six years, leaving few prospects for the city's growing tide of new arrivals.

In spite of the hardships, Hone remarked, "honest, manful laborers who are not afraid of toil will have cause to rejoice." The outlook was not as bright for honest women, for whom manful labor was not an option. In Connecticut, Phoebe Rogers and her young daughter had been secure and socially prominent, the descendants of several important New England families—including the Mather and Rogers clans, who were among the first settlers of New London County. In New York, by contrast, the two of them were alone and nearly friendless, facing an uncertain future with very few prospects.

It cannot have been how Phoebe Rogers imagined her declining years. Born in 1778, she was not quite eighteen when she married

Ezra Mather, a descendant of Increase Mather, the legendary Puritan leader, and his son Cotton Mather, who had played a significant role in the Salem witch trials of 1692. Phoebe's new husband was a successful merchant in his own right. Ezra Mather owned property in Lyme and the surrounding communities, and even a Pearl Street lot in New York City. The couple lived comfortably and were well regarded in the community.

By 1808 the marriage had produced four sons and a daughter, and the family appeared firmly settled into a life of convention and prosperity. That same year, however, Ezra Mather fell ill and died suddenly at the age of thirty-eight. Phoebe Mather, not quite thirty years old at the time, was now a widow with five children in her care. Fortunately her husband had left a considerable estate: His will provided for the support and education of the children, and insured that his widow would be well cared for until such time as she should remarry.

Phoebe Mather could easily have lived out the rest of her life in comfort. Six years later, however, she married again, relinquishing the generous bequest from her first husband. Daniel Rogers, a man eleven years younger than his new wife, came from one of the leading families in New London's thriving shipbuilding community. Like the Mathers, the Rogers family had featured in the early history of the region, but where the Mathers had been Puritans, the Rogers family had been of a more rebellious turn of mind, forging a religious sect known as the "Rogerenes" that stood in direct opposition to the established orthodoxy of the Puritans. Sometimes this opposition took the form of creative civil disobedience, with members appearing "nearly or quite naked" at public assemblies, and behaving in "a wild and tumultuous manner" so as to disrupt the Puritan solemnities. Apparently this unruly streak was passed down through the generations: James Rogers, Daniel's grandfather, once found himself trading blows with a constable over a barrel of beef that had been set aside for a minister's wages. The conflict ended only when Rogers threw scalding water on the officer and made off with the spoils.

Although the progression from the Puritan Mathers to the rebellious Rogers family may have been unconventional, Phoebe Rogers's second marriage appears to have been a happy one. Mary Rogers was born in 1820, probably in Lyme, Connecticut, when the marriage was in its sixth year. Curiously, the official records of the birth are missing or destroyed, though the births of the five children from Phoebe's previous marriage are well documented in a variety of forms. It is possible that this discrepancy reflects a decline in social status from the first to the second marriage, but another explanation suggests itself. Phoebe Rogers would have been forty-two years old in 1820, a notably advanced age for childbearing at the time. This fact, coupled with the absence of official birth records, has led to speculation that Mary was not the daughter of Phoebe Rogers at all, but was instead her granddaughter—possibly the illegitimate child of Phoebe's twenty-one-year-old daughter by her first marriage, taken in by Phoebe and Daniel Rogers to be raised as their own. The Rogers family would not have been the first to resort to this means of concealing the pregnancy of an unmarried daughter.

Whatever the circumstances of Mary's birth, her early years in Connecticut were marked by loss. By the time she was fourteen years old, three of the older children from Phoebe Rogers's first marriage had died in the space of only five years. To compound the family's grief, a steamship explosion on the Mississippi River claimed the life of Daniel Rogers, Phoebe's second husband, in 1834.

Twice widowed, Phoebe Rogers remained in Lyme with her young daughter under increasingly straitened circumstances for three more years. As the financial panic of 1837 took hold, however, the two women were forced to sell up and try their luck in New York City. The fact that Phoebe had a sister in New York would likely have been a factor, though it is also possible that John Anderson, who may have had business dealings with Ezra Mather, lent some assistance with the move. Whatever the reasons for the move, the transition from the tranquil and familiar world of rural Lyme to the bustling streets of New York must have been wrenching. At nearly sixty years of age, Phoebe Rogers left behind the only world she had ever known. In Lyme, at least during her first marriage, she had enjoyed a life of prosperity and social position. Now she found herself alone and unprotected, and charged with the care of a young daughter while seeking to make an entirely new life in a strange and chaotic city. Acquaintances in New York would describe her as grim, withdrawn, and "deserving of our earnest compassion." In the circumstances, this cannot be seen as entirely surprising.

Where Phoebe Rogers inspired sympathy, the vivacious Mary awakened more complicated feelings in the many men whose paths she crossed. As the beautiful young daughter of an elderly widow, she appeared to have stepped from the pages of Dickens, complete with ambiguous lineage and a tragic aura. "We look upon this girl as we would our own daughters," one admirer would declare, but this paternal instinct seems to have been in the minority. A far greater number of men expressed their admiration in terms of courtship. Mary's Puritan ancestors would have recoiled at the sight of her passing out cigars in Anderson's Tobacco Emporium, but at a time when many able-bodied men were losing their jobs, she was fortunate to have found such a congenial position.

Mary seems to have understood from the beginning what was expected of her, and as time passed she began to show a certain flair. One hopeful suitor spoke of passing an afternoon at the cigar store for no other purpose than to exchange "teasing glances" with the captivating girl behind the counter, who seemed able to fan the flames of his ardor without giving false hope. A poem published in the New York *Herald* gives some indication of the effect she exerted:

> She moved amid the bland perfume
> That breathes of heaven's balmiest isle;
> Her eyes had starlight's azure gloom
> And a glimpse of heaven—her smile.

John Anderson paid his employee a generous wage to provide this glimpse of heaven for his customers. Undoubtedly Mary enjoyed the attention and preferred these light duties to the scullery work she might otherwise have been doing to support herself and her mother. After a few months behind the cigar counter, however, she found herself at the center of a strange and disturbing episode. In October of 1838, barely a year after her arrival in New York, Mary suddenly went missing from her post behind the cigar counter. Later that day, Phoebe Rogers discovered that her daughter had left behind a suicide note.

At the time Mary and her mother were still living at the home of Mrs. Hayes, Phoebe's sister, on Pitt Street. On October 6 the New York *Sun* reported, under the heading of "Something Mysterious," that Phoebe Rogers had discovered a letter on her daughter's dressing table bidding her "an affectionate and final farewell." Horrified, Phoebe "sent messengers in all directions" to search for her daughter, but no trace could be found. The New York *Journal of Commerce* took up the story, relating that Mrs. Hayes promptly carried the letter to the office of the New York coroner, who agreed that the young woman's message revealed a "fixed and un-alterable determination to destroy herself." The *Sun* added that the "cause of this wayward freak of the young lady is supposed by her friends to be disappointed love—she having recently received the addresses of a certain widower, who, it is said, has deserted her and by his desertion has brought upon her a state of mind which has prompted her, it is feared, to commit self-destruction." Readers were urged to report any sightings of the young lady, in the hope of preventing "the fulfillment of her dreadful purpose."

Mary returned home safely a short time later—within a few hours, according to some accounts. The following day's issue of the *Times and Commercial Intelligencer* dismissed the matter as a hoax: "A Correspondent who says he is well acquainted with the parties in the 'Love and Suicide' affair published yesterday gives a quite different version of it and states that the story is without the least foundation." According to this unidentified informant, the tale had been "got up by some evil-disposed person who addressed a letter to the mother amounting in substance to that published yesterday." In fact, the article went on to report, "Miss R. only went on a visit to a friend in Brooklyn. She is now at home with her mother."

This innocuous explanation failed to put an end to the matter. According to some accounts, the report of Mary's safe return was itself a hoax—as evidenced by Mary's failure to return to work—designed to discourage unwanted attention to the matter while she remained missing. When Mary eventually reappeared, apparently none the worse, another paper insisted that the disappearance had been a publicity stunt engineered by John Anderson: "After the smoke of the extra cigars sold during the excitement had cleared away," declared the reporter, "the young woman returned as good as new." Still others insisted that the suicide story had been fabri-cated to cover the fact that Mary had run off with one of her young suitors: "Some penny-a-liner trumped up a tale that she had eloped," insisted a weekly paper called *Brother Jonathan*, though this story also went unsubstantiated.

The true facts of Mary's brief disappearance remained muddled and contradictory, and would grow more so in years to come. Years later, an account in the *Sunday News* would dismiss the affair as a "cruel and unjustifiable hoax" practiced by one or more of the journalists who frequented the cigar store. This is entirely possible, as journalistic hoaxes had become a familiar tradition in the newspapers of the day. A few years earlier, in 1835, the *Sun* had created a sensation—and sold thousands of extra newspapers—with a breathless front-page account of the discovery of life on the moon. The "scientific dispatch" told of herds of bison thundering across the lunar surface, and blue unicorns clustered on its hilltops, while a colony of intelligent "bat-creatures" disported themselves in a mysterious golden temple. This "Great Astronomical Finding," usually attributed to Richard Adams Locke, came to be known as the "Great Moon Hoax," and it inspired numerous imitations.

If the story of Mary's disappearance and suicide bid began as a journalistic hoax, it may well have had an element of personal malice behind it. In her early days at the cigar store Mary received the attentions of a young newspaperman named Canter. On one occasion, according to the *Herald*, Canter was "severely beaten . . . by three or four rivals, in consequence of visiting her." It is possible that Canter found his revenge in print, as the account in his newspaper, the *Times and Commercial Intelligencer*, took a decidedly bizarre tone toward the affair: "It seems that Miss Rogers was employed in Anderson's segar store in Broadway," the paper noted. "There she met and fell in love with a gallant gay Lothario, whose name did not transpire. After a month's course of billing and cooing across the counter of Anderson's store, which ended like the smoke of one of that gentleman's segars (not however to speak disparagingly of their departed worth) in thin air. The Lothario was one morning found missing and that is the reason why Miss Rogers is now missing. When she left she took with her a shilling, as it is supposed, with the intention of purchasing poison."

It seems curious that a young woman's threatened suicide should have been an occasion of such mirth in the offices of the *Times and Commercial Intelligencer*. If the article was the work of a wounded lover, intended as a barbed hoax, the joke fell wide of its mark.

Whatever the truth of the episode, all accounts agree that Mary herself was mortified by the attention. One report had her fainting with horror upon her return to work, overcome by a crowd that had gathered for a glimpse of the celebrated cigar girl. "Concerned hands bore her back to her lodgings," reported the *Sunday News*, "where she remained for some time." Tearfully, Mary told her mother that she would never show herself again at the cigar store, and only the earnest pleadings of John Anderson—and a generous increase in wages—could induce her to return. Nothing more was heard of the suicide note she was supposed to have left, or of the "gallant gay Lothario" who was said to have led her astray.

Soon enough the commotion surrounding the disappearance faded and Mary resumed her work behind the cigar counter as if nothing had happened. Still, the incident had tempered her enthusiasm and she no longer felt quite so comfortable in the public gaze. A short time later, when an opportunity to leave Anderson's presented itself, she seized it. It emerged that Mary's half-brother (Phoebe Rogers's surviving son by her first marriage) had gone to sea and managed to accumulate a large sum of money by means that some described as "a foreign business venture" and others referred to as "plunder." In any case his pockets were lined with money when he next passed through New York in the spring of

1839. Upon learning of Mary's recent notoriety, he resolved at once that a tobacco store was not a fit place for a young woman to earn her keep, and provided his mother with the funds to open and maintain a boardinghouse on Nassau Street. With her son's help Mrs. Rogers leased the property from a man named Peter Aymar, who owned several buildings in the neighborhood, and immediately began advertising for lodgers. Over John Anderson's strong objections, Mary stepped out from behind the cigar counter, never to return.

As it happened, Phoebe's generous son would not live to see the results of this new venture. Within a few months, a lurching sail would knock him off the deck of his ship and he would drown before his crewmates could fish him out of the water. The news of his death would add yet another sorrow to Phoebe Rogers's already heavy burden. She had now outlived four of her five older children.

For the moment, her son's generosity appeared to offer a safe haven, providing Phoebe and Mary with a place to live and also a steady source of income. The three-story red brick building was one of several boardinghouses along Nassau Street, all of which catered to business travelers and office workers. Boardinghouses were a relatively new phenomenon in New York at the time, reflecting the unsettled nature of its workforce. For previous generations, room and board had often been provided as a condition of service, with long-term assistants and apprentices attaching themselves to the households of their employers. As that way of life vanished, boardinghouses sprang up to meet the needs of a far more transitory worker. Providing rooms and meals to these workers offered a rare opportunity for a widow such as Mrs. Rogers, who would have had few other avenues of income open to her. "The kindly matrons who open their doors to New York's working man give much-needed warmth and succor," wrote the New York *Gazette*. "They give sanctuary to the noble working man." Perhaps so, but for Phoebe Rogers, scrubbing potatoes and washing linens for a group of tradesmen and office clerks marked a considerable descent from her vastly more comfortable life back in Connecticut. As if to underscore the decline in her fortunes, her new boardinghouse was only a few hundred yards from the Pearl Street lot once owned by Ezra Mather, her first husband.

The federal census of 1840 lists seven people living at 126 Nassau Street, including Phoebe and Mary Rogers, which suggests that the number of boarders at any given time would have been about four or five, though their names are not recorded. Although Phoebe was able to hire a servant girl to help with some of the household chores, the bulk of the daily duties fell to Mary, as her mother's declining health left her unable to cope with the heavy lifting of running a household.

Although Mary's circle of admirers had shrunk considerably from the heady days of Anderson's Tobacco Emporium, she continued to exert a powerful fascination. It seems that none of the men who boarded on Nassau Street was impervious to her charms. A sailor named William Kiekuck was among the early lodgers, and though he would later claim that his relationship with Mary had been merely "one of tender friendship," he continued to call on her for several months after he had left the premises.

Alfred Crommelin, who was variously described as "courtly" and "officious," came on the scene in December of 1840. Tall and gaunt-faced, Crommelin impressed Phoebe Rogers with his fastidious table manners and polite manner of speaking. The exact nature of his occupation remains obscure, though it seems to have involved a clerkship of some type, possibly in a law office, and he appears to have been reasonably successful at it. His efforts at courtship also showed promise. On arrival at Nassau Street Crommelin found himself deeply smitten with Mary and began to plead his case almost from the moment he set down his valise. Mary found him agreeable, and for a short while she encouraged his attentions.

Archibald Padley, who formed a close friendship with Crommelin, found Mary to be a "worthy girl," but there is no evidence that he ever pursued her, possibly out of respect for Crommelin's feelings. Whatever Padley's own intentions may have been, both he and Crommelin were soon cut out by the jovial Daniel Payne, who came to occupy the central place in Mary's affections.

Daniel Payne worked as a cork cutter, a flourishing trade that served not only vintners and brewers but also doctors and chemists, who required durable and airtight stoppers for their glass bottles and ceramic jugs. Apart from his ability to cut cork, Payne had little to offer. He was known to be a heavy drinker even by the impressive standards of the day, when many considered alcohol to be a healthful alternative to disease-ridden water. At a time when it was not unusual to dispatch two or three bottles of claret at a single sitting, Payne's habits were thought to be excessive, and he was often described as a "bibber" and a "tosspot." Possibly he made an agreeable change, in Mary's eyes, from the more straitlaced Crommelin. Whatever the case, in a very short time Payne had come to think of himself as Mary's future husband, though it is by no means clear that he actually made a formal offer of marriage.

Alfred Crommelin was slow to accept that he had been replaced in Mary's affections by Payne, a man he described as "dissipated." Crommelin's ill will toward his rival caused considerable discomfort around the breakfast table, with Padley describing the relations between the two men as "frosty." Seeking an ally, Crommelin expressed his disapproval to Phoebe Rogers, hoping that their united approbation would force Mary to see the error of her ways. If anything, the plan had the opposite effect. Mary remained bound to

Payne, and was often seen strolling arm in arm with him on Broadway. Crommelin, much to his distress, found himself treated as if he were a kindly uncle.

By June of 1841, Crommelin's festering resentments came to a crisis. Returning from work one evening, he found Payne and Mary engaged in "unseemly intimacies" in the front parlor. Crommelin drew himself up into an indignant rage and began lecturing Payne on the duties and obligations of a gentleman. Payne responded first with a grin and then a sneer, which only increased the volume of Crommelin's tirade. Finally Payne was moved to remark, while placing a hand on Mary's knee, that Crommelin would do well to mind his own affairs, as he himself had better things to do.

This proved to be too much for Crommelin. Gravely affronted, he stormed upstairs and packed his bag. Reappearing a few moments later with his belongings in hand, he offered another string of cautions on the wages of sin while Payne sat grinning up at him. At length, when his indignation had spent itself, Crommelin turned and made a theatrical exit from the house. Somehow Crommelin's friend Archibald Padley found himself caught up in the drama and was obliged to follow in Crommelin's stormy wake. On the front steps, Crommelin paused and turned back to the house, where Mary stood watching. He declared himself to be "sorry for the step she was taking" and added that he still cared for her. He told her that "if she were ever in trouble" she was to call upon him for help. The declaration was undoubtedly heartfelt, but in the weeks to come, when Mary did in fact call upon him, Crommelin would fail her thoroughly.

With the departure of Crommelin, Daniel Payne settled into his new role as Mary's unchallenged suitor, though he would have little time to enjoy it. Phoebe Rogers disapproved of the young cork cutter. Though Payne was unfailingly cordial and eager to please, Phoebe considered him a wastrel. Her daughter, she believed, could do better for herself. For the moment, however, Payne was unaware of the gathering storm.

Although Mary no longer entertained the young men who came to "preen and squawk" in Anderson's Tobacco Emporium, the quarrel between Payne and Crommelin indicates that life on Nassau Street was not substantially quieter than it had been at the cigar store. If further reminders were needed, Mary's employment as the "beautiful seegar girl" had left a considerable legacy of turgid prose and bad poetry in the newspapers of the day. A typical example could be found in the *Sunday Morning Atlas* in September of 1838, which displayed an engraving of "The Cigar Girl" on its front page, as part of a series of New York character sketches called "Portraits of People." The illustration showed Mary in profile, with careful attention given to the "captivating eyes" and "perfectly symmetrical features" mentioned in other publications, as well as the pleasing figure that had so delighted Anderson's customers. The *Atlas* accompanied the engraving with a brief and largely irrelevant history of cigars before turning to the real business at hand: a thinly veiled cautionary tale based on the notoriety of an attractive cigar vendor. The story concerned the misfortunes of a lovely young woman named Ellen Somers, who, finding herself in reduced circumstances, is obliged to take a position in a cigar emporium, over the earnest objections of her mother: "You would be exposed to the gaze of every creature, who in laying out his beggarly trifle, expected that the exhibition of a pretty girl was included in his charge, and that he had paid for the privilege of staring you out of countenance."

Under the looming threat of absolute destitution, Ellen reluctantly assumes her post at the cigar shop, only to find her virtue under assault by a pair of leering young customers "known in common parlance as gentlemen," while a "gentle, modest" suitor named Henry Wilkinson watches with mounting concern. The two young cads even go so far "as to bet upon who should be the happy man to make the divine creature his goddess of pleasure," but the virtuous Ellen repels their advances. Having shown herself to be "a superior being," Ellen performs her daily tasks with maidenly decorum, only to find herself abducted by Henry Wilkinson, who proves to be a wolf in sheep's clothing. Lying in wait outside the shop, he bundles her into his coach and speeds off through a dark and stormy night. Ellen, fearing death and "perhaps worse," pleads for her release. "I have gone too far to recede," Wilkinson snarls. "It is useless for you to oppose my wishes. What can you do?"

The cigar girl's reply is chillingly prophetic:

"I can die," she answers.

II

I Tremble for the Consequence

AT 169 BROADWAY, no more than a dozen blocks south of Anderson's Tobacco Emporium, stood a dark and forbidding bookseller's shop known as the Long Room. The proprietor, an eccentric Scottish immigrant named William Gowans, preferred to deal with "readers of serious intent" rather than common browsers, and it was known in the neighborhood that "freedom of Gowans's bookstore was not presented to every passer-by." The chosen few who gained admittance found a massive but haphazard inventory, ranging from rare texts on Greek horology and Roman funerary practices to the latest European novels. Gowans opened the shop in January of 1837 and soon filled the floor-to-ceiling oak plank shelves to capacity. As additional volumes accumulated they were stored first in wooden crates stacked on a pair of battered deal tables, then on chairs scavenged from a previous tenant, and finally in teetering stacks on the floor. The impression created, recalled one early visitor, was that of a "Minotaur maze of books."

In time, Gowans would become one of the most respected book dealers in the city, renowned as "one of the most truthful and uncompromising of men." In the early days of his business, however, he had few friends or acquaintances, and kept mostly to himself. One of his few companions was his landlady's son-in-law,

Edgar Allan Poe, also known to some members of the household as "Eddy."

"During that time I saw much of him, and had an opportunity of conversing with him often," Gowans wrote many years later, "and I must say, that I never saw him the least affected with liquor, nor even descend to any known vice, while he was one of the most courteous, gentlemanly, and intelligent companions I have met with during my journeyings and haltings through divers divisions of the globe. Besides, he had an extra inducement to be a good man as well as a good husband, for he had a wife of matchless beauty and loveliness; her eyes could match that of any houri, and her face defy the genius of a Canova to imitate."

If Gowans sounded defensive of his young friend's character, he had good reason to be. Though not yet thirty, Poe had already made powerful enemies in New York, many of whom dismissed him as an unreliable drunkard. Poe had already begun to publish his poetry and tales, but his modest reputation at that time rested chiefly on his literary criticism, published in Richmond's *Southern Literary Messenger* and elsewhere.

Poe was a gifted critic, but a controversial one. Although his skill and insight were undeniable, many readers were put off by the astonishing venom he displayed when he went on the attack. He became so notorious for his bile that a contemporary caricature showed him brandishing a tomahawk. "I have scalped him!" he would say after completing an especially vicious review, adding that "feeble puffing is not my forte. It will do these fellows good to hear the truth, and stimulate them to worthier efforts." In Poe's view, the criticism of the time suffered from an excess of bland civility. He believed that his broadsides would rouse his fellow critics from their stupor and attract the notice of the insular literary establishment of New York and Boston.

The strategy succeeded to a certain extent. Poe's tirades soon found favor with the editor of a new journal called the *New York Review*, who invited Poe "to fall in with your *broad-axe* amidst this miserable literary trash which surrounds us." With his wife and mother-in-law in tow, Poe moved to New York from Richmond in February of 1837. By some accounts, the three of them were subjects of curiosity as they wandered the streets in their "Southern garb," looking for lodging. The new arrivals eventually found rooms in a dilapidated building at the corner of Sixth Avenue and Waverly Place.

Soon enough, however, Poe's hopes of employment vanished amid the upheavals of the banking panic of that year, a consequence of the same grim economic conditions that had brought Mary Rogers and her mother to the city. Several newspapers and magazines suspended publication as a result, including the *New York Review*. Over the course of fifteen months in New York, Poe would manage to publish only two stories. As his prospects dwindled, he considered abandoning literature altogether and training for a career in lithography. At times, the household subsisted on bread and molasses for days at a stretch.

Circumstances improved marginally when the family moved from Waverly Place to a small house at 113½ Carmine Street, near Washington Square. There, Poe's mother-in-law, Maria Clemm, hit upon an idea to help the family stay afloat. "The hard times of 1837, with insistent force, had been knocking at Poe's door," wrote one early chronicler, "until Mrs. Clemm found it wise to turn her attention to keeping a few boarders to meet the expenses of daily needs." Like Phoebe Rogers, Mrs. Clemm believed that running a boardinghouse would offer a measure of stability in worsening times.

Among Mrs. Clemm's boarders was the affable William Gowans, who seems to have taken a warm interest in the family's welfare.

"For more than eight months one house contained us," Gowans would recall, and "one table fed us." Gowans, who came to regard Poe as a "gifted but unfortunate genius," soon offered to use his connections to introduce the young critic to the New York literary set. On March 30, 1837, Gowans brought Poe as his guest to a formal Booksellers' Dinner at the City Hotel on lower Broadway. The event drew a number of literary notables, including Washington Irving and the poet Fitz-Greene Halleck. Gowans recalled that the evening "was a brilliant one and marked the first appearance of the young Southern critic and poet among the Knickerbockers." Conscious of the opportunity to make an impression, Poe stood and proposed one of the evening's toasts, raising his glass to "The Monthlies of Gotham—Their distinguished Editors, and their vigorous Collaborateurs."

It is reasonable to suppose that Poe made other attempts to ingratiate himself with his distinguished and vigorous colleagues. If so, there would have been a number of avenues open to him. In addition to the famous Shakespeare Tavern, the newly opened Anderson's Tobacco Emporium was fast establishing itself as a literary gathering place. Poe may well have called in to mingle with other men of letters, and perhaps make purchases from Mary Rogers, the haunting young woman behind the cigar counter. A young police constable named George Walling, later to become New York's chief of police, would recall that Poe had been one of a host of literary men who were "acquainted with the dainty figure and pretty face where they bought their cigars," though it is worth noting that Walling had not yet joined the police force at that time. Even so, it is pleasant to imagine Poe rubbing elbows with Irving and Cooper, and perhaps basking in the "glimpse of heaven" afforded by Mary Rogers and her dark smile. If so, he could little have imagined, as he would later write, "the intense and long-enduring excitement" that would soon develop over the beautiful cigar girl's fate, or how intimately his own fortunes would be bound up in hers.

"I THINK," Poe once wrote, long before his arrival in New York, "that I have already had my share of trouble for one so young." It was one of the few occasions where he might have been accused of understatement. It is often said that Poe lived a life as bizarre and tortuous as one of his own tales of the imagination, though perhaps the story would have fit more comfortably in a Gothic melodrama. David Poe, Edgar's father, had been destined for a career in law when he spied a young actress named Eliza Arnold across the footlights of a theater in Norfolk, Virginia. Instantly smitten by the "fetchingly girlish" performer, he abandoned his legal studies and gave himself over to life on the stage, much to his father's displeasure. In time, David Poe managed to join Eliza Arnold's theatrical troupe, where he wooed and won the recently widowed actress.

Eliza Arnold Hopkins was only nineteen at the time, but she was already a ten-year veteran of the stage. A celebrated beauty, her only known portrait shows a round yet fragile face, with large, liquid eyes framed by dangling curls. Reviews often made mention of her "interesting figure" and "sweetly melodious voice." The appearance of David Poe was also pleasing to critics, but it seems that his abilities as an actor left much to be desired. Writing in 1806, the year of the Poes' marriage, one critic observed that "the lady was young and pretty, and evinced talent both as singer and actress; the gentleman was literally nothing."

In January of 1807, nine months after the marriage, the young Mrs. Poe gave birth to a son, Henry. Two years later, on January 19, 1809, Edgar was born in a boardinghouse near the Boston Common, not far from where the troupe was appearing. By this time a heavy strain was evident in the Poes' marriage. David Poe, resentful of his wife's success, proved to be quick-tempered and hard-drinking, especially when affronted by criticism of his acting skills. On one occasion he berated an audience from the stage, and on another he presented himself at the home of a critic to take issue with a hostile notice. As his behavior grew more and more erratic, the burden of providing for the family fell on Eliza, who was obliged to continue performing until the week of Edgar's birth, and to resume some two weeks later.

A third child, Rosalie, arrived the following year. By this time Henry had been sent to live with his paternal grandparents, while Edgar and his newborn sister spent much of their time in the care of nursemaids, one of whom, according to a family friend, "fed them liberally with bread soaked in gin" and "freely administered . . . other spirituous liquors, with sometimes laudanum." This, the nurse believed, would "make them strong and healthy."

David Poe abandoned his wife and three children in July of 1811 and is said to have died, alone and destitute, five months later. By this time the unhappy circumstances had also taken a toll on Eliza. For a brief time she struggled alone in failing health, only to die of tuberculosis in Richmond, Virginia, on December 8, 1811, with her children at her side. Edgar was not quite three.

During their mother's final illness, Edgar and his sister Rosalie had been under the care of kindly actor friends by the name of Usher, but the couple were unable to take permanent custody. The children's maternal grandparents had died years earlier, and the paternal grandparents, who already had custody of Henry, had suffered a financial reverse that made it impossible to accept responsibility for the two younger children. A home was found for Rosalie with a Richmond family by the name of Mackenzie, while Edgar was taken into the care of an enterprising merchant named John Allan.

John Allan would become the closest thing to a father that the young Poe would ever know. His wife, Frances, a nervous and sickly woman, had been unable to have children of her own. A Scottish immigrant, Allan was a man of cultured tastes and a reputation for acts of charity, but he was also known to be hot-tempered and imperious. "Mr. Allan was a good man in his way," a family friend wrote of him. "He was sharp and exacting, and with his long, hooked nose, and small keen eyes looking from under his shaggy eyebrows, he always reminded me of a hawk." At the time Allan was also extremely wealthy, having established a complex of offices and warehouses in Richmond's business district from which he brokered tobacco, services, and other goods in a network of trade that stretched across America and Europe.

At a stroke, young Edgar went from a life of wandering and struggle to a world of wealth and indulgence. The Allans lavished attention on their new charge, and assured the family of David Poe that they would provide a first-rate education befitting a young gentleman. From the first, however, John Allan's benevolence was conditional. Although he added the family name to Edgar's as a kind of honorific, he never formally adopted the boy.

The newly christened Edgar Allan Poe proved to be a charming and precocious child, with many of his late mother's theatrical tendencies. Dinner guests were occasionally treated to the spectacle of the boy standing on the dining room table in his velvet suit and stockinged feet, declaiming passages of poetry.

At the age of five Edgar accompanied his foster parents on a five-year sojourn in Britain. While John Allan tended to his business, the boy was enrolled in a series of excellent boarding schools and shown off to Allan's relatives in Scotland. Allan took visible pride in his young charge's academic accomplishments, and showered him with gifts and extravagant sums of pocket money. Poe was "a quick and clever boy," according to one schoolmaster, "and would have been a very good boy if he had not been spoilt by his parents."

Returning to Richmond in 1820, the eleven-year-old Edgar continued his schooling and was soon able to read Horace in Latin and Homer in Greek. Already the seeds of his future career were taking shape; he filled his notebooks with poems, some of which were thought to be so accomplished that the doting Allan considered having them published. "His imaginative powers seemed to take precedence of all his other faculties," another schoolmaster recalled, while a cousin of Allan's remarked that Poe was "fully imbued in his early youth with an idea that he would one day become a great writer."

By all accounts, the aspiring writer was also a fine athlete, and much given to reckless feats of daring. At age fifteen he made a swim of six miles in the James River against "the strongest tides ever known in the river," trailed by a boat filled with cheering friends. Poe likened this exploit to Byron's swimming of the Hellespont. "It would have been a feat comparatively easy to swim twenty miles in still water," he boasted. "I would not think much of attempting to swim the British Channel from Dover to Calais."

For all his swagger, he was remembered as holding himself apart from his peers. A teacher recalled him as sensitive and somewhat aloof, but added that he would "strain every nerve to oblige a friend." As Poe entered his teens and grew more conscious of the workings of Richmond society, he became keenly aware of his own tenuous social position. "Of Edgar Poe it was known that his parents were players," a classmate would say, and that he was "dependent on the bounty" of his foster father. Worse, that bounty had become increasingly uncertain. As the boy grew older and more willful, Allan's devotion began to wane. "I know that often when angry with Edgar he threatened to turn him adrift," a friend said of Allan, "and that he never allowed him to lose sight of his dependence on his charity."

Allan's charitable impulses were undoubtedly shadowed by a series of business reverses that had dogged his return to Richmond. As his finances grew more precarious, his foster son's increasingly willful behavior struck him as all the more thankless. "The boy possesses not a Spark of affection for us," Allan complained, "not a particle of gratitude for all my care and kindness toward him." Uncertain of his position in the household, Poe began to look elsewhere for affection. He formed an intense attachment to Jane Stanard, the mother of a Richmond classmate, whom he would later recall as "the first, purely ideal love of my soul." It is said that the aspiring young poet read his verses aloud to her and basked in the warmth of her praise and encouragement. She was, Poe would recall, "an angel to my forlorn and darkened nature." By all accounts Mrs. Stanard was a beautiful and tragic figure, much given to fits of melancholy, and Poe watched with mounting despair as she slowly succumbed to a wasting illness. She was not yet thirty years old when she died in April of 1824, a few months past Edgar's fifteenth birthday. With its echo of Eliza Poe's early death, the loss of Jane Stanard cut deeply. The grief-stricken Edgar could often be found at her graveside keeping a vigil with her son Robert.

Poe's transparent and sometimes theatrical grief over Jane Stanard served to widen his rift with John Allan, who interpreted the behavior as a display of ingratitude toward himself and his wife. Poe, meanwhile, had found a new outlet for his roiling emotions. Within a year of Jane Stanard's death, the forlorn young poet had fallen in love with Sarah Elmira Royster, the fifteen-year-old daughter of one of the Allans' neighbors. Poe was keenly aware that her father considered him an unsuitable match, owing largely to his uncertain position in the Allan household, but he managed to persuade her to agree to a secret engagement.

In March of 1825 John Allan's diminished fortunes were suddenly restored—and vastly extended—by an enormous inheritance from a wealthy uncle. Financially secure for the first time in years, Allan bought a luxurious new home on Richmond's Main Street, with commanding views of the capitol building and the James River. At the very moment that Allan received this windfall, Thomas Jefferson's "academical village," the University of Virginia, opened its doors in Charlottesville, sixty miles away. As Poe approached his seventeenth birthday, Allan made plans to enroll him, both as a statement of his own wealth and position, and as a means of honoring his earlier promise to provide an education. Privately, Allan felt relief at having his quarrelsome foster son out of the house, and hoped that college life would help to settle him.

Poe arrived in Charlottesville in February of 1826 and had to contend with the hardships of the university's ongoing construction, including crowded, unheated buildings and questionable sanitation. There were, however, numerous compensations. Thomas Jefferson, then eighty-three, was very much in evidence as the university's first rector. Poe would have dined with him on several occasions, and would have been among the mourners when the former president died on July 4 of that year.

Popular legend holds that Poe was a wild and dissolute rebel among sober young academicians. In fact, the opposite appears to have been true, at least in his earliest days. Jefferson had designed an educational system with the sons of wealthy Virginia planters in mind. In the belief that these "spirituous fellows" would chafe at a discipline similar to that of Harvard or Yale, he established a code of behavior that set aside restrictive rules in favor of self-governance. The experiment was not a success, culminating in a student uprising during the first year, with books, bricks, and bottles of urine thrown at the professors. In his first letter home, Poe would tell John Allan that fights among students were "so trifling an occurrence" that no one took any notice. He went on to describe a more noteworthy brawl in which a student, having been struck on the head with a rock, "drew a pistol (which are all the fashion here) and had it not missed fire would have put an end to the controversy."

Against this background, the less combative Poe proved a model student, and wrote home to Richmond of his hopes of succeeding, "if I don't get frightened." Initially, at least, Poe excelled, though he was known to rely on his sharp intellect and keen memory—often spending just a few moments preparing before a class—rather than careful study habits. Even so, he flourished. One professor would recall an occasion on which Poe had been the only member of the class to complete a suggested assignment, translating a portion of the Italian Renaissance poet Tasso into English verse. In December of his first year Poe was examined at length by two former presidents of the United States, James Madison and James Monroe, and received the highest honors in both ancient and modern languages.

Poe's classmates offered conflicting accounts of him. Some remembered Poe as being given to periods of lassitude and melancholy, while others described manic fits of "nervous excitability." Poe could cut a flamboyant figure when he wished, favoring his classmates with snatches of poetry and covering the walls of his room with charcoal sketches of "whimsical, fanciful and grotesque figures." Once he invited a group of students to hear a story he'd written, pacing back and forth in front of the fireplace as he read aloud. When one of his classmates ventured a word of criticism, Poe turned and flung the pages into the fire.

From his first days in Charlottesville, Poe struggled with a chronic shortage of money, and his letters to Richmond were filled with increasingly desperate requests for books, soap, clothing, and other basics. By accident or design, John Allan had sent Poe off to the university with insufficient funds. This made a dramatic change from Poe's early days in the Allan household, when the doting foster father had spared no expense to provide a fine European education. Now, at a time when Allan was considered one of the wealthiest men in Virginia, he kept a tight hold on the purse strings and placed Poe in a situation that would soon prove ruinous.

Within weeks, Poe found himself unable to pay his room and board. In a bitter letter to Allan written four years later, the details were still vivid in his memory: "I will boldly say that it was wholly and entirely your own mistaken parsimony that caused all the difficulties in which I was involved while at Charlottesville. The expenses of the institution at the lowest estimate were $350 per annum. You sent me there with $110. . . . I had, of course, the mortification of running in debt . . . and was immediately regarded in the light of a beggar. You will remember that in a week after my arrival, I wrote to you for some more money, and for books—You replied in terms of utmost abuse—if I had been the vilest wretch on earth you could not have been more abusive."

Allan may have hoped that a tight budget would teach Poe self-reliance, as his own early struggles had done. Instead, the "mortification" awakened Poe's worst instincts. He turned to gambling to make up the shortfall, only to sink further into debt. As his losses mounted, he turned to alcohol for consolation. "Poe's passion for strong drink was as marked and as peculiar as that for cards," a friend recalled. "It was not the taste of the beverage that influenced him; without a sip or smack of the mouth he would seize a full glass, without water or sugar, and send it home with a single gulp."

Not surprisingly, Poe found that alcohol and cards were a poor mix. He soon racked up staggering losses, estimated in some accounts to have exceeded $2,000—or more than five times his yearly expenses. In December, after Poe had completed only ten months of college life, John Allan descended on Charlottesville, paid off a few of the debts that he considered to be legitimate, and withdrew his foster son from the university, all but dragging him back to Richmond by the ear.

Poe's remaining debts followed him back to Richmond, and each day brought another demand for payment and threats of legal action. Allan imposed a further punishment by setting Poe to work without pay in his firm's counting house. Adding to Poe's distress, he now had to contend with the ruin of his courtship of Elmira Royster, the beautiful young woman to whom he had been secretly engaged. Poe had written to her often from Charlottesville, but she had failed to answer. It would be many years before he discovered the reason: Elmira's father had intercepted the letters, so as to derail the courtship. In later life Elmira would claim, in spite of her promise to marry Poe, that she had not realized the depth of his feelings for her. In the absence of any evidence to the contrary, she assumed that he had forgotten her once he went off to the university. One account holds that Poe, on his return to Richmond, attended a party at her home in hopes of a reunion, only to discover that the gathering was a celebration of her engagement to another man. While this incident may be apocryphal, Elmira would be married within two years, an occasion that inspired Poe to write the poem "Song" (better known as "I saw thee on thy bridal day") in which he spoke of a "burning blush" of "maiden shame," suggesting that the bride's feelings for him had never faded.

After two months in John Allan's counting house, Poe's festering resentments boiled over into an open confrontation. After a bitter argument, Allan threw Poe out of the house. Sheltering in a friendly tavern, Poe fired off a remarkably ill-judged letter: "My determination is at length taken—to leave your house and endeavor to find some place in this wide world, where I will be treated—not as *you* have treated me." After accusing Allan of blasting his hopes for a college education, and taking delight in his failure, Poe requested, "if you still have the least affection for me," that his clothes and books might be sent on immediately, along with enough money to see him safely out of town. "If you fail to comply with my request," Poe wrote darkly, "I tremble for the consequence."

Allan responded with an angry catalogue of Poe's sins, and ridicule for the manner in which his high-handed statement of independence was followed by a plea for cash: "after such a list of Black charges," Allan wrote, "you Tremble for the consequence unless I send you a supply of money."

When it became clear that the door to Allan's home was truly closed to him, Poe wandered the streets of Richmond in a state of mounting desperation, penniless and starving. One account has him falling into a round of drinking with a childhood friend and wheedling his way onto a ship bound for England. Another has him setting off for Greece in the tradition of Lord Byron, so as to fight for independence. Still another finds him sending a series of letters reporting on his progress in St. Petersburg. Allan himself confessed his uncertainty, and indifference, in a letter to his sister: "I'm thinking Edgar has gone to sea to seek his own fortunes."

The truth was notably more prosaic. Unable to pay for food or shelter, Poe somehow talked his way onto a coal vessel bound for Boston, probably working for his passage. It is likely that Poe gravitated toward Boston as the center of America's literary establishment.

He had a thin sheaf of poems in hand as he made his way north, clutched all the more tightly because Allan had scorned his literary aspirations. Unquestionably there was an even more personal reason pulling him toward Boston; one of the few mementos he had of his mother was a sketch of Boston Harbor, on the back of which she had written: "For my little son Edgar, who should ever love Boston, the place of his birth, and where his mother found her best, and most sympathetic friends."

Poe found few sympathetic friends in Boston. Arriving in April of 1827, he served brief stints as an office clerk and a reporter. One acquaintance recalled a landlady who "lost patience with a boarder who sat up nights writing on paper which he could not afterward sell. She soon turned him into the street." Another spoke of being bustled into an alleyway by a shabbily dressed Poe, who urged him not to speak his name aloud, explaining that "until he hit it hard"— or until he made good—"he preferred to remain incognito."

After several weeks, Poe had still not managed to "hit it hard." Finally, finding himself at loose ends, he enlisted for a five-year stint in the United States Army, listing his name as "Edgar A. Perry" and giving his age as twenty-two. In fact, he was eighteen.

It is difficult to know what possessed Poe to join the army, though sheer desperation must have played a part. At the very least, the army promised to provide him with three square meals a day. He may also have wished to demonstrate to Allan the lengths to which he was prepared to go in order to make something of himself. In any event, it marked a dramatic change in his fortunes. At the University of Virginia he gambled away hundreds and perhaps thousands of dollars. In the army, his salary was five dollars a month.

"Private Perry" would spend six months with Battery H of the First Artillery, stationed at Fort Independence in Boston Harbor. He adapted quickly to the harsh regimen of army life, serving various functions as a company clerk, commissary worker, and messenger. It is unlikely that there were many other recruits in Battery H who were able to translate Cicero and Homer, and fewer still who had published a collection of verse. In the summer of 1827, just two months after Poe joined the army, a forty-page pamphlet entitled *Tamerlane and Other Poems* appeared in Boston. Poe had arranged for the publication before his enlistment, somehow paying for the private printing with funds cobbled together from his various jobs. Still incognito, Poe presented the volume as the anonymous work of "a Bostonian." It drew heavily on his thwarted romance with Elmira Royster, with many of the poems addressing the follies of youth and lost love. In a brief preface, the young poet proclaimed that many of the verses had been composed "when the author had not completed his fourteenth year," adding that "why they are now published concerns no one but himself." If by any chance the volume failed to succeed, Poe assured his readers that "failure will not at all influence him in a resolution already adopted" to succeed as a poet. This was just as well. Poe's limited resources had restricted the printing to a meager fifty copies—too few to attract serious attention from critics or readers. On publication, the collection drew almost no notice at all.

Meanwhile, "Private Perry" found himself thriving under military discipline. After six months at Fort Independence, Poe's battery shipped out to South Carolina in November of 1827. Poe would spend more than a year stationed at Fort Moultrie on Sullivan's Island in Charleston Harbor, followed by a move in December of 1828 to Fortress Monroe near Hampton, Virginia. By this time Poe had been promoted to artificer, charged with the preparation of artillery shells, with a rise in pay to ten dollars a month, plus a ration of spirits per day. A commanding officer would praise his exemplary conduct, noting that the young private kept entirely "free of drinking." On New Year's Day of 1829 Poe was promoted to sergeant major, the highest possible rank for a noncommissioned officer.

By this time, however, Poe had grown weary of army life, especially after the tedious stretch on Sullivan's Island, which he would describe as offering "little else than the sea sand." With three years remaining on his five-year term of enlistment, Poe realized that he had reached a dead end. He confided in his sympathetic commanding officer, Lieutenant Howard, revealing not only the unhappy circumstances that led to his enlistment, but also his true age. The lieutenant allowed as how a discharge might be possible, but it carried a condition that Poe must have dreaded: a reconciliation with John Allan, whose permission was required.

Clearly the prospect was unwelcome to Poe, no matter how much he may have wished to escape the drudgery of three more years in the army, so it fell to Lieutenant Howard to write and broach the subject with Allan. Apparently Poe's long absence had stirred no fondness in Allan's heart. He coldly informed Lieutenant Howard that Poe "had better remain as he is until the termination of his enlistment."

It was hardly the reconciliation Poe might have wished for. Nevertheless, he now undertook to write to Allan directly, attempting over the course of several letters to make a case for leaving the army and returning home. "I am altered from what you knew me," he insisted, attempting to distance himself from the sins of Charlottesville, "and am no longer a boy tossing about on the world without aim or consistency." However, like the boy he had been, Poe was not above resorting to veiled threats that he would be "driven to more decided measures if you refuse to assist me."

When these letters went unanswered, Poe changed tactics. Instead of leaving the army, he now sought Allan's help in advancing further through the ranks. Acting on the advice of Lieutenant Howard and others, Poe asked Allan's support in securing a place at the United States Military Academy at West Point. Having already completed artillery training, and shown himself to be a capable soldier, Poe expected to complete his cadet training in only six months. Unfortunately, the new plan of action carried a familiar refrain: "Under the certain expectation of kind news from home I have been led into expenses which my present income will not support," he wrote, adding that he was "at present in an uncomfortable situation." Worse yet, he ended with another of his dark threats. He would await Allan's response with impatience, he declared, for it meant a choice between "the assurance of an honourable & highly successful course in my own country—or the prospect—no *certainty* of an exile forever to another."

Perhaps the only grace notes of Poe's letters to Richmond had been his consistent and genuine concern for the well-being of Frances Allan, his foster mother: "My dearest love to Ma—it is only when absent that we can tell the true value of such a friend—I hope she will not let my wayward disposition wear away the love she used to have for me." Mrs. Allan's health, always fragile, had gone into a slow and painful decline during Poe's army stint. In March of 1829 Poe received the unhappy news that she had died at the age of forty-four. In her final illness, she had repeatedly expressed the desire for a reunion with her foster son.

Poe secured a leave from the army and traveled to Richmond, where the grieving John Allan welcomed him in a spirit of reconciliation, even buying him a suit of mourning clothes. By the time Poe returned to duty, Allan had given his consent to the plan to leave the army and enter West Point. On his discharge forms, Poe declared himself to be John Allan's "son & heir."

All that remained was to finalize the discharge, a task Poe mishandled. Regulations required him to arrange for a substitute to serve the remaining years of his enlistment. Although the standard payment for this service was only twelve dollars, Poe would have had to remain until his superiors returned from furlough to secure a man at this price. Unwilling to wait, he rashly offered seventy-five dollars to an ex-soldier to take his place immediately. The substitute received twenty-five dollars in cash and a promissory note for the balance. As with his departure from the University of Virginia two years earlier, Poe now left the army with a debt he had no means of honoring. When John Allan learned of this, the truce with his prodigal foster son began to unravel.

Fourteen months would elapse before a place opened up at West Point. John Allan made it clear that Poe was not especially welcome in Richmond—"I am not particularly anxious to see you," he wrote—so Poe passed several months in Baltimore, living mostly at the home of a cousin. He spent much of his time assembling his West Point application materials and letters of recommendation, at one stage walking some thirty-seven miles to Washington to plead his case to John H. Eaton, the secretary of war.

Poe also devoted time to a second collection of poetry, even placing a few of his verses in literary journals, where they drew some backhanded praise: "though nonsense, rather exquisite nonsense." In May of 1829 Poe wrote to Allan with "a request different from any I have ever yet made," asking for one hundred dollars to indemnify a publisher against loss if they agreed to publish his new volume of poems. In this way, Poe believed, he could "cut out a path to reputation" without derailing his plan to enter West Point.

The request was not entirely outlandish—guarantees of this type were fairly common at the time—but John Allan, who had chided Poe for studying literature at the University of Virginia, made an unlikely patron of the arts. Allan not only refused, he wrote to Poe and strongly censured his conduct. Undeterred, Poe took the manuscript to a small Baltimore firm whose owners did not require a surety. The seventy-two-page *Al Aaraaff, Tamerlane, and Minor Poems* was published at the end of 1829 in an edition of only 250 copies. The twenty-year-old poet set aside the anonymous "Bostonian" pseudonym of his earlier collection and published the work as Edgar A. Poe. This was the name he would use henceforth, neither abandoning nor fully acknowledging his uncertain claim on the name of Allan.

The new collection fared slightly better than Poe's first effort, even drawing a small smattering of reviews, and Poe now described himself as "irrecoverably a poet." By this time, however, his application to West Point had advanced through the bureaucracy. As he had promised Allan, he would not allow the demands of poetry to divert him. In June of 1830, Poe traveled to New York to enter the United States Military Academy.

It is commonplace to observe that this fragile and melancholy poetic genius was ill suited to the rigors and harsh discipline of West Point. During Poe's time, regulations specifically forbade cadets to "read novels, romances or plays," suggesting that the academy was inhospitable to the artistic temperament. As he sought to restore himself to his foster father's good graces, however, Poe had few options. It was natural that he should attempt to capitalize on his earlier success as an enlisted man, and West Point seemed to offer, as he told Allan, the promise of achieving distinction.

Upon arrival, Poe was immediately thrown into the difficult period of summer encampment: sleeping rough in crude tents and undergoing a seemingly endless round of drills and weapons training beginning each day at 5:30 A.M. When the academic year began in September, Poe and his fellow cadets moved into spartan barracks and divided their time between class work and military exercises until ten at night. Not surprisingly, Poe excelled on the academic side, but after the comparatively light duties of his army service, he found the training to be intolerably difficult. He was not alone in this opinion; the class size would dwindle from 130 to some eighty-seven cadets in barely six months.

A fellow cadet named Timothy Jones would recall that Poe seemed "given to extreme dissipation" shortly after arrival. "At first he studied hard and his ambition seemed to be to lead the class in all studies," Jones noted, but after a few weeks "he seemed to lose interest in his studies and to be disheartened and discouraged." Poe sought refuge in a nearby tavern, whose proprietor he would recall as the "sole congenial soul in the entire God-forsaken place."

Poe had expected, as he told Allan, to "run thro'" his training in a mere six months. Now he faced the deadening realization that he, like all the rest of the cadets, would be required to spend four full years before receiving his commission. If three more years in the army had seemed intolerable, four years at West Point was the stuff of nightmares.

Worse yet, Poe's fragile détente with Allan had begun to fray. Although Allan had permitted a brief visit to Richmond once Poe's appointment to West Point was secure, the visit had gone poorly, with old grievances boiling to the surface. Allan, meanwhile, had other calls on his attention. Barely a year after the death of Frances Allan, he made plans to marry Louisa Patterson, a woman twenty years younger than himself, with whom he would go on to have three children. Almost at the same time, another of Allan's paramours, his longtime mistress, gave birth to twin sons.

For Poe, toiling away at West Point, the implications were obvious. Although he had identified himself as Allan's "son & heir" on his army discharge papers, he now found himself in a crowded field.

Apparently Allan was anxious to get on with his new life and marriage, and felt fully prepared to consign Poe to a place among his late wife's discarded effects. By the end of the year, he had engineered a final rupture, hastened by his anger over the unnecessarily large sum Poe had paid his substitute when leaving the army. The substitute, a man named "Bully" Graves, had sent several letters to Poe attempting to collect the balance of the money owed to him. Poe, in attempting to explain his inability to pay, offered some ill-advised comments, claiming that Allan always "shuffled off" his requests for help, and was "not very often sober—which accounts for it." Somehow these remarks found their way back to Allan, who sent Poe a furious letter in which he requested "no further communication with yourself."

Poe, the trained artificer, loaded up his heavy artillery. In the past he had always made some effort, no matter how clumsily handled, to preserve the flickering embers of his benefactor's goodwill. Now, seeing that Allan had truly turned his back, Poe fired off a blistering four-page tirade, cataloguing complaints and accusations dating back to childhood: "Did I, when an infant, solicit your charity and protection, or was it of your own free will that you volunteered your services in my behalf?" He concluded with a typically dramatic and self-destructive flourish: "You sent me to W. Point like a beggar. The same difficulties are threatening me as before at Charlottesville—and I must resign."

Although Poe had already soured on the idea of four full years at West Point, it is likely that he perceived his resignation as a final means of punishing Allan. Unfortunately his withdrawal required

Allan's signature, and Poe warned that if his foster father failed to grant "this last request" he would actively court dismissal by neglecting his duties. Poe had already accrued an impressive number of bad conduct points by this time, and it is possible that he launched this threat as a means of accounting for misconduct already committed. Be that as it may, when Allan failed to respond, Poe mounted an active campaign of negligence, failing to report for duty on numerous occasions, and missing classes. On January 28, 1831, Poe was brought up on charges of neglect and disobedience. He offered no defense, thereby assuring his discharge. "I have been dismissed," he wrote to Allan, "when a single line from you would have saved it."

Astonishingly, Poe's former West Point classmates now extended aid where John Allan had refused. In his early days at the academy Poe had established himself as a satirist, lampooning West Point's commanders and traditions in verse. A fellow cadet recalled that "he would often write some of the most forcible and vicious doggerel, have me copy it with my left hand in order that it might be disguised, and post it around the building." Apparently these efforts made quite an impression. After Poe's departure, more than a hundred of his classmates contributed to a fund to underwrite his third collection of poems, amassing more than $150. The resulting volume, entitled simply *Poems*, appeared in May of 1831 in an edition of five hundred copies. Although it featured a grateful dedication to the "United States Corps of Cadets," the volume was met with disappointment in the barracks, as it contained none of Poe's military spoofs. "This book is a damn cheat," wrote one cadet.

In time, the disgruntled cadet's outburst came to be the minority opinion. The volume reflected Poe's growing maturity, forged in the crucible of desperate circumstances. With chilling clarity, the twenty-two-year-old poet announced the themes that would dominate his life and career:

> *And so, being young and dipt in folly*
> *I fell in love with melancholy,*
> *And used to throw my earthly rest*
> *And quiet all away in jest—*
> *I could not love except where Death*
> *Was mingling his with Beauty's breath—*
> *Or Hymen, Time, and Destiny*
> *Were stalking between her and me.*

Although barely out of his teens, Poe had managed to give voice to a sense of loss and wretchedness that would echo in nearly every poem and story he would ever write. Poe's early bereavements—the desertion of his father and the death of his mother—had created a wound that was not permitted to heal under John Allan's wavering affections. "For God's sake pity me," Poe had once written to his foster father, "and save me from destruction." It is impossible to say whether anyone could have saved Poe from his own self-destructive impulses—what he later termed "the human thirst for self-torment"—but there can be little question that the upheavals of his early years had created a vision of the world in which beauty and death would always shadow one another. It was a theme that Poe would find in every corner of his life, and it would soon lead him, perhaps inevitably, to Mary Rogers, the most celebrated and tragic young beauty of the age.

III

Left Home on Sunday

ON THE MORNING OF SUNDAY, July 25, 1841, with the temperature climbing toward 93 degrees, Mary Rogers rose before dawn and helped to prepare breakfast for the lodgers in her mother's Nassau Street boardinghouse: boiled eggs, oatmeal porridge, and milk toast. Next, she saw to the morning laundry, stoked the fires, and swept the halls. After three hours, with her morning chores completed, she prepared to go out for the day. She dressed in her Sunday finest: a white cotton frock with a bright blue scarf tied at her neck. Anticipating a hot day, she chose a light straw hat and carried a summer parasol.

"The quiet of a Sabbath morning in the city is in marked contrast to the confusion and hubbub of the week," wrote a diarist of the time. "On Sundays it is as quiet as a cathedral. Broadway, on which Old Trinity stands sentinel at one end, and aristocratic Grace at the other, is swept clean and is deserted. An occasional coach, bringing to the hotels a Sabbath traveler, or a solitary express wagon loaded down with baggage, is all that breaks the solitude. The broad, clean pavement of Broadway glistens with the morning sun, and is as silent as the wilderness. The revelers, gamblers, the sons and daughters of pleasure, who ply their trade into the small hours of the morning, sleep late; and the portions of the city occupied by them are silent as the tomb."

Shortly before ten o'clock, Mary knocked at the door of her fiancé Daniel Payne's room. Payne, who was in the middle of shaving, spoke to her through a half-opened door. Mary informed him that she had made plans to visit her aunt, Mrs. Downing, and accompany her family to church. Mrs. Downing lived on Jane Street, fifteen minutes away by omnibus (the horse-drawn coach that carried commuters up and down Broadway). Mary told Payne that she planned to return in the early evening, so he arranged to meet her at the corner of Broadway and Ann, in front of Barnum's Museum, so that he might escort her safely back to Nassau Street.

Nothing in Mary's behavior struck Payne as out of the ordinary. She appeared to be, as he would later insist, "cheerful and lively as usual" and very much looking forward to her day out. "Very well, Mary," said Payne. "I will look out for you." With that, Mary went down the stairs and stepped out onto Nassau Street.

Although Payne had no reason to be suspicious, there was much about Mary's story that would not have stood up to scrutiny. It would subsequently emerge that she had not told Mrs. Downing of her plan to visit, and, in fact, her aunt was not at home that morning. Perhaps Mary had planned to drop in unannounced, but it is worth noting that this pretext for leaving the house—a visit to Mrs. Downing—was the same excuse she had used to cover her disappearance three years earlier, when her unexplained absence from Anderson's Tobacco Emporium had caused such a stir.

Whatever else may have been in Mary's mind that morning, it's clear that she was having second thoughts about Daniel Payne. Phoebe Rogers disliked the hard-drinking cork cutter, and two days earlier Mary had been overheard making a "positive promise" to her mother that she would break off their relationship. Alfred

Crommelin, whose stormy departure from the premises had occurred the previous month, may have been mentioned as a more suitable prospect.

On the same day that Mary promised to stop seeing Payne, Crommelin received a note asking him to call at the boardinghouse. The message struck him as odd: It was written in Mary's hand but signed with Phoebe's name. Uncertain of what to do, he showed the note to his friend Archibald Padley as the two men walked together toward Crommelin's office. Whatever Mary wished of him, it must have been a matter of some urgency—when Crommelin arrived at his office, there was a second message written on the chalk slate that hung beside the door. This time the message was signed by Mary, and it repeated the request to call at the earliest convenience. As a further token of her visit, and perhaps as a signal of her feelings toward him, Mary placed a red rose through the keyhole of the door.

If there was romantic significance in this gesture, Crommelin failed to apprehend it. Only a few weeks earlier he had stood on the front stoop of the boardinghouse and pledged his unwavering devotion, urging Mary to call on him if she were ever in need. Now, confronted with a clear, urgent, and perhaps amorous summons, Crommelin balked. Later, he would explain that he "had been coldly received when last there," leaving him ill disposed toward the possibility of further indignities. He also mentioned, in passing, that he felt no great desire to see the smirking face of Daniel Payne, who still believed himself to be the victorious suitor. Crommelin claimed that he briefly considered paying a call on Sunday—unaware that Mary planned to be out for the day—but on further reflection he decided against it. Instead, he remained at home, in his new boardinghouse on John Street, and passed the day in the company of Padley.

Daniel Payne was also enjoying a day of ease. Having learned of Mary's plans at ten o'clock, he set off an hour later and walked to his brother John's house on Warren Street, a few steps across City Hall Park. The two of them visited a market called Scott's Bazaar on Dey Street, idly picking over the various goods on offer, then parted in front of St. Paul's Church on Broadway. Payne continued on to Bickford's Tavern on James Street, where, in keeping with Sunday tradition, the saloon's owner made a "compromise with the day" by putting his employees into clean shirts and closing up the wooden shutters halfway. Payne would later testify that he sat and "read the papers until 2 o'clock." This done, he continued to a Fulton Street eating house and took a solitary lunch. Afterward he returned to the boardinghouse and, perhaps exhausted from his study of the newspapers, took a three-hour nap.

As evening fell, Payne rose, refreshed himself at the washbasin, and set out to keep his rendezvous with Mary. Walking along Broadway, he ran across his brother coming in the opposite direction with his wife and children. He exchanged pleasantries for several minutes before continuing on to the omnibus stop beside Barnum's Museum. Only then did it occur to him that the omnibuses did not run on Sundays. Payne paused to wonder how Mary had traveled uptown to her aunt's house in the absence of her usual mode of transportation, but the question was soon driven from his head by the approach of a violent summer thunderstorm. Payne assumed, based on past experience, that Mary would not venture out in a driving rain shower, and would instead pass the night at her aunt's house and return in the morning. As the storm bore down, Payne took shelter once again at Bickford's Tavern, where he remained until nine o'clock. As the skies cleared, he returned to Nassau Street. In the front parlor he encountered Mrs. Hayes, another of Mary's aunts, who agreed with him that Mary was not likely to return until morning. Payne went upstairs to his room and retired for the night.

The following morning when Payne came down to breakfast he found Phoebe Rogers in a state of high anxiety. Mary still had not returned, and Mrs. Rogers now believed that something catastrophic had occurred. Mrs. Hayes, who had stayed the night, offered her assurances that Mary had simply lost track of time and would be along shortly. Payne shared Mrs. Hayes's view of things. Although concerned, he still believed that Mary's absence was well within the realm of normal behavior, and he thought it likely that she would return at any moment. After saying as much to Mrs. Rogers, he headed off to work as usual.

When he returned to the boardinghouse for lunch, Payne discovered that Mary was still missing. With Mrs. Rogers growing ever more alarmed, Payne volunteered to mount a search. It is probable that Payne was merely humoring Mrs. Rogers at this stage, as his search seems to have been conducted in taverns and dram shops. "It was hoped," ran one account, "that some genial companion might offer a clew as to the lady's whereabouts."

When these inquiries failed to bring results, Payne progressed up Broadway to Jane Street, where he knocked on the door of Mrs. Downing's house. There he learned that Mary had never arrived the previous day, nor had she been expected—the family had been out for the entire day.

Payne now realized that something was seriously amiss. With a gathering sense of foreboding, he launched a remarkably wideranging search, calling at the homes of various friends and relations in a trek that took him as far as Harlem and Staten Island. No one had seen Mary, or had any word of her.

By late Monday afternoon Payne realized that further measures were needed. Stopping at the offices of the New York *Sun*, he placed a missing persons ad. Unwilling to risk a repeat of the news-paper sensation caused by Mary's earlier disappearance, Payne decided to withhold her name. Instead he gave a full description of the clothing she had been wearing:

> Left her home on Sunday Morning, July 25, a young lady, had on a white dress, black shawl, blue scarf, leghorn hat, light colored shoes and parasol light colored; it is supposed some accident has befallen her. Whoever will give information respecting her at 126 Nassau Street shall be rewarded for their trouble.

This done, Payne returned to the boardinghouse and reported on his efforts to Mrs. Rogers, who had now sunk into a state of brooding lethargy. Payne retired to his room and passed an uneasy night, resolving to resume his search in the morning.

On Tuesday, in response to the newspaper notice, Payne received word from a tavern keeper on Duane Street that a young woman and her escort had passed several hours on the premises on Sunday afternoon. Payne rushed out of the house, but when he arrived at the tavern he found that the description of the young woman bore no resemblance to Mary. Undeterred, he resumed his efforts, casting his net even wider than he had the previous day. He walked to the Barclay Street ferry launch and crossed the Hudson to Hoboken, stopping to ask strangers at the ferry landing, and at three different homes in the vicinity, if they had seen a dark-haired young woman pass by. Continuing along a winding path to a wooded area known as Elysian Fields, Payne stopped to make inquiries of various people along the way, but he learned nothing of any use. Frustrated, he recrossed the Hudson and put in a brief appearance at the shop where he worked, resuming his search that evening.

Alfred Crommelin learned of Mary's disappearance on Monday, but he took no action and carried on with business as usual until Wednesday, when he was shown the previous day's missing persons notice in the *Sun*. The brief notice had a galvanizing effect. Although Crommelin had ignored Mary's earlier requests to call, he now hurried directly to Nassau Street, where he found a glassy-eyed Phoebe Rogers sitting in her parlor with Payne standing at her side. At the sight of Crommelin, Payne turned on his heel and left the room without a word, leaving Phoebe Rogers to offer a halfhearted excuse on his behalf. Payne, she murmured, had "gone to Bellevue." Payne may, in fact, have made a stop at the Bellevue hospital, which at that time dealt mainly with disease victims, but he spent most of the morning following up on several other notes that had arrived in response to his notice, all of which proved fruitless.

Crommelin, meanwhile, questioned Mrs. Rogers about the details of Mary's disappearance, and soon formed a decisive plan of action. He hurried directly to the police office, as the *Herald* would later report, "with the fixed intent of seeing Hays." This would have been Jacob Hays, known far and wide as "Old Hays," the celebrated high constable of New York, known not only for his prowess as a detective, but also for his inventive manner of controlling unruly gangs. A short and stocky man, Hays would hurl himself into the midst of even the most vicious street fight and use his gold-tipped walking stick to knock the hats from the heads of the brawlers. When the gang members bent down to pick up their hats, Hays knocked them off their feet and ordered them to go home. "He held the monopoly on catching thieves," wrote one admirer. "He was about the only constable in the state who did any business." Unfortunately, the constable was unavailable on the morning Crommelin went looking for him, and Crommelin refused to wait, believing that every moment was essential. After leaving a message for Hays, Crommelin began a search on his own, unwittingly retracing many of the steps Payne had made the previous day, including the tavern on Duane Street and the home of the friends in Harlem.

When these inquiries brought no results, Crommelin enlisted his friend Archibald Padley, proposing to carry the search to Hoboken, just as Payne had done a few hours earlier. By some accounts the two suitors missed crossing paths by a matter of minutes, though Crommelin was unaware of Payne's efforts as he made his way to the Barclay Street launch.

Although at that time Hoboken was known chiefly for its attractive greenery and "health-bearing breezes," the city also offered less wholesome diversions for those who were so inclined. Later, Crommelin would declare that if Mary Rogers had gone to Hoboken on the Sunday in question, she could only have been "decoyed there by malice." Jacob Hays and his contemporaries would have understood the inference. As Crommelin would later elaborate, something in Mrs. Rogers's account of her daughter's absence had led him to conclude that Mary was being "forcibly detained in some assignation house or some other place." Although he never said so explicitly, it is likely that Crommelin went to Hoboken intending to call in at various houses of ill repute.

As Crommelin knew, New York and its environs had a thriving and varied trade in prostitution at this time. In addition to the seedy "concert saloons of ill repute" to be found in Five Points and elsewhere, the city also offered a decidedly more refined class of brothel for the well-to-do. "No hotel is more elegantly furnished," wrote a diarist of the time. "Quiet, order and taste abound. The door swings on well-oiled hinges. The bell is answered by an attentive servant. The lady boarders in these houses never walk the streets nor solicit company. They are selected for their beauty, grace and accomplishments. They dress in great elegance, and quite as decorously as females generally do at balls, parties or at concerts."

Another commentator addressed the troubling question of how these lady boarders came to be employed in this manner: "From whence comes this unceasing supply of brilliant, well-educated, accomplished, attractive and beautiful young girls? They come, many of them, from the best homes in the land. . . . Men and women are employed in this nefarious work as really as persons are round the country to hunt up likely horses; and when the victim is uncommonly attractive the pay is large. No system is better arranged with bankers, express-men, runners and agents. . . . They hang about hotels, under pretense of being strangers to New York; they get acquainted with young lady visitors, invite them to church, to a walk, to the opera, and, when confidence is gained, they are invited to call at the house of an acquaintance; and, after a pleasant evening, they wake up in the morning to know that they have been drugged and ruined, and that their parents are in despair."

With thoughts of a drugged and ruined Mary preying on his mind, Crommelin hurried down the gangway of the Hoboken ferry and made his way north along the shoreline. Padley, trailing a few steps behind, had to hurry to catch up with his friend. He would later recall that Crommelin seemed gripped by a sense of urgency, as though Mary were not merely missing but in some immediate peril. It seemed to Padley that his friend's conscience was troubling him greatly, though he could not be certain why this should be.

Payne, meanwhile, had returned to Nassau Street, where he found Phoebe Rogers sitting ashen-faced in the parlor, twisting a linen handkerchief in her hands. Payne reported on his efforts and insisted that Mary would likely return home at any moment. Perhaps, he offered, Mary had gone to visit some friend in the country. Perhaps she had even tried to send word to that effect. The city had only two post offices, and it was not unknown for letters to miscarry.

Mrs. Hayes, who had been through this at least once before during Mary's earlier disappearance, did her best to echo Payne's reassurances. She hovered at her sister's side, patting her hands and offering words of comfort. Mary was simply off enjoying herself, she said. Like before. She would be along shortly.

Phoebe Rogers would not be comforted. She simply stared through the front windows and twisted at the square of cloth in her hands. Her life had been a catalogue of loss—four children, two husbands, and whatever small comforts she might have wished for in old age. Sighing deeply, she reached up and took her sister's hand. When she spoke, her tone was grim but resigned and matter-of-fact, as though she were pointing out the approach of a thunderstorm.

"I fear," she said, "that we shall never see Mary again."

IV

Very Clever with His Pen

IN DECEMBER OF 1835, a strange mechanical marvel, described as "the greatest and most baffling wonder of this or any other age," appeared at an exhibition hall in Richmond. Variously known as "The Turk" or the "Automaton Chess Player," the device's owner claimed that it would "engage and defeat scores of human chess players" and would "defy all attempts at explanation" of its mysterious inner workings. For Edgar Allan Poe, the appearance of the Turk would mark a turning point. In approaching the problem of the chess-playing machine, Poe demonstrated the first stirrings of what he would later call "ratiocination," or the science of deduction. Poe took up the matter as if he were a detective interrogating a suspect.

At the time of its appearance in Richmond, the chess-playing automaton already had a long and storied history. Created in 1769 by a Hungarian nobleman, the device appeared to be nothing more than a mannequin in Turkish robes and a turban sitting behind a polished wooden cabinet. Doors at the front of the cabinet opened to show a complex array of gears and cylinders. A chessboard sat on top. At the turn of a key the Turk pushed its chess pieces across the board, and moved and nodded its head as it followed the play of opponents. Sometimes, if a human player made a particularly egregious blunder, the Turk would even roll its eyes. The device created a sensation in Europe; in Paris, no less a figure than Benjamin Franklin lost a spirited match against the device.

By the time Poe saw the chess-player it had passed into the hands of a talented showman named Johann Maelzel, who burnished the device's fame with a much-publicized match against Napoleon Bonaparte. As Maelzel toured throughout Europe and the Americas, any number of treatises and so-called exposés appeared, all of them focusing on the question of whether the Turk was a legitimate mechanical marvel or an elaborate hoax, with a human operator concealed inside the cabinet to control the movements. Poe, who had recently won a position as the assistant editor of Richmond's *Southern Literary Messenger*, resolved to settle the argument once and for all, in hopes of bringing national attention to both himself and the magazine.

"Perhaps no exhibition of the kind has ever elicited so general attention as the chess-player of Maelzel," Poe declared. "Whenever seen, it has been an object of intense curiosity to all persons who think. Yet the question of its *modus operandi* is still undetermined." Poe then offered a brief discussion of other celebrated mechanical marvels, including the "calculating machine of Mr. Babbage," the precursor of the modern computer. In Poe's view, Charles Babbage's "analytical engine," however impressive, was nothing more than a mathematical machine, while the Turk was able to apprehend and counter the moves of its human opponent, a far more complicated and subtle process. If the device truly was a "pure machine," he reasoned, "we must be prepared to admit that it is, beyond all comparison, the most wonderful of the inventions of mankind."

But Poe was not prepared to make this admission, and pointed to its original presenter's description of the device as "a *bagatelle* whose effects appeared so marvelous only from the boldness of the conception, and the fortunate choice of the methods adopted for promoting the illusion." That being the case, Poe asserted, it was "quite certain that the operations of the Automaton are regulated by *mind*, and by nothing else. . . . The only question then is the *manner* in which human agency is brought to bear."

In discussing the theory of an earlier writer, Poe made an observation that would loom large in his future work: "We object to it as a mere theory assumed in the first place, and to which circumstances are afterward made to adapt themselves." In other words, as a later writer would remark, "It is a capital mistake to theorize before one has data. Insensibly one begins to twist facts to suit theories, instead of theories to suit facts." To avoid this trap in the case of the chess-player, Poe determined to clear his mind of any preconceptions about how the device might work, and draw his conclusions based solely on what he had seen with his own eyes. Dupin, Poe's detective, would take much the same approach to the problem of Mary Rogers.

Poe began with an elaborate recounting of the exhibitions he had witnessed, lingering on the manner in which Maelzel opened the doors at the front and back of the cabinet to reveal "wheels, pinions, levers, and other machinery," then held a burning candle at the rear opening to throw a bright light through the interior, "which is now clearly seen to be full, completely full, of machinery." Poe then described the movements of the Turk during the chess matches, emphasizing the manner in which the left arm and gloved hand grasped the chess pieces from above and moved them to the appropriate positions. "At every movement of the figure machinery is heard in motion," Poe reported. "During the progress of the game, the figure now and then rolls its eyes, as if surveying the board, moves its head, and pronounces the word *echec* (check) when necessary. . . . Upon beating the game, he waves his head with an air of triumph [and] looks round complacently upon the spectators."

Occasionally, Poe noted, the Turk's mechanical hand failed to grasp one of the chessmen. In these instances, the empty hand continued on to the intended position "as if the piece were in the fingers," leaving Maelzel to complete the move as the automaton had intended. In Poe's view, this was just one of several irregularities put in practice "with a view of exciting in the spectators a false idea of the pure mechanism in the automaton."

Having laid this groundwork, Poe went on to catalogue some of the "bizarre attempts at explanation" by earlier commentators, including a prevalent theory that the Turk's cabinet was designed to conceal a dwarf or small child, which Poe dismissed as "too obviously absurd to require comment." Poe's own explanation, however, was not a significant departure from this notion. "Some person *is* concealed in the box during the whole time of exhibiting the interior," Poe allowed, but he discounted the notion that this human operator must be undersized. The dimensions of the cabinet, he insisted, were larger than they seemed and "fully sufficient for the accommodation of a man very much above the normal size." He went on to describe the manner in which it would be possible for Maelzel to open and shut the doors of the cabinet, apparently displaying a solid mass of interior workings, while a human operator inside shifted his position and manipulated a series of cleverly designed clockwork panels, creating the illusion of a cabinet jammed full of complicated machinery.

Poe bolstered his argument by identifying a man named Schlumberger, a member of Maelzel's entourage who "attends him wherever he goes," but was always found to be mysteriously absent during the Turk's performances. On one occasion, Poe observed, "Schlumberger was suddenly taken ill, and during his illness there was no exhibition of the Chess-Player. . . . The inferences from all this we leave, without farther comment, to the reader."

"Maelzel's Chess-Player" offers a clear template for the deductive thinking that Poe would shortly use to great effect: a careful elaboration of the background of the case, a step-by-step recitation of the known facts, and a cunning conclusion based on an imaginative leap. Of more immediate importance for the struggling young editor, the piece received widespread attention and was reprinted many times, helping to establish Poe's reputation as a rising figure in the world of letters.

The success of Poe's essay formed a rare bright spot in a period of almost constant struggle. The appearance of a third collection of his poems in 1831 had failed to "cut out a path to reputation" as he had hoped. In the aftermath of his break with his foster father, Poe had washed up in Baltimore and sought out his aunt, Maria Clemm, one of the few remaining links to the family of his father, David Poe. Although Maria's husband, William Clemm, had been prominent in Baltimore society, his death five years earlier had left the family in financial straits. Aunt Maria had been reduced to taking in sewing and boarders to augment a modest pension drawn by her elderly mother, Edgar's grandmother, Elizabeth Poe.

Aunt Maria, known to the family as "Muddy," was a sturdy and sweet-natured woman who bore her hardships with "martyr-like fortitude," according to Poe. In addition to her bedridden mother, she cared for her two children—thirteen-year-old Henry and nine-year-old Virginia—as well as a steady stream of more peripheral relations who were down on their luck. Even so, Aunt Maria welcomed Edgar with open arms. Coming to the household after the unhappiness of Richmond, Poe formed an intense attachment to his aunt and would later describe her as "dearer than the mother I knew."

Eager to provide for his new family, Poe tried his hand at short stories. A friend would describe him as "constantly occupied by his literary labors," inspired at least in part by a one-hundred-dollar prize on offer in a Philadelphia newspaper contest. Although he failed to win, Poe's work impressed the editors greatly. Five of his stories would appear in the newspaper in 1832, including "Metzengerstein," which tells of a noble orphan who exacts a supernatural vengeance on those who have wronged him.

Although Poe had turned to writing short stories out of necessity, it was a form in which he would show uncommon ability. A later essay, a review of Nathaniel Hawthorne's *Twice-Told Tales*, showed that he had given a great deal of thought to the "short prose narrative." Poe believed that the success of these shorter tales depended on brevity—"requiring from a half-hour to one or two hours in its perusal"—to permit the necessary "unity of effect or impression," and he laid down a famous dictum that would inspire generations to come: "In the whole composition there should be no word written, of which the tendency, direct or indirect, is not to the one preestablished design."

While Poe bent to his labors, Maria Clemm took it upon herself to act as an intermediary between her nephew and local publishers. "I attended to his literary business," she later recalled, "for he, poor fellow, knew nothing about money transactions. How should he, brought up in luxury and extravagance?" Poe literally could not afford to be discouraged. The following year, when Baltimore's *Sunday Visiter* offered a fifty-dollar award for the best prose tale submitted, he fired off six submissions, claiming the prize with the now-famous "MS. Found in a Bottle," the haunting story of a ghostly ship and its spectral crew who find themselves at the brink of a terrifying abyss. The prospect of passing into an unknown realm both horrifies and stimulates the unnamed narrator: "It is evident that we are hurrying onward to some exciting knowledge," he declares, "some never-to-be-imparted secret, whose attainment is destruction."

Poe, who was living in fear of debtor's prison, desperately needed the *Visiter* prize. "The impression made," noted one of the magazine's judges with considerable understatement, "was that the award in Mr. Poe's favor was not inopportune." In spite of his gratitude and relief, however, Poe also felt a stinging sense of injustice, believing that he should also have won a twenty-five-dollar prize offered for poetry. He became so incensed when he discovered that the prize had gone to one of the paper's editors, who had submitted under a pseudonym, that the two men came to blows in the street. Though only twenty-three, Poe had already cultivated a lifelong habit of quarreling with editors.

Soon enough, Poe was forced to swallow his pride and appeal to John Allan for assistance. He sent several letters in an effort to repair the breach, declaring himself "ready to curse the day when I was born," and describing conditions of abject poverty. "I know that I have no longer any hopes of being again received into your favour," he wrote, "but, for the sake of Christ, do not let me perish for a sum of money which you would never miss." Well aware that Allan had become hardened to his pleas, Poe also had Aunt Maria write on his behalf, describing him as a worthy soul who had fallen into temporary difficulty. In time Allan relented, asking a Baltimore friend to inquire into Poe's debts and offering twenty dollars "to keep him out of further difficulties."

In February of 1834, Poe learned that Allan was seriously ill. Fearing the worst, he traveled to Richmond in hopes of a final reconciliation. According to one account, Allan's second wife,

Louisa, answered Poe's knock, but did not recognize the shabby and haggard figure who stood before her. Upon being told that Allan was too ill to receive callers, Poe forced his way past and burst into the sickroom. At the sight of Poe, Allan brandished his walking stick and threatened to strike if he came within reach. For a long moment the old man simply glared at his foster son; then he ordered him from the house.

Six weeks later, John Allan was dead. Any hopes Poe might have had for reconciliation, or even a token bequest in deference to the wishes of Frances Allan, were dashed. Poe received nothing: Allan had made good on his oft-stated threat to cast Poe out "without a shilling." In one of his last letters, Poe had written that "when I think of the long twenty-one years that I have called you father, and you have called me son, I cry like a child to think that it should all end in this."

Returning to Baltimore, Poe sank still further into destitution. At one stage he was reported to be laboring in a brickyard. When a friend, John Pendleton Kennedy, invited him to Sunday dinner one evening, Poe found himself in the embarrassing position of having to refuse "for reasons of the most humiliating nature": His clothes were simply too threadbare. The sympathetic Kennedy resolved to lend assistance, and recommended Poe as "very clever with his pen" to Thomas Willis White, the publisher of Richmond's *Southern Literary Messenger*. In time White offered Poe an editorial position at a salary of fifteen dollars a week, and held out a tentative prospect of advancement.

As desperate as he was, Poe had mixed feelings about trading the warmth of Aunt Maria's household in Baltimore for the painful associations of Richmond. He knew that life as a hired hand on the *Messenger* would mark a considerable decline from the life he had known when he lived in the Allan household. He would no longer be able to move about in Richmond society, or mix freely with the friends of his youth. Worse yet, he knew that there were still whispers about him and his past behavior, both real and imagined. One story even had him stealing silver and linens after the funeral of Frances Allan.

Nevertheless, by the summer of 1835 Poe had reestablished himself in Richmond, intending to help the *Southern Literary Messenger* make good on its stated intention "to stimulate the pride and genius of the South." Poe soon made his mark, impressing Thomas White with his talent and editorial ability. Over the course of his tenure Poe would oversee every aspect of production—dealing with printers, editing copy, soliciting submissions, and writing reviews, poetry, and editorial filler. From the first Poe demonstrated a shrewd grasp of the principles that would distinguish his own fiction. When White objected to a macabre story Poe had submitted, the young assistant wrote of the value to be found in "the ludicrous heightened into the grotesque: the fearful coloured into the horrible: the witty exaggerated into the burlesque: the singular wrought out into the strange and mystical." He allowed as how White "may say all this is bad taste," but, he insisted, "to be appreciated you must be *read*, and these things are invariably sought after with avidity."

Almost immediately, however, Poe felt an overpowering sense of loneliness at his separation from his Aunt Maria and cousin Virginia, whom he hoped would join him in Richmond. When word reached him that another cousin, Neilson Poe, had offered to become Virginia's guardian, and perhaps bring Maria into his home as well, Poe fell into despair. In his view Neilson's offer threatened to cut him off from the only true family he had ever known, isolating him not only from Aunt Maria but also Virginia, whom he now intended to make his "darling little wifey."

It is difficult to track the stages by which Poe developed romantic feelings for his young cousin, who was barely nine years old when he began living under Aunt Maria's roof. He is thought to have looked elsewhere for companionship when he first arrived in Baltimore—and one account has the young Virginia acting as a courier for his love letters—but the penniless and unemployed suitor did not find favor with the families of the young ladies he courted. Although it was fairly common for close cousins to wed, Virginia had only recently turned thirteen when Poe began at the *Messenger*, and her extreme youth placed the idea of marriage outside the conventions of the time. Neilson Poe's offer of guardianship may well have been an expression of his discomfort over the suitability of the match.

Although Maria Clemm had made no decision about accepting Neilson's offer, Poe responded to the possibility in terms of devastating loss and betrayal. He wrote an anguished (and likely drunken) letter to his aunt, begging her to refuse. "Oh, Aunty, Aunty you loved me once," he wrote, "how can you be so cruel now?" Writing as he had once done with John Allan, he dangled the prospect of suicide—"I have no desire to live and *will not*"—and he finished the letter with a direct appeal to Virginia: "My love, my own sweetest Sissy . . . think well before you break the heart of your cousin."

With this distress weighing him down, Poe threw himself into a round of heavy drinking, much to the alarm of Thomas White, who had founded his magazine on principles of moral rectitude and the "chaste empress" of temperance. White had become fond of Poe and tried to show compassion. For a time Poe was assigned to lighter duties in the hopes that he would recover his "more amiable" nature. When this failed, White discharged him amid grave misgivings about Poe's mental state. "I should not be at all astonished," he admitted, "to hear that he had been guilty of suicide."

In desperation Poe returned to Baltimore in September of 1835 and managed to persuade the Clemms to reject the comfort and stability of Neilson Poe's offer in favor of a decidedly less certain future with him. According to some accounts, Poe put the seal on his obligation by taking out a marriage license at the Baltimore County courthouse.

The following month Poe brought Virginia and Maria to Richmond, and took pride in having the family "residing under my protection." Poe's departure had left the *Messenger* short-staffed, so Thomas White readily agreed to give him a second chance, but with the understanding that Poe would give up the bottle. "No man is safe who drinks before breakfast!" White cautioned. Determined to mend his ways, Poe threw himself into the work of reviewing and editing. By the end of December, White had increased his responsibilities, noting with satisfaction that Poe "still keeps from the Bottle." The editorial burden was heavy. Although Poe reprinted some of his own early stories, he had little time to write new ones. Significantly, one of the few original efforts he wrote during this period was based on a true crime, anticipating his interest in the Mary Rogers saga.

The Beauchamp-Sharp murder case, more widely known as "The Kentucky Tragedy," unfolded in 1825 when a young woman named Ann Cooke was seduced and cast aside by Colonel Solomon P. Sharp, the Kentucky solicitor general. After giving birth to Sharp's child, the aggrieved Cooke turned to another suitor, an attorney named Jeroboam O. Beauchamp, and promised that she would marry him if he agreed to avenge her honor. When Sharp refused Beauchamp's challenge to a duel, the attorney donned a mask and stabbed his rival to death. After a lengthy and sensational trial, Beauchamp received a death sentence. On the eve of his execution, Cooke joined him in his cell and the star-crossed lovers attempted suicide with both laudanum and self-inflicted stab wounds. Cooke died that night, but Beauchamp survived long enough to be hanged the next day.

The drama would inspire works by several of Poe's contemporaries—including Charles Fenno Hoffman, William Gilmore Simms, and Thomas Holley Chivers—and a century later it would provide inspiration for Robert Penn Warren's *World Enough and Time*. With its Southern setting and tragic young heroine, the case would also seem to have been an ideal subject for Poe and the *Messenger*. Mysteriously, Poe chose to present it as "Politan," an Italian-themed drama set in sixteenth-century Rome, written in blank verse. Even Poe's admirers were baffled. When early portions of the work appeared in the *Messenger*, John Pendleton Kennedy, Poe's early benefactor, gently suggested that he might find a more congenial form in French farce. Duly chastened, Poe left the drama unfinished.

Poe had better luck with the literary criticism he wrote for the *Messenger*. In addition to his other duties, he wrote nearly one hundred critical pieces over the course of some ten months. An especially notable review centered on a novel by Theodore Fay called *Norman Leslie*, which took its inspiration from a sensational New York murder case. Poe dismissed the work as "the most inestimable piece of balderdash with which the common sense of the good people of America was ever so openly or so villainously insulted." In fact, the good people of America had rather liked the book, which had been a runaway bestseller, and it had enjoyed particular praise in the pages of the New York *Mirror*. As it happened, the author Theodore Fay was also one of the editors of the *Mirror*, a fact Poe lost no time in pointing out. Whatever justification Poe may have felt in exposing this self-aggrandizement, the ferocity of his review caused the literary establishment to rally to Fay's side. Poe would be made to suffer for his impudence.

In May of 1836, after several months in Richmond, Poe and Virginia Clemm were officially married in a small ceremony performed at their boardinghouse. A witness would attest that the bride was twenty-one years of age, though in fact she was not yet fourteen. By all accounts, Virginia had a cherubic face, dark brown hair, and captivating violet eyes. Friends often spoke of her gentle manner and uncanny ability to bring out her moody groom's better nature. In her presence, an admirer declared, "the character of Edgar Allan Poe appeared in its most beautiful light."

Mindful of his cousin Neilson's promise of security and education, Poe made every effort to compensate. A friend recalled that he "devoted a large part of his salary to Virginia's education, and she was instructed in every elegant accomplishment at his expense. He himself became her tutor at another time, when his income was not sufficient to provide for a more regular course of instruction. I remember once finding him engaged, on a certain Sunday, in giving Virginia lessons in Algebra." On the rare occasions when finances allowed, Poe would provide her with a piano and a harp.

Whatever Virginia's talents as a student and musician, Poe is reported to have felt considerable discomfort over her youth. One frequent visitor of the time recorded that "although he loved her with an undivided heart he could not think of her [at first] as his wife, as any other than his sister, and indeed he did not for two years assume the position of husband, still occupying his own chamber by himself." It has been suggested that this arrangement persisted until the bride reached the age of sixteen.

Not surprisingly, elements of Poe's unorthodox marriage would soon make themselves felt in his work. In "Eleonora," the most unequivocally romantic story he ever wrote, the narrator speaks of his obsession with the beauty of "the sole daughter of the only sister of my mother long departed," with whom he lived innocently for many years until, one fateful evening "at the close of the third lustrum of her life," they fell into one another's arms. In fact, Virginia was well short of completing her third lustrum, or five-year period, at the time of their marriage. Be that as it may, the awakening of love in Poe's story is expressed as both a release and an imprisonment: "A change fell upon all things," he wrote, as if "the God Eros" himself had conspired in "shutting us up, as if forever, within a magic prison-house of grandeur and of glory."

Significantly, there was room for three in the magic prison-house: "I, and my cousin, and her mother." Whatever else may have attracted Poe to his cousin, he embraced the fact that his marriage to Virginia had forged a deeper bond with Aunt Maria. Having successfully transferred the Baltimore household to Richmond, Poe declared himself confident of a bright future: "My health is better than for years past, my mind is fully occupied, my pecuniary difficulties have vanished, I have a fair prospect of future success—in a word, all is right."

It would not remain so for long. Despite his happiness at home, Poe developed feelings of resentment toward the *Messenger* and its editor, Thomas White. Although Poe's efforts had helped to increase the magazine's readership sevenfold, and brought a profit in excess of ten thousand dollars, Poe continued to be paid what he considered a "contemptible" wage. Poe would later complain that "my best energies were wasted in the service of an illiterate and vulgar, although well-meaning man, who had neither the capacity to appreciate my labors, nor the will to reward them." Despondent, Poe once again found solace in alcohol, drawing a series of rebukes from White. "Mr. Poe was a fine gentleman when he was sober," observed a clerk at the *Messenger*. "But when he was drinking he was about one of the most disagreeable men I have ever met." In January of 1837, Poe and the *Southern Literary Messenger* parted ways, with White declaring, "I am as sick of his writings as I am of him."

Whatever the justice of Poe's grievances, his failure at the *Messenger* was largely his own doing, establishing a pattern he would repeat again and again throughout his career. As his literary talent flowered, so too did his genius for self-destruction, with the result that nearly every triumph was immediately nullified by an alcoholic binge or other reckless behavior. Having struggled so earnestly to win the position in Richmond and succeed in his duties, he chafed against the creative restrictions placed upon him. His resentment grew when he found himself "debased and degraded" by having to ask White repeatedly for more money, as he so often had done with his foster father. "Men of genius ought not to apply for my aid," Allan had once told him. The remark had been intended as a jibe, but Poe sincerely believed a talent such as his ought to be placed above such things. He knew that Thomas White had profited handsomely through their relationship; it galled him that he could barely feed himself or his family.

With nothing to hold him in Richmond, Poe gathered up his household and moved to New York in February of 1837, drawn by the same economic forces that had also brought Mary Rogers and her mother to the city that year. For both Poe and the cigar girl, like the thousands of others who flowed into the city that year, New York held out the promise of a bright new beginning.

PART TWO

The Unpleasantness at Sybil's Cave

". . . and when I came to my senses, I found she was dead."
A woodcut illustration from *A Confession of the Awful and Bloody Transactions in the Life of Charles Wallace,* a fictional account of the Mary Rogers case published in 1851.

Courtesy of American Antiquarian Society

———⊰⊱———

Really—really, the newspapers are becoming the only efficient police, the only efficient judges that we have.
—James Gordon Bennett, the New York *Herald*,
August 9, 1841

The nose of a mob is its imagination. By this, at any time, it can be quietly led.
—Edgar Allan Poe, marginalia

———⊰⊱———

V

A Person of Chastity

BY THE SUMMER OF 1841, according to an editorial in New York's *Daily Graphic*, the "infernal crowding and overbuilding" of lower Manhattan had reached a crisis. Any further construction, the newspaper warned, must be rejected for fear that Wall Street and its environs might "literally sink beneath the crushing weight of new arrivals." Indeed, only a few years earlier, a pair of enterprising hucksters had caused a sensation with a scheme to sever the "afflicted area of the city" by means of a giant crosscut saw. In this manner, it was supposed, the offending section would be transformed into a free-floating, heavily populated raft, which could then be rowed out between Governors and Ellis islands by means of enormous wooden oars attached at the east- and west-side gunwales. Once downstream, the floating city would be turned end-for-end and safely reattached to the mainland, effectively redistributing its weight.

Although this ambitious plan never came to fruition, it reflected a growing fear that New York would soon burst at the seams. By 1841, the population of the city stood at just over 300,000, having swelled from 123,000 over the course of only twenty years. In hot weather, residents complained, the conditions were fast becoming intolerable. "The heat of a New York crowd is stultifying," wrote one newsman in the summer of 1841. "Together with the funk of teeming humanity and free-roaming animals, it forms a wet, suffocating blanket."

"Warm weather!" wrote Charles Dickens, making his first visit to the city the following year. "The sun strikes upon our heads at this open window, as though its rays were concentrated through a burning-glass. . . . Was there ever such a sunny street as this Broadway! The pavement stones are polished with the tread of feet until they shine again; the red bricks of the houses might be yet in the dry, hot kilns; and the roofs of those omnibuses look as though, if water were poured on them, they would hiss and smoke and smell like half-quenched fires." The scant "refreshment from the heat" Dickens found lay "in the sight of the great blocks of clean ice which are being carried into shops and bar-rooms; and the pineapples and water-melons profusely displayed for sale."

For many others, refreshment from the heat could be found across the river in New Jersey, a short steamboat ride across the Hudson from the Barclay Street launch. There, on a poplar-lined strip of the Hoboken shore known as Elysian Fields, courting couples strolled arm in arm along winding pathways, while children darted among the trees and threw pebbles at straw targets. As the afternoons wore on, the ladies raised their parasols against the hot sun, and the men fetched cooling water from the open pavilion at Sybil's Cave, on a rocky outcropping known as Castle Point, where a natural spring bubbled up within a chamber of hewn rock. It formed "a beautiful promontory," according to one visitor, and a perfect place in which to "lave the parched lip of youth." Local officials liked to claim "healthful, restorative properties" for the waters drawn from the spring at Sybil's Cave, and frequently likened it to the fountain of youth. For those whose tastes ran to something stronger, ales and whiskeys could be had in the taproom at nearby Mansion House, a local hostelry, or farther afield at road-houses such as Nick Moore's Tavern, up the River Walk in Wee-hawken.

The idyllic setting also provided a venue for entertainments of various sorts. P. T. Barnum staged an ambitious "Grand Buffalo Hunt" in June of 1843, complete with a lasso-twirling horseman sporting Indian war paint. The event was free, and a staggering 24,000 people crossed from New York to see the spectacle—with half of the steamboat profits going to the canny Barnum. "Unfortunately for the seekers after excitement," wrote one spectator, "the sedative qualities of Hoboken's atmosphere produced such an effect on the 'wild untamable' animals that they refused utterly to be disturbed in their meditations, and the only real hunt that took place at the time was that for sufficient refreshment with which to regale the famished multitude."

The tranquil atmosphere proved better suited to a popular new game called "town ball," or baseball. In 1846, Elysian Fields would host the first "official" baseball game, which offered a great deal of action, if not much competition, as the New York Nine gave the rival Knickerbockers a 23–1 drubbing.

Baseball and buffalo hunts aside, Elysian Fields offered the "heated and tired inhabitants of the metropolis" with a place to "enjoy the pleasures and health-bearing breezes of the Country," noted the New York *Tribune*, "without purchasing them at the dear rate of sweating over country roads." For many, the lush greenery offered sanctuary of a different sort: "All the unfortunate beings that crowd a large city seem to go to Hoboken to get rid of their sorrows," offered the *Herald*. "The beauty of its groves—the picturesqueness of its cliffs and creeks—the deep mystery of its wild woods seem to charm all unfortunates to find their solace there."

Such was the case on Wednesday, July 28, 1841, when New Yorkers awoke yet again to scorching heat, with the temperature threatening to break 90 degrees for the tenth consecutive day. By midafternoon Elysian Fields was swarming with refugees from the city. One young stock clerk, driven from his office by the stifling conditions, recalled an atmosphere of "snappish enervation," as though the heat had now taken the form of "an unwanted house-guest."

Henry Mallin, a young vocalist and music instructor, debarked at the Hoboken ferry landing shortly after three P.M. With him were two friends, James Boulard and H. G. Luther, and perhaps one or two others. Together the group strolled north along the river toward the pavilion at Sybil's Cave. "The walk is beautiful," noted one visitor. "On the left are the steep marble cliffs, bare in most places, and overhung with deep green trees of the forest. On the right, the waves of the Hudson, rippling up the shore with a gentle murmur."

As the group neared Sybil's Cave, Mallin and Boulard spotted a strange object floating in the river. It appeared, as they later testified, to be "a body floating between two tides, two or three hundred yards from shore." Rushing to a nearby boathouse, they jumped into a wooden scull and rowed out from shore. As they drew near, there came "an evil shock": The body proved to be that of a young woman, hideously bruised and waterlogged, floating on her back with her arms crossed stiffly at her chest, and a cloud of dark hair pulsing like seaweed in the water.

Reluctant to touch the corpse, Mallin and Boulard snatched up a wooden plank from the bottom of the boat and attempted to use it as a hook to tow the body back to shore. After several attempts they managed only to strike a series of flailing blows, tearing at the white fabric of the dead woman's dress. Tossing the plank aside, they managed at last to fix a length of rope under the corpse's chin. The two men then rowed back to shore, trailing the body behind the boat. Unwilling to risk contact with the rotting flesh, they declined to drag their cargo out of the water. Instead they fastened their towrope to a heavy boulder and anchored the body to shore, so it would not float back out into the river. This done, the pair spent several moments watching the battered corpse bob up and down at the end of its tether. After half an hour or so, Mallin and Boulard decided that there was nothing more to be done. Leaving the body anchored to the boulder, they rejoined their friends and wandered off along the water's edge.

During this time, a large crowd had gathered along the shoreline. With the departure of Mallin and Boulard, a pair of stouthearted bystanders screwed up their courage and waded into the water to pull the body onto land. A reporter from the *Herald* happened to be on the scene as the young woman was dragged ashore. "The first look we had of her was most ghastly," he wrote. "Her forehead and face appeared to have been battered and butchered to a mummy. Her features were scarcely visible, so much violence had been done to her. On her head she wore a bonnet—light gloves on her hands, with the long watery fingers peering out—her dress was torn in various portions—her shoes were on her feet—and altogether she presented the most awful spectacle that the eye could see."

On shore, the body suffered further indignities as a long line of morbidly curious bystanders filed past. Some of them prodded the corpse with their feet while others poked at it with sticks. One "rude youth" went so far as to reach down and lift one of the legs, offering "unfeeling remarks" to his companions.

At this moment, Alfred Crommelin and Archibald Padley, the two former tenants of the Rogers boardinghouse, were making their way up the River Walk. As they hurried north, a small boy ran past in the opposite direction, shouting the news that a girl's body had been brought ashore at Castle Point. Wordlessly, Crommelin and Padley changed direction and hurried to the spot. As they approached the outcropping and saw the knot of bystanders huddled around the sodden corpse, Crommelin felt his throat constrict. As he pushed his way to the water's edge, the crowd parted to let him through, sensing the urgency of his manner. As Crommelin's eyes ran the length of the body, he felt a combination of revulsion and dread. Kneeling beside the corpse, he took the extraordinary step of ripping open the sleeve of the dead woman's dress. For a moment he rubbed the discolored skin of the bare arm, then gently lowered it, apparently having satisfied himself on some final point of identification. "Dear God!" he cried. "This is Mary Rogers! Oh, God—the news may kill her mother!" Ashen-faced, he crouched protectively over the body until the crowd dispersed.

Dr. Richard H. Cook, the New Jersey coroner, was the first official on the scene, arriving within an hour of the discovery of the body. Cook was accompanied by two jurors, in anticipation of a coroner's inquest. According to New Jersey law, however, it was necessary that a justice of the peace take charge of the investigation. It soon emerged that the nearest available candidate, the Honorable Gilbert Merritt, was several miles away in Secaucus. While a messenger summoned Justice Merritt, Dr. Cook fretted over the corpse. The excessive July heat was causing the remains to "consume themselves" at a greatly accelerated rate. If an autopsy was not performed soon, Cook feared, there would be nothing left to examine.

Indeed, according to one bystander who saw the body coming ashore, it was difficult to imagine that the "ruined figure" bore any relation to the beautiful young woman from Anderson's Tobacco Emporium. After three days in the water, followed by several hours in the hot sun, the body appeared to Dr. Cook to be "nightmarish in its injuries," and he watched in despair as the dead woman's features putrefied before his eyes. So horrible were the ravages of exposure that Alfred Crommelin had identifed her not so much by her battered face as by her clothing and by the delicate shape of her feet. Crommelin's seemingly strange action of tearing open the dead woman's sleeve had allowed him to recognize a distinctive pattern of hair on her arm, confirming his identification.

At last, shortly after 7:00 in the evening, Gilbert Merritt arrived on the scene. After receiving a terse report from Dr. Cook, the justice of the peace ordered that the body be removed to a nearby building. There, while Merritt began assembling witnesses for an inquest, Dr. Cook began his autopsy.

Cook's first concern was to establish the cause of death. Justice Gilbert had assumed on arrival that the young victim had fallen off a boat and drowned, but Cook had reason to doubt the conclusion. The doctor had previously examined some sixteen or seventeen drowning victims, and the case before him differed from the earlier instances in several key respects. "The face when I examined it was suffused with blood—bruised blood," he later testified. "There was frothy blood still issuing from the mouth, but no foam, which issues from the mouth of persons who die by drowning. Her face was swollen, the veins were highly distended. If she had been drowned there would not have been those particular appearances that I found in the veins." To confirm his findings, Cook used a scalpel to make an incision along one of the veins in the arm. "The blood was so much coagulated," he noted, "that it was with difficulty I could get it to follow the lancet at all. If she had been drowned the discoloration would have been in the cellular tissue and not in the veins." Furthermore, the position of the arms was inconsistent with death by drowning. Both arms were found bent over the chest, and remained so on the examining table—so rigid that considerable force had been required to straighten them. In drowning cases, Cook noted, the arms were invariably extended.

Further conclusions were made difficult by the appalling condition of the face—the skin had now turned a purplish black—but Cook was able to make out signs of bruising along the neck. He discovered a deep bruise about the size and shape of a man's thumb on the right side of the neck, near the jugular vein, and several smaller bruises on the left side resembling the shape of a man's fingers. These marks, Cook stated, "led me to believe she had been throttled and partially choked by a man's hand."

As he made to examine the marks more closely, Cook's fingers brushed up against a small mass behind the left ear. "This for some time escaped my attention," he later admitted. "I observed a crease round the neck [and] passing my hand behind her ear, I accidentally felt a small knot; and found that a piece of lace . . . was tied so tightly round her neck as to have been hidden from sight in the flesh of the neck; this was tied in a hard knot under the left ear." Now, only one conclusion was possible: Mary Rogers had been strangled to death.

As he undressed the body, Cook made a further discovery: The lace cord used to strangle Mary Rogers had been torn from the trimming of her underskirt. This finding, coupled with the thumb and finger marks around her neck, led the coroner to conclude that Mary Rogers had, in essence, been strangled twice. First, he reasoned, the attacker had grabbed her by the throat with one hand, choking off her air until she lost consciousness. Then, as she lay senseless, the attacker tore a strip of fabric from her skirts and pulled it "fast round her neck"—so tightly that the thin cord sank deep into the flesh—insuring that she would never regain consciousness.

Having found the victim's undergarments in disarray, Cook's examination now turned to matters of "so delicate a nature," as the *Herald* would report, that they could not be fully reported in the columns of a respectable newspaper. The coroner's fears were quickly confirmed: A cluster of bruises and abrasions in the "feminine region" forced him to conclude that Mary Rogers had been "abducted, brutally violated by no fewer than three assailants, and finally murdered."

A grim sequence of events now came into focus. The dead girl's arms, Cook concluded, were positioned "as if the wrists had been tied together, and as if she had raised her hands to try to tear something from off her mouth and neck, which was choking and strangling her." Abrasions on the left wrist, along with corresponding marks on the upper side of the right wrist, confirmed that her hands had been lashed together with sturdy rope. "The hands had been tied, probably, while the body was violated," Cook concluded, "and untied before she was thrown in the water." Though the ropes had been removed, a loop of fine muslin—carefully torn from another of the undergarments—was found hanging loosely at the young woman's throat. Cook reasoned that the fabric had been used as a gag. "I think this was done to smother her cries," he said, "and that it was probably held tight around her mouth by one of her brutal ravishers."

Cook also found large patches of raw skin on the victim's back and shoulder bones, which he believed to be the result of "the young girl struggling to get free, while being brutally held down on her back, to effect her violation." Cook felt confident in stating that these marks had been made before death, because "coagulation had been found in the cellular tissues." He concluded that "this outrage was effected while she was laid down upon some hard substance, a hard board floor, the bottom of a board, or something similar. It convinces me fully that the outrage was not effected on a bed."

Cook could not state with any confidence whether the murder had taken place during or after the assault, nor could he say whether or not the young woman had been conscious when the lace cord had been tightened about her throat. Following the murder, however, it was clear that the body had been dragged along the ground for some distance. A foot-wide strip of the white dress had been ripped from the hem to the waist, then wound three times around the body and tied as a "sort of hitch," to serve as a handle by which the corpse could be pulled to the riverbank. Although several items of clothing were missing, the corpse had evidently been dressed with some care after death: "I consider that her hat was off her head at the time of the outrage," Cook noted, "and that after her violation and murder had been completed, it was tied on." Cook took special pains to emphasize that the hat's ribbons had been fastened under the dead woman's chin with "a slip knot, not a lady's knot . . . a sailor's knot." The phrase would loom large in the later stages of the investigation.

The coroner conducted his examination with remarkable speed, but even so it was well past eight o'clock by the time he finished. Given the lateness of the hour, it would undoubtedly have been best to postpone the official inquest. In the circumstances, however, Justice Merritt could not be certain of reassembling his witnesses the following day, so he proceeded as soon as Dr. Cook emerged from the examining room. Apart from Cook himself, only four witnesses were called—Alfred Crommelin and Archibald Padley, who had identified the remains, and John Bertram and William Walker, who had watched the drama unfold as the body was brought ashore. Strangely, the men who actually fished the corpse out of the river were not called to the stand. Henry Mallin had presented himself at the scene only to be told that he would not be required to testify.

The testimony of Bertram and Walker left only a faint imprint on the official record, though Walker asserted with apparent pride that he had "been of some use" in securing the body to a boulder. Alfred Crommelin, by contrast, had a great deal to say, detailing how he had immediately recognized the body of the "drowned female" and had "made use of every proper means" to identify her—including tearing open her sleeve and rubbing her bare arm. By this time Crommelin had evidently decided that he would serve not only as the spokesman for the Rogers family, but also as the guardian of the dead woman's memory. He spoke in glowing terms of her character, describing her as "the officiating member of her family" and "the main support of an infirm and aged mother—with the whole charge of conducting the boardinghouse." Furthermore, he insisted, he had "never heard her virtue questioned in the least."

Archibald Padley's testimony followed, confirming Crommelin's sentiments in every respect, but the bulk of the proceedings were given over to Dr. Cook, who gave a detailed summary of his autopsy findings. At one stage, a wave of sentiment seems to have overwhelmed the doctor's scientific impulses. He declared that the murdered girl had "evidently been a person of chastity and correct habits." The conclusion, as many critics would note, seemed difficult to verify given Cook's earlier assertion that she had been "violated by no fewer than three men." It is probable that Cook's gentlemanly, if unscientific, conclusions owed something to the concern Alfred Crommelin had expressed for the dead woman's reputation. If so, Cook would regret the impulse. Though he could not have realized it at the time, his statements would draw considerable fire in the weeks to come, with accusations ranging from medical incompetence to cruel insensitivity.

In fact, weighed against the standards of the day and the unusually rapid deterioration of the corpse, Cook's autopsy was remarkably thorough. As he told Justice Merritt and the other jurors, the conclusion was inescapable: Mary Rogers had been savagely beaten, tied down, and "horribly violated by more than two or three persons." Either during or after the assault she had been partially choked by one of her attackers, and finally strangled to death with a makeshift garrote torn from her own clothing. Her body was then dragged some distance over hard ground and dumped into the Hudson River, apparently in the hope that it would never be found. Without question, Cook stated, this was the most "bestial" crime of his experience.

The jurors deliberated briefly before returning a verdict that the death had been caused by "violence committed by some person or persons unknown." The inquest adjourned shortly before nine o'clock. Due to the late hour and "in consequence to the great heat," Justice Merritt and Dr. Cook oversaw a hasty burial of the body in a crude double coffin, under only two feet of earth. In this manner, as they would later explain, they preserved the possibility of a second examination at a later time.

Even now, the coroner apparently felt some reservations over the identification of the body, in spite of Alfred Crommelin's certainty in the matter. Accordingly, Cook provided Crommelin with an assortment of personal effects to carry back to Phoebe Rogers. Although Crommelin viewed them as simple keepsakes intended to comfort a bereaved mother, the broad range of items—including various swatches of clothing, the flowers from the straw hat, a garter, a shoe, and a lock of hair—indicate that Cook was seeking a second confirmation of the victim's identity.

With these items wrapped in brown paper and tucked under his arm, Crommelin set out for the Hoboken ferry landing. He reached the pier shortly before eleven o'clock, only to find that the last ferry had already gone. He made his way to a second ferry landing in Jersey City, but the boats there had also stopped running. With no other means of getting back to his rooming house in New York, Crommelin put up in the Jersey City Hotel for the night.

Earlier, Crommelin had sent Archibald Padley back to the city to convey the sad news to Mrs. Rogers. By the time Padley reached the boardinghouse, however, he found that Mrs. Rogers had already been notified. Henry Mallin and his friends—the group that had pulled the body from the river—had returned to New York several hours earlier, upon learning that they would not be called to testify at the inquest. One of the men, H. G. Luther, presented himself on Nassau Street to deliver the unhappy news.

Luther arrived at seven o'clock that evening and found a grim-looking Phoebe Rogers seated in her drawing room, with Daniel Payne hovering protectively at her side. Taking his hat in his hands, Luther steeled himself to say what he had come to say. Neither Mrs. Rogers nor Payne had ever met Luther before. Mary had been missing for three days at this stage, and it was perhaps natural that her mother and fiancé would have braced themselves for bad news. Even so, Luther found the pair's reaction inexplicable. He would later report that they had received the news with a curious lack of emotion, amounting almost to polite indifference. Stranger still, Payne took no action that evening. The hour was still early enough that he could have gone to Hoboken if he had wished. It would have been natural enough in the circumstances to hope that a mistake had been made, and that the body pulled from the river had not been Mary's after all. Even if he had learned of Crommelin's presence at the scene, and accepted his rival's identification of the body, it seemed peculiar that he should not have hurried to the side of his dead fiancée, if only to see to the disposition of her remains. Instead, he remained at Nassau Street, and left it to others to bury the woman he loved.

Luther, for his part, would never forget the strangely bloodless response to his devastating news. "Neither of them seemed much distressed by it," he would later recall. "I distinctly felt that the news was not unexpected."

VI

The Dead House

DRESSED IN BLACK, and with a dark wool shawl wrapped tightly around her head, Phoebe Rogers stepped onto the front stoop of her boardinghouse and stood blinking in the hot sun. Leaning heavily on the arm of Daniel Payne, her late daughter's fiancé, Mrs. Rogers appeared far older than her sixty-three years. "It was impossible to trace the lineaments of the daughter's beauty and vivacity in the features of the sorrowing mother," wrote one observer. The lined face, stooped shoulders, and faltering step gave Mrs. Rogers "the air of an inexpressible burden," as though her recent loss had "extinguished any will toward life."

With Payne at her side, Mrs. Rogers walked slowly up Nassau Street toward City Hall. Passing to the rear of the building, she made her way to the so-called Dead House, a small wooden building that served as a makeshift examining room. As the grieving woman approached, a stir passed through the small knot of reporters and other bystanders gathered outside. As Mrs. Rogers mounted the steps, the men straightened and removed their hats.

Robert Morris, the recently elected mayor of New York, was absent from the city in the days following Mary Rogers's murder. Morris, an outspoken advocate of police reform, had been supervising a fire crew's response to a burning building when gang members commandeered a pumper wagon and turned its hoses on him. Although he was not injured, Morris felt it wise to remove himself to a distant and presumably drier locale for a fortnight. In his absence, it fell to Elijah Purdy, his lieutenant, to respond to growing disquiet over the death of the beautiful cigar girl.

Purdy's actions were unusually decisive, and calculated to show that City Hall had taken charge. On August 11, 1841, at Purdy's request, a trio of gravediggers exhumed the body of Mary Rogers from its shallow grave in Hoboken. The remains were then handed over to officials of the New York Coroner's Office and carried back across the river for a more rigorous examination. As a further signal of City Hall's resolve, Phoebe Rogers was summoned to make a positive identification.

Purdy's request marked the end of nearly two weeks of apparent indifference toward the fate of Mary Rogers. "A fortnight has now elapsed since the perpetration of one of the most daring and murderous outrages ever perpetrated in a community calling itself civilized," wrote the *Herald*. "Yet we hear of no clue arrived at, and but very little exertion made for the discovery and punishment of the brutal ravishers and murderers." To a large degree, this inertia stemmed from a simple border dispute between New York and New Jersey. In the view of New York's officials, Mary Rogers's murder had occurred in Hoboken, and was therefore the responsibility of New Jersey. In Hoboken, meanwhile, the New Jersey police were quick to absolve themselves of the burden on the grounds that Mary Rogers was a resident of New York. To bolster their position, New Jersey authorities put forward a theory that the young woman had been murdered in New York and set adrift in the Hudson, only to have the remains float across jurisdictional boundaries into New Jersey. The dispute soon escalated, and within a few days the two cities began arguing over river currents:

"It is well known that at the time the body was first discovered, there was, and had been a prevalence of north and north-easterly winds for almost a week previous," declared a New Jersey partisan. "In all such cases a very powerful current is produced. Now then, had the murder, as alleged, been committed in Hoboken, the body could not possibly have *left* the shore such a distance, while so strong a current was setting against it. For proof it is only necessary to point you to the numerous instances in which decomposed substances thrown from the docks in the upper part of the city are found lying upon the opposite shores."

Below the surface, the clash had more to do with money than shifting currents. Both jurisdictions were well aware, but unwilling to admit, that there could be little hope of progress in the Mary Rogers case without the offer of a generous reward. "It is well known," complained a writer in the *Sun*, "that in the present inefficiently organized state of our Police Department, little will be done towards detecting the authors or perpetrators of this awful crime without the promise of a cash bounty." Gilbert Merritt, the New Jersey justice of the peace, was well aware of the problem. The day after he presided over the coroner's inquest, Merritt wrote to the governor of New Jersey to request that a large sum be earmarked for the capture of the murderers. He was flatly refused. In New York, Elijah Purdy also declined to put up city funds, insisting that he did not "deem it necessary." Both sides clung to the belief that the responsibility, financial and otherwise, lay on the opposite side of the Hudson.

The stalemate pointed up the dismal state of New York's law enforcement, which had not progressed much beyond the seventeenth-century "rattle watch," the brigade of uniformed men who patrolled the streets with noisemakers, calling out the hour and the latest weather report. At the time of the Mary Rogers murder, New York did not have a centralized, full-time profes-sional police force. Instead, a pair of constables was assigned to each neighborhood, together with roundsmen and marshals who cobbled together a living out of court fees and private rewards. Their efforts were supplemented by a patchwork corps of watch-men, made up of moonlighting day laborers and retired ser-vicemen, who patrolled the streets and stood guard outside sentry boxes. "They were known as 'Leatherheads,' a nickname which arose from the fact that they wore leather helmets, something like an old-fashioned fireman's helmet, with a broad brim behind," wrote George Walling, who joined the force in 1847. "Twice a year these hats received a thick coat of varnish, and after a time they became almost as hard and heavy as iron. The only insignia of office which these old fellows had, besides the leather helmet, was a big cloak and a club; at night they also carried a lantern."

To the city's gang members, the leatherheads were little more than a source of amusement. "Youthful and exuberant New York-ers considered that an evening out was not spent in the Orthodox manner unless they played some rough practical jokes on the poor, old, inoffensive Leatherheads," Walling recalled. "It is recorded of such a staid young man as Washington Irving, even, that he was in the habit of upsetting watch-boxes if he caught a 'Leatherhead' asleep inside; and on one occasion, so it is said, he lassoed the box with a stout rope, and with the aid of companions dragged it down Broadway, while the watchman inside yelled loudly for help."

Adding to this sense of ignominy were the meager fees offered for serving warrants and summoning juries, which left many on the force looking for alternative sources of income. It was not un-common to find large rewards offered to constables for the return of stolen property, which in turn led to charges of collusion be-tween criminals and police over the spoils. The *Herald* charged that

New York's police were "mere loafers on the public—selling their duties to the highest bidder—and only suppressing crime or catching rogues when private individuals come forward to offer money for the performance of public duties."

Against this backdrop of political infighting and police inefficiency, the Mary Rogers investigation stagnated until pressure from the New York press forced City Hall to take action. By that time, however, Mary Rogers's remains had festered for eleven days in a coffin of rough pine, rendering a second coroner's examination largely meaningless. Even so, the New York inquest went forward as planned, if largely for the sake of appearances.

"Difficult it would be for the most imaginative mind to conceive a spectacle more horrible or humiliating to humanity," observed the New York *Journal of Commerce*. "There lay, what was but a few days back, the image of its Creator, the loveliest of his works, and the tenement of an immortal soul, now a blackened and decomposed mass of putrefaction, painfully disgusting to sight and smell. Her skin, which had been unusually fair, was now black as that of a negro. Her eyes so sunk in her swollen face as to have the appearance of being violently forced beyond the sockets, and her mouth, which 'no friendly hand had closed in death' was distended as wide as the ligaments of the jaw would admit, and wore the appearance of a person who had died from suffocation or strangulation. The remainder of her person was alike one mass of putrefaction and corruption on which the worms were reveling at their will."

Mercifully, Phoebe Rogers was spared this spectacle, as the advanced state of decomposition was thought too horrific for the aged woman to bear. Daniel Payne, however, was judged to be of sterner stuff. While Mrs. Rogers waited in an antechamber, the young man was led away to the examining room. The *Times and*

Commercial Intelligencer described the scene in language usually re-
served for the "yellow-back" novels of the day: "And as if nothing
should be wanting to send the moral home to men's hearts, and
render it more painfully impressive, the young man who was to
have been, in a few days, married to her, now stood beside the
rough box in which all that remained of her he loved was lying.
Her whom but a few days back, he had seen 'exulting in her
youth,' filled with life, hope and animation, whom he so ardently
wished to make his wedded wife, to fold to his bosom, to press to
his 'heart of hearts,' now lay before him an inanimate mass of matter, so hideous, horrible and offensive that the bare idea of coming
into contact with it was almost sufficient to make the gorge rise."

Payne, by one account, could manage only a stiff nod to acknowledge that the moldering remains were indeed those of his
fiancée. Meanwhile, a coroner's assistant prevailed upon Phoebe
Rogers to identify the long white dress her daughter had been
wearing on the day of her disappearance. Even this, according to
the *Journal of Commerce*, was not for the faint of heart, being "so
discolored and half-rotten as to render it almost impossible to be
identified, and so impregnated with the effluvia from her person
that scarcely any person would venture to touch or examine it."
Apparently Mrs. Rogers weathered the ordeal with some distinction, identifying the dress "beyond the shadow of a doubt" on the
strength of an old tear in the fabric, which she and her daughter
had repaired with a distinctive pattern of stitchwork.

Although the official identification was now complete, Daniel
Payne's troubles were far from over. Earlier that day he had given a
lengthy deposition to city magistrates, acquitting himself honor-
ably in the eyes of the police, but the press scented blood. The following day, as Mary's remains were reinterred behind a church on
Varick Street, reporters picked over Payne's account of his actions

in tones ranging from outrage to ridicule. Payne had testified that Mary intended to visit her aunt, Mrs. Downing, on the Sunday morning of her disappearance, but she had not said so to her mother or anyone else. Was this, the press wondered, a deception on the part of Mary—who, by some accounts, was later seen in the company of another man—or was Payne lying to cover his own guilt? His alibi for the afternoon in question, a three-hour nap, was far from convincing. His story of arranging to meet Mary at an omnibus stop was also held up to suspicion, as was his statement that he did not keep the appointment because of a thunderstorm. "Far be it from me to cast any suspicion upon anyone," wrote a correspondent in the *Tribune*, but "Payne's evidence is very inconclusive and unsatisfactory on many points—he fancies the omnibuses run on Sundays, and because it rained he would not go and meet her to whom he was engaged to be married."

Speculation mounted as a new detail came to light. A few days before her disappearance, Mary and her mother had a heated exchange that ended with Phoebe extracting a promise that her daughter would not marry Payne. The quarrel had been overheard by the housemaid, and soon made its way into the press, fueling rumors that Mary had broken the engagement. It was thought by some that Payne might have killed her in a jealous rage.

Even Payne's supporters were forced to concede that he had not behaved in a gentlemanly fashion. "Some persons think that Payne should be arrested," said a writer in the *Atlas*. "If the authorities have satisfied themselves of the *truth* of his statement, which they ought to have done, we cannot see what suspicion can lie against him. The only curious circumstance was that on hearing of the murder the lover did not go to see his betrothed. This may be accounted for by the subsequent testimony of Alfred Crommelin, which states that Payne is a dissipated man."

Under fire, Payne responded with indignation. On August 13 he wrote a letter to the *Times and Evening Star* objecting to the manner in which the newspaper had conspired "to throw a doubt on the mind of the public" as to his whereabouts on the fatal Sunday. He promised to produce affidavits that would "entirely exculpate me with regard to this horrible affair." Three days later, Payne presented himself at the newspaper's offices carrying sworn statements from his brother and from three of the tavern keepers and restaurant owners who had served him on the Sunday in question. In addition, Payne brought letters from Phoebe Rogers and her cousins, Mrs. Hayes and Mrs. Downing, attesting to the "earnest nature" of his efforts to locate Mary after her disappearance. Taken together, the seven affidavits corroborated every word of Payne's deposition to the authorities. The *Times* immediately backpedaled. "No one can read the affidavits," the paper stated, "without feeling that Mr. Payne stands exonerated from even a shadow of suspicion." The other newspapers quickly followed suit.

It is significant that Payne felt obliged to plead his case to the newspapers, and that they required a higher standard of proof than the police. "It is certain that the public look more to this paper now," boasted the *Tattler*, "rather than to the police, for an elucidation of the mystery." If the tone of the coverage grew a little smug, the city's editors had cause for satisfaction: Their efforts had goaded City Hall into action. Many of them had been patrons of Anderson's Tobacco Emporium when Mary held court there, and felt personally invested in the capture of her killers. "Who caused any stir to be made to discover the murderers of Mary C. Rogers?" thundered the New York *Atlas*. "Why, the Press!"

For all of that, even the press had been slow to take notice. In the days immediately following the discovery of the body there had been no mention in any of the newspapers, and little reason to suppose that the murder would stand out among the dozens of other unreported and unsolved cases of stabbing, drowning, and domestic violence that had occurred over the course of the summer months. Almost a week elapsed before the first scattered reports of the crime appeared, and even then the notices were buried in the back columns, under neutral headings such as "Police Office" and "City Affairs." It was not until the first week of August that the Mary Rogers case was singled out and promoted to front-page news. "The murder is of such an atrocious character," declared the *Daily Express*, "as to demand that it be taken forth from the ordinary police reports, to be made a matter of especial attention, in order, if possible, to arouse inquiry as to the murderers."

The reasons for calling for "especial attention" had more to do with personal agendas than with the crime itself. Each of the city's editors had a private grievance against City Hall, with concerns ranging from police powers and judicial reform to universal temperance and moral rectitude. In each case the tragedy of Mary Rogers seemed to provide a potent symbol. To some, she was an innocent lamb led to the slaughter, illustrating the failures of law enforcement. "Our city is all but helpless," wrote the *Commercial Advertiser*. "Whose sister or daughter will be next?" To others, Mary Rogers was a "fallen woman" led astray by the weaknesses of the flesh, an emblem of New York's descent into depravity. "One word to the young ladies into whose hands this paper may fall," wrote the *Advocate of Moral Reform*, "a voice from the grave—from an untimely and dishonored grave—speaks to you in tones of warning and entreaty. Had Cecilia Rogers loved the house of God—had she reverenced the Sabbath—how different had been her fate!"

As the press drumbeat gathered force, a thriving if morbid carnival atmosphere sprang up at Elysian Fields. "The curiosity and crowds continue at Hoboken," noted the *Herald*, "and the name of poor Mary Rogers is on every lip." Families and courting couples spread out their picnic lunches on the spot where the body came ashore. The headmistress of a New York girls' school brought a delegation of her young charges to Castle Point, where she delivered a cautionary lecture on the wages of sin.

As the drama took hold of the public imagination, the apparent indifference of the police and public officials brought renewed protests. "Nothing tending to elucidate the mystery hanging over the murder of poor Mary has yet transpired at the Police Office," wrote the *Herald*. Instead, the public appetite for news was being fueled by "stories made to suit the gullibility of the gaping crowd . . . but, on enquiry, they are all found to be like the baseless fabric of a vision." Each new rumor, no matter how baseless, commanded several columns of newsprint. One story held that Mary Rogers had been spotted on the fatal Sunday near Theater Alley, walking arm in arm with a young man with whom she appeared to be on intimate terms. Another had it that a "well known person" had fled the city to escape arrest. Accounts of similar crimes in distant cities were circulated in the hope that they might throw light on the case.

The newspapers rose to new heights of indignation when Alfred Crommelin, Mary's rejected suitor, came forward with his theory that she had been carried off to a house of ill repute and murdered there. "Was it not perpetrated in one of the hundred assignation houses which are permitted to exist by our grave administration of criminal justice?" asked the *Herald*. "Ought not every one of these dens to be searched at once for traces of violence, murder and blood? More than one person has been engaged in this horrid crime—it cannot hide forever."

"Murder will out," insisted the New York *Sunday Mercury*, and the press would be the instrument "adopted to help it out." The

Mercury liked to claim credit for being the first newspaper to bring attention to the crime. "We must remember," one editorial noted, "that it was in these pages the ghastly matter first came to public notice." While it was true that the *Mercury* was among the first— with an article that managed to botch the victim's name and address, along with the date of the crime—the real force behind the reporting of the Mary Rogers murder lay with James Gordon Bennett, the editor of the *Herald*, a man once described by an envious competitor as having "no more decency than a rutting pig."

No less a figure than Walt Whitman would describe Bennett as a "reptile marking his path with slime wherever he goes and breathing mildew at everything fresh and fragrant." But even his most bitter critics were forced to admit that Bennett's path was bold and innovative, having made the *Herald* "impudent and intrusive" at a time when the more established sixpenny press had receded into bland uniformity. Often described as the father of yellow journalism, Bennett claimed with characteristic bluster that his paper would "outstrip everything in the conception of man." Later, he expanded on the point: "What is to prevent a daily newspaper from being made the greatest organ of social life? Books have had their day—the theaters have had their day—the temple of religion has had its day. A newspaper can be made to take the lead of all these in the great movements of human thought. . . . A newspaper can send more souls to heaven, and save more from Hell, than all the churches and chapels in New York—besides making money at the same time." Bennett was in no doubt as to the role he himself would play in this revolution: "Shakespeare is the great genius of the drama, Scott of the novel, Milton and Byron of the poem—and I mean to be the genius of the newspaper press."

Born in Scotland in 1795, Bennett emigrated to the United States at the age of twenty-four. He would later claim to have been seized by a sudden impulse to see the birthplace of Benjamin Franklin, though he seems also to have been seeking an escape from family pressure to enter the priesthood. Tall and gangly, Bennett had long hair, a small chin-beard, and a pair of crossed eyes that left him acutely self-conscious about his appearance. In later years he liked to recall how he had once been chased out of a bordello, having been informed by the ladies of the evening that he was "too ugly to come amongst us."

On his arrival in America, Bennett spent several years living hand-to-mouth as a proofreader, translator, and freelance journalist. In 1827, at the age of thirty-one, he joined the staff of the New York *Enquirer*, where much of his time was spent covering the "hollow-heartedness and humbuggery" of political life in the early days of Tammany Hall. His outspoken style earned him a stint as the paper's Washington correspondent, where he offered a blunt and entertaining commentary on the city's political landscape and social pretensions: "Do you see that lady at the Northwest corner of the second cotillion?" one dispatch ran. "The caputography of her head would puzzle a corps of engineers."

By 1835 the combative Bennett had left the *Enquirer* and burned his bridges with nearly every other editor in town. With a grubstake of five hundred dollars, he decided to strike out on his own. He found a cheap basement office on Wall Street, stretched out some pine boards across a pair of flour barrels, and sat down to compose the first issue of the New York *Herald*. The new journal, Bennett promised, would offer "good sound, practical common sense, applicable to the business and bosoms of men engaged in every-day life. We shall endeavor to record facts on every public and proper subject, stripped of verbiage and coloring, with comments when suitable, just, independent, fearless and good tempered. If the *Herald* wants the mere expansion which many journals possess, we shall try to make it up in industry, good taste, brevity, variety, point, piquancy, and cheapness."

Priced at one cent, Bennett's *Herald* joined the "Penny Press" tradition of Benjamin Day's *Sun*, which set its sights on the working classes and relied on street sales at the hands of newsboys, as opposed to the annual subscriptions offered by the larger, upper-class "blanket" sheets such as the *Commercial Advertiser* and the *Evening Post.* "Everybody wonders how people can buy these receptacles of scandal, the penny press," wrote the diarist Philip Hone, "and yet everybody does encourage them; and the very man who blames his neighbors for setting so bad an example, occasionally puts one in his pocket to carry home to his family for their and his own edification."

From the first, Bennett aimed at the widest possible audience—"the journeyman and his employer—the clerk and his principal"—in the belief that he could attract the wealthy society readership as well as the man on the street. He resolved to "astonish some of these big journals that now affect to look down on us with scorn." From his first issue, Bennett courted controversy. "The man was never happier than when he was firing broadsides at his betters," noted a rival journalist. "He was born for a scrap." From time to time Bennett's clashes boiled over into actual combat, with the result that on one occasion a parcel labeled "For Mr. Bennett Only" was found to contain a crude bomb, rigged to detonate when opened. Bennett escaped injury when he noticed grains of black powder trickling out of the box.

Every so often a disgruntled reader would confront Bennett on the street and express his dissatisfaction by lashing the editor with a horsewhip. Once, when an assailant's whip snapped in two across Bennett's shoulders, the editor politely picked up the pieces and handed them back to his attacker. Even his former employer James

Watson Webb of the *Enquirer* felt moved to violence on several occasions. Webb, who had a habit of touting favored stocks in return for under-the-table "considerations," was indignant to find his integrity questioned in the pages of the *Herald*. Not content to flail away with his walking stick, Webb forced Bennett's jaws open and spat down his throat. Bennett responded with unflappable humor: In attempting to bash open his head, Bennett suggested, Webb "no doubt wanted to let out the never-failing supply of good humor and wit which has created such a reputation for the *Herald*, and appropriate the contents to supply the emptiness of his own thick skull."

Webb later took his revenge in the form of a boycott of the *Herald* and the "moral pestilence" of its editor, uniting the city's rival newspapers in a campaign designed to drive Bennett out of business. Advertisers were urged to withdraw their patronage, and hotel owners were advised to refuse service to anyone seen carrying a *Herald*. "The creed of us *all*," wrote Webb, "should be—*purchase* not, *read* not, *touch* not."

In Bennett's view, this "Moral War," as it came to be known, sprang from his denunciation of "the affected prudery of society." He found it "ridiculous and false" that journalists such as himself were obliged to observe the vapid pieties of the day, resorting to such tortured euphemisms as "the branches of the body" in reference to arms and legs, and "inexpressibles" for personal articles of clothing. With gleeful verve, Bennett prepared to do battle: "Petticoats—petticoats—petticoats—petticoats—there—you fastidious fools—vent your mawkishness on that!"

In truth, Bennett's offenses were not quite so trivial as he liked to pretend. Webb's outrage had less to do with intimate garments than with Bennett's religious provocations. In May of 1840 Bennett had seized on a religious charity event to denounce the Pope as a "decrepit, licentious, stupid Italian blockhead" and to ridicule the doctrine of transubstantiation as "the delicious luxury of creating and eating our divinity." Not surprisingly, the city's clergy took issue. Bennett watched with satisfaction as a "Holy Alliance" of church and press railed against him, recalling that a similar campaign of name-calling had helped to propel Martin Van Buren into the White House. "These blockheads are determined to make me the greatest man of the age," he wrote. "Newspaper abuse made Mr. Van Buren chief magistrate of this republic—and newspaper abuse will make me the chief editor of this country. Well—be it so, I can't help it."

No less controversial was Bennett's claim to have advanced the cause of journalism by "discovering and encouraging the popular taste for vicarious vice and crime." Polite society was scandalized when the *Herald* presented a sensationalized account of the murder of Helen Jewett, a "beautiful but erring" twenty-three-year-old prostitute. The young woman had plied her trade in a luxurious brothel known as "The Palace of Passions" on Thomas Street, three doors down from a police station. On a Sunday morning in April of 1836, an unknown assailant bludgeoned her to death with a hatchet and then attempted to set the body on fire. Four neighborhood watchmen responded to the disturbance and doused the smoldering corpse with water from a backyard cistern, while various clients—*en deshabillé*, in Bennett's phrase—sought to remove themselves from the premises.

As one might expect in a journalistic climate that quailed at the mention of body parts, the other newspapers did not see the Jewett murder as a fit subject. Bennett felt otherwise. The *Herald* had been in business for less than a year at the time, but Bennett had already blazed a path in the virtually uncharted realm of crime reporting. Six years earlier, as a reporter for the *Enquirer*, Bennett covered a sensational murder trial in Salem, Massachusetts, involving two young men charged with the murder of a retired sea captain. The case drew national interest, with no less a figure than Daniel Webster joining the prosecution, but as the press gathered at the courthouse, the state attorney general dictated a set of restrictive guidelines intended to preserve the "solemn dignity" of the process. Bennett recoiled in anger, expressing his indignation in terms that would mold his future: "It is an old, worm-eaten Gothic dogma of Courts to consider the publicity given to every event by the Press as destructive to the interests of law and justice. . . . *The press is the living Jury of the Nation.*"

The sentiment would remain close to Bennett's heart throughout his career. At the same time, as he soon came to appreciate, there was nothing quite like a "gripping and horrific" murder to sell newspapers. From the moment he caught wind of the Helen Jewett story, Bennett sensed its explosive potential. Eager to capitalize, he took the unprecedented step of visiting the scene personally to report on the crime. His firsthand account, written in a breathless, immediate tone, gave him an excuse to linger over the salacious details, such as the moment when a police officer lifted a linen covering to allow him a glimpse of the corpse: "What a sight burst upon me! I could scarcely look at it for a second or two. Slowly I began to discover the lineaments of the corpse as one would the beauties of a statue of marble. It was the most remarkable sight I ever beheld. I never have and never expect to see such another. 'My god,' I exclaimed. 'How like a statue! I can scarcely conceive that form to be a corpse.' Not a vein was to be seen. The body looked as white, as full, as polished as the purest Parisian marble. The perfect figure, the exquisite limbs, the fine face, the full arms, the beautiful bust, all, all surpassed in every respect the Venus de Medici."

The dead woman, Bennett soon discovered, had been no ordinary "daughter of the pave." Born in Maine to a destitute family,

Helen Jewett had been taken in and given an education in the home of a local judge, only to lose her "honor and ornament" and fall into the ways of sin. Arriving in New York at the age of nineteen, she found her way into the service of Rosina Townsend, whose house on Thomas Street was thought to be one of the most orderly and genteel brothels in the city. Jewett soon cultivated a devoted circle of patrons, offering them companionship that extended beyond the usual services of such an establishment. She accompanied her gentlemen callers to the theater, darned their socks, and wrote them letters—as Bennett would report—filled with "apt quotations from the Italian, French and English poets." Bennett expressed a hope that the murderer of this "remarkable but wayward" young woman would soon be brought to justice.

By the morning following the discovery of the body, the police had recovered a bloody hatchet wrapped in a long blue cloak at the rear of the Townsend house. Within hours, a nineteen-year-old clerk named Richard Robinson had been seized at a boardinghouse on Dey Street. The son of a prominent Connecticut family, Robinson had come to New York to gain experience in business, and soon gained a reputation as a young rake. Initially, the case against him appeared inarguable. Rosina Townsend and several others testified that he had been with Helen Jewett in her room on the night of the crime. The hatchet used in the murder matched one that had gone missing from the shop where Robinson worked. The blue cloak found at the scene appeared identical in style to one that Robinson had worn on the night in question, though he denied owning such a garment until confronted with the testimony of witnesses.

Reporting on the case in the *Herald*, Bennett assumed at first that Robinson was guilty, and the discovery of a diary, under the name of "Frank Rivers," that purported to describe the young man's sexual exploits seemed to guarantee Robinson's conviction. But as the evidence mounted, the contrarian Bennett decided to swim against the tide. Robinson, he proclaimed, was in reality a "young, amiable and innocent youth" who had been wrongly accused by a corrupt police force "which is rotten to the heart." Bennett attempted to explain away the bloody hatchet and cloak, and laid out a dubious theory that a scorned woman had committed the crime. "How could a young man perpetrate so brutal an act?" he asked. "Is it not more likely the work of a woman? Are not the whole chain of circumstances within the ingenuity of a female, abandoned and desperate?" Bennett fixed his suspicions on Rosina Townsend, whom he described as an "old miserable hag who has spent her whole life seducing and inveigling the young and old to their destruction."

It is impossible to say whether Bennett actually believed his own rhetoric or simply recognized that taking a contrary position would boost the sales of the *Herald*. In either case, his competitors were quick to condemn him not only for championing Robinson but also for dwelling on the lurid details of the murder. William Cullen Bryant declined to discuss this "disagreeable subject" in the *Post*, while James Watson Webb wrung his hands over the *Herald*'s "moral leprosy." To protect the delicate sensibilities of female readers, a new paper called the *Ladies Morning Star* came into being, promising to offer a more palatable version of the events.

As the *Herald*'s circulation took a dramatic climb, however, the other newspapers were soon forced to follow Bennett's lead. With no fresh details emerging, the press began to fill pages with conflicting theories, false accusations, and dubious conclusions. One clergyman, who described the victim as beyond redemption, actually expressed approval of the murder. Other commentators traced Helen Jewett's moral degradation to the effects of popular literature. Bennett himself noted with concern that a portrait of Lord Byron hung in her bedroom, while a copy of the poet's *Don Juan* was found among her effects. He declared that the book "has no doubt produced more wretchedness in the world than all the other moral writers of the age can check." Other newspapers took up the cry. "Avoid the perusal of novels," advised the *Journal of Public Morals*, for "it is impossible to read them without injury."

Meanwhile, the attacks against Bennett gained force. A rumor circulated that he had extorted thirteen thousand dollars in hush money from a man who had literally been caught with his pants down at the scene of the crime. "The whole story is too ridiculous to be entertained for a single moment," Bennett complained. If his rivals imagined that impugning the editor's integrity would undercut the *Herald*'s sales, they were sadly mistaken. Over the course of the Helen Jewett affair, Bennett's circulation topped fifteen thousand—passing most of his competition—and he predicted, correctly, that it would soon double.

By the time the case came to trial in June of 1836, New York was bitterly divided. Those who believed Robinson was guilty reviled him as a symbol of society's decay, while those who thought him innocent complained that he had been made a scapegoat because of his "sporting" lifestyle. Robinson's supporters packed the courtroom wearing a type of hat favored by the defendant, which came to be known as a "Frank Rivers cap." They cheered lustily for Robinson's defense witnesses, and sent up catcalls at every statement by the prosecution. Robinson's attorney portrayed the young man as an innocent led astray, and dismissed the considerable evidence against him—much of it based on the testimony of Rosina Townsend—as fatally flawed. "I am not going to say that a prostitute's oath is not legal in a court of justice," he said, "but I am going to say that eminent judges have held it very doubtful as to the credit that should belong to it." Following a three-hour summation, Robinson was acquitted after only fifteen minutes of jury deliberation.

An exultant Bennett provided his own summation of the case: "The evidence in this trial and the remarkable disclosures of the manners and morals of New York is one of those events that must make philosophy pause, religion stand aghast, morals weep in the dust, and female virtue droop her head in the dust. . . . the publication and perusal of the evidence in this trial will kindle up fires that nothing can quench." Bennett was no less grandiose in reviewing his own role in the proceedings: "Instead of relating the recent awful tragedy . . . as a dull police report, we made it a starting point to open up a full view upon the morals of society—the hinge of a course of mental action calculated to benefit the age—the opening scene of a great domestic drama that will, if properly conducted, bring about a reformation—a revolution—a total revolution in the present diseased state of society and morals."

Bennett's concern for social welfare rings a bit hollow when measured against the fact that, in all likelihood, he helped to free a guilty man. Robinson, whom a later writer branded "the Great Unhung," would spend the rest of his days coyly hinting that he had gotten away with murder. Nevertheless, although Bennett later reversed his opinion of the case, his reporting had ushered in a journalistic revolution. Crime had been plucked from the dull, matter-of-fact columns of the police reports and spun into public drama. The old guard newspapers would grouse about impropriety for years to come, but Bennett's sales figures showed that his readers had a taste for blood. It is too much to say that he created the sensational press—Benjamin Day's *Sun* and others had already opened the door—but Bennett had turned the penny press into a force that could no longer be ignored. For good or ill, the floodgates had opened.

Bennett would spend the next five years attempting to duplicate the sensation that had surrounded the murder of Helen Jewett, filling the pages of the *Herald* with murders, suicides, grisly accidents, and catastrophic fires. At times, when New York did not provide a broad enough canvas, he drew on bloodshed from overseas—a guillotine execution in France, a knifing in Russia, scenes of torture from South Africa. Bennett could scarcely have imagined that the next great newspaper phenomenon was quite literally waiting around the corner.

VII

The Sable Divinity of Night

ARRIVING IN NEW YORK at the outset of the banking panic of 1837, Edgar Allan Poe sank to new extremes of desperation. With New York and much of the rest of the country entering a six-year economic depression, Poe found that opportunities for work, literary and otherwise, were in short supply. Visitors to his lodgings would recall an atmosphere of threadbare gentility. "The rooms looked neat and orderly," remarked one friend, "but everything . . . wore an air of pecuniary want." Much the same could have been said about Poe himself. He wandered the streets in a worn black suit that Virginia and Aunt Maria kept carefully brushed—"his linen was especially notable for its cleanliness"—but few doors were open to him. A friend observed that Poe "carried himself erect and well, as one who had been trained to it. . . . Coat, hat, boots, and gloves had very evidently seen their best days, but so far as brushing and mending go, everything had been done, apparently, to make them presentable. On most men his clothes would have looked shabby and seedy, but there was something about this man that prevented one from criticizing his garments."

William Gowans, the friendly bookseller who lodged with the family, would attest that Poe spent much of his time in New York toiling away at his writing table. For some months Poe had labored to find a publisher for a collection of stories to be called *Tales of the Folio Club*. The publishing firm of Harper & Brothers gave serious consideration to the volume but eventually sent a rejection, along with a word of advice: "I think it would be worth your while, if other engagements permit, to undertake a Tale in a couple of volumes, for that is the magical number."

Poe seems to have taken the message to heart, and immediately set aside his stories to work on a novel, *The Narrative of Arthur Gordon Pym*, which he hoped would be published in the popular two-volume format of the day. Drawing on Defoe, Swift, and his own "MS. Found in a Bottle," Poe envisioned the work as a first-person account of a perilous sea voyage to the South Pole. Early portions of the work had already appeared in the *Southern Literary Messenger*, but Poe set it aside as his relations with White began to fray. Now, in New York, he resolved to finish the manuscript and Harper & Brothers agreed to publish it on terms they described as "liberal and satisfactory."

Poe envisioned the story in epic terms, as evidenced by the novel's sprawling subtitle: *"Comprising the Details of Mutiny and Atrocious Butchery on Board the American Brig Grampus, on Her Way to the South Seas, in the Month of June, 1827. With an Account of the Recapture of the Vessel by the Survivers; Their Shipwreck and Subsequent Horrible Sufferings from Famine; Their Deliverance by Means of the British Schooner Jane Guy; the Brief Cruise of this Latter Vessel in the Atlantic Ocean; Her Capture, and the Massacre of Her Crew Among a Group of Islands in the Eighty-Fourth Parallel of Southern Latitude; Together with the Incredible Adventures and Discoveries Still Farther South to Which That Distressing Calamity Gave Rise."*

As Richard Adams Locke and other artful hoaxsters had done, Poe took a special delight in obscuring the line between fact and fiction, even withholding his own name from the title page. Instead the book was presented as the work of "A. G. Pym," whose preface identified "Mr. Poe" as one of a group of gentlemen from Virginia who had expressed interest in the tale. Pym went on to explain that Poe's earlier account of the adventure, as published in the *Messenger*, had been adapted "under the garb of fiction" from an early portion of the narrative. Poe bolstered his conceit with mock diary extracts, logbook entries, and even hieroglyphic inscriptions. At a time when little was known about the Antarctic, some editors and readers accepted the fanciful narrative as fact. In a few places, extracts from the novel were reprinted as breaking news, as if Pym were a genuine pioneer sending back dispatches from a distant realm.

Reviews were mixed when the novel appeared in July of 1837, in part because the literary elite of New York and Boston had not forgotten Poe's critical thunderbolts from Richmond. Though Poe's career had barely begun, he had managed to blacken his name with a powerful cabal of literary figures, including Theodore Fay, whose novel *Norman Leslie* had been lambasted by Poe a few months earlier. Lewis Gaylord Clark, a supporter of Fay's, attacked *Pym* for its "loose and slip-shod style, seldom chequered by any of the more common graces of composition." Poe may well have heard echoes of his own attack on Fay: "There is not a single page of Norman Leslie in which even a school-boy would fail to detect at least two or three gross errors in Grammar, and some two or three most egregious sins against common-sense."

In spite of the ambivalence of the critics, Poe had reason to hope that Harpers would now consider publishing a collection of his stories. The following year, however, he managed to squander whatever goodwill he had accrued with an ill-considered piece of hack work. Harpers had recently published an expensive and lavishly illustrated book on sea creatures called *The Manual of Conchology*, prohibitively priced at eight dollars. The author, Thomas

Wyatt, hatched plans to bring out an abridged version of the work at a lower price, in hopes that it might be sold in schools. When Harpers objected, not wanting to undermine the sale of their more expensive edition, Wyatt decided that he would publish the abridgment under the name of "some irresponsible person whom it would be idle to sue for damages."

Enter Edgar Allan Poe, who assisted in editing the book and contributed a preface and introduction. Although he had withheld his name from the title page of *The Narrative of Arthur Gordon Pym*, he now accepted billing as the author of *The Conchologist's First Book: Or a System of Testaceous Malacology*. The book sold well, but Poe did not share in the royalties. Instead he received a flat fee of fifty dollars and earned the lasting enmity of Harpers. It marked a low point of his career, and charges of plagiarism and copyright infringement would dog him for years to come.

Poe now sank even deeper into what he invariably called "a state of pecuniary embarrassment." Soon enough he would declare himself ready to accept any type of work, no matter how menial— *"any thing, by sea or land"*—to lift himself out of the "literary drudgery" in which he felt trapped. He was keenly aware that he had "no other capital" apart from "whatever reputation I may have acquired as a literary man," but even this modest resource had now been squandered. After only a few months in New York, Poe found himself unable to get work of any kind. For the moment, he concluded, he would do better to try his luck elsewhere. In the early months of 1839, he abandoned New York for Philadelphia, eventually settling with his wife and mother-in-law in a small house on Sixteenth Street.

It had been more than two years since Poe left the *Southern Literary Messenger*. Although his fortunes had foundered badly in the interval, he felt reluctant to submit himself to the tastes and whimsies of another magazine publisher. Even so, in May of 1839, with no other options emerging, Poe made a tentative overture to William Burton, the publisher of Philadelphia's *Burton's Gentleman's Magazine*, about the possibility of being taken on in an editorial position.

Poe's approach to Burton provides a fair index of his desperation. By this time Poe had become an assiduous reader of reviews of his own work ("No man living loved the praises of others more than he did," one colleague remarked), and he never forgot a critical slight. Perhaps the most scathing of all the notices for *The Narrative of Arthur Gordon Pym* had come from the pen of Burton. "A more impudent attempt at humbugging the public has never been exercised," the editor declared. "We regret to find Mr. Poe's name in connexion with such a mass of ignorance and effrontery."

After two years of scrabbling, however, Poe felt he had no choice but to swallow his pride and come to Burton asking for a job. To his relief, he found the editor in a receptive frame of mind. Burton, an Englishman who had made a name for himself in Philadelphia as a comic actor, bore a passing resemblance to two of his more popular roles, Falstaff and Sir Toby Belch. A man of extraordinary energy and wide interests, he entered into the magazine business with the intention of creating a publication "worthy of a place upon every parlour table of every gentleman in the United States." When Poe arrived on the scene, only a few hundred gentlemen had seen fit to clear a space on their parlor tables for Burton's magazine, and the publisher, who divided his time between the editor's desk and the stage, needed help in the daily maintenance of the enterprise.

In June Poe's name appeared alongside Burton's as the magazine's assistant editor. Although the title was impressive, the salary was not. Claiming that his expenses were "woefully heavy," Burton started Poe off at ten dollars a week, promising a raise if the arrangement bore fruit. Burton expressed confidence that the duties would be light, requiring no more than two hours a day, leaving Poe free to pursue other "light avocation" in his spare time. Poe was in no position to bargain; Burton's wages, however meager, marked a substantial improvement. Poe's earnings over the previous two and a half years averaged less than five dollars per week.

Initially the duties were much the same as they had been at the *Messenger*. Poe contributed various filler pieces while performing basic proofreading and other technical chores. Poe also resumed the savage criticism of his *Messenger* days, and weighed in on topics ranging from mundane housekeeping tips to help with romantic quandaries.

When he was not dispensing advice to the lovelorn, Poe returned his attention to his own work and began to turn out a new series of short stories. In "The Man That Was Used Up," a military officer whose magnificent and commanding figure has been whittled away by numerous battle injuries is methodically reassembled by means of false limbs, chest and shoulder pieces, and other prosthetics. In "The Journal of Julius Rodman," an unfinished novella, Poe presented another imaginary travelogue in the style of *The Narrative of Arthur Gordon Pym*, transplanting the action to the Rocky Mountains. Once again Poe's fiction, which drew heavily on the reports of Lewis and Clark, became mistaken for fact in some quarters, with the unexpected result that portions of the story were later incorporated into a government report on the Oregon Territory.

With "The Fall of the House of Usher," published in the September 1839 issue of *Burton's*, Poe seized on the conventions of Gothic horror and spun them into an expression of psychological torment. In the process he found the notes that would form a major chord of his career. In the story the decay and ultimate destruction of an isolated mansion both mirrors and obscures the anguish of its strange inhabitant, Roderick Usher, who suffers from "a morbid acuteness of the senses." The story drew wide praise when it appeared, and brought Poe some welcome notice as a writer of serious fiction. As a result, in December of 1839 the Philadelphia publishing house of Lea & Blanchard brought out *Tales of the Grotesque and Arabesque*, a two-volume collection of all of Poe's stories to date, many of them revised for the occasion. In spite of the success of "Usher," however, the publisher had little confidence in the book and granted no advance payment or royalties. Instead, Poe had to be content with receiving twenty free copies. Reviews were mixed, with some praising the collection's "opulence of imagination" while others bemoaned the lack of "anything of elevated fancy or fine humor." The book sold poorly, and when Poe later suggested a revised edition, the publisher declined on the grounds that the original had "not yet returned to us the expense of its publication."

By this time Poe had become disenchanted with William Burton and his magazine. Where Thomas White had deferred to Poe in most matters of editorial judgment, Burton had a robust confidence in his own literary talents and seemed to regard Poe as little more than an office boy. Although the magazine had garnered a great deal of attention for "The Fall of the House of Usher" and other contributions by Poe, Burton took issue with his assistant's "morbid tone" and "jaundiced" frame of mind, which were at odds with the otherwise cheery tone of the magazine. Poe, for his part, resented the fact that Burton was not more generous with his compensation and was slow to recognize that Poe's duties were far heavier than expected. Once again, Poe found himself in the embarrassing position of having to beg his employer for loans.

By May of 1840 Burton's theatrical aspirations had progressed to the point of hatching plans to build a national theater in

Philadelphia. As his new preoccupation took hold, Burton recognized that he would no longer be able to divide his time between literature and the stage. Accordingly, he formed plans to sell the magazine. Burton, it seems, did not inform Poe, who only caught wind of the impending sale when he spotted a newspaper advertisement offering an unnamed magazine "of great popularity and profit." Realizing that his job was in peril, Poe scrambled to capitalize on his position before he lost it. He drew up a prospectus for a new literary monthly, to be called *The Penn Magazine*, in hopes of fulfilling a long-cherished dream of becoming the editor of his own journal. Poe promised a magazine that would operate "without reference to particular regions" and would be free of "any tincture of the buffoonery, scurrility, or profanity" prevailing in other publications.

Burton exploded when he learned of Poe's scheme. Recognizing that Poe's departure would undercut the sale price of *Burton's*, he bitterly rebuked his assistant and gave him his notice. By one account Poe became so enraged that he shouted abuse at Burton and stormed out of the offices. Not content to let the matter rest, Poe followed up with an angry screed: "Your attempts to bully me excite in my mind scarcely any other sentiment than mirth. . . . If by accident you have taken it into your head that I am to be insulted with impunity, I can only assume that you are an ass."

To friends and colleagues, Poe attempted to cast his departure as a matter of high principle, claiming he could not countenance Burton's underhanded editorial dealings. Burton offered a similarly self-serving version of the break, complaining that his employee's "infirmities"—a reference to Poe's drinking—had caused considerable annoyance. It was a charge Poe hotly denied. "I could obtain damages," he told one colleague. "I pledge you, before God, the solemn word of a gentleman, that I am temperate even to rigor. . . . My sole drink is water." Poe's denial is suspect to say the least, as there are several accounts of him drinking liberally in Philadelphia. On one occasion a friend reported finding him sprawled in a gutter.

Spurred on by his quarrel with Burton, Poe redoubled his efforts to launch his own journal. "I have been led to make the attempt of establishing it through an earnest yet natural desire of rendering myself independent," he wrote. "I mean not so much as regards money, as in respect to my literary opinions and conduct." Elsewhere he insisted that "if there is any impossibility about the matter, it is the impossibility of *not* succeeding." In the end, however, failure proved not only possible but inevitable. A fresh bank panic cut off whatever resources Poe might have gathered—just at the moment, as he would later claim, that his magazine was being readied for the presses.

While Poe's plans foundered, William Burton's moved ahead. In October of 1840 he sold his magazine to a Philadelphia lawyer named George Graham for $3,500. Graham already owned a magazine called *Casket*, which he now proposed to combine with *Burton's*, giving his new *Graham's Lady's and Gentleman's Magazine* a healthy subscriber base of five thousand readers.

It is often reported that Burton took a paternal interest in Poe's welfare during the sale, instructing the new owner to "take care of my young editor." In light of Burton's strained relations with Poe at the time, it seems more likely that he warned Graham of Poe's shortcomings. If so, Graham was not put off; soon after taking control of the magazine, he offered Poe a job. In spite of Poe's yearning for independence, he recognized a promising opportunity. In February of 1841 he signed on as an editor, receiving a salary of eight hundred dollars a year, a healthy increase over his earnings at *Burton's*. Graham gave him a warm welcome in the pages of the new magazine: "Mr. POE is too well known in the literary world to require a word of commendation." Better still, Poe was no longer expected to handle the entire load of proof-reading and other drudgery. Graham himself solicited and chose much of the material that ran in the magazine, a job he handled with a canny appreciation of public taste, leaving Poe free for more "elevated" contributions. It was agreed that each issue would feature an original Poe story, for which he would receive a contributor's payment on top of his salary.

On this encouraging note, Poe threw himself into his work and seems to have cultivated a genuine affection for his genial and outgoing employer. At twenty-seven, Graham was four years younger than Poe, which may have helped to place the relationship on a more collegial footing. Poe admired his young editor's willingness to spend money to make a success of the magazine, commissioning original illustrations and shunning reprinted articles and stories in favor of fresh material. Under Graham's more lenient stewardship Poe's experience and innovation came into full flower, helping to transform the magazine into an immediate success. Over the first year, the circulation took an astonishing leap from five to forty thousand subscribers.

At first, Poe appeared sympathetic to Graham's aim of attracting a broader, perhaps less aesthetic audience than he had envisioned for his own *Penn Magazine*. He initiated a popular series of articles on cryptography, resurrected from earlier freelance work, which resulted in readers submitting reams of coded messages for him to solve. Poe also resumed his literary criticism. Although he claimed to have set aside the "causticity" of his younger days, his work at *Graham's* showed little softening. Other critics, he believed, were too quick to praise, with the result that each new writer and poet who came along was lauded as a genius. "Our very atmosphere is redolent of genius," he protested. "All our poets are Miltons."

Poe's vehemence on this point owed much to his belief that his own genius had been overlooked in favor of these lesser talents. Poe's critical broadsides brought him a great deal of notice—and attacks on his perceived arrogance—but his work for *Graham's* rose to an undeniably high standard and included several of his most exceptional short stories. In "The Man of the Crowd," Poe again took up the theme of the workings of the criminal mind, as he had in "Politan" and other stories. The new story opens as an unnamed narrator sits in a London coffeehouse pondering the "tumultuous sea of human heads" that surrounds him, and marvels at the feeling of "solitude on account of the very denseness of the crowd around." Presently he spots a decrepit old man whose ragged cloak reveals a dagger and a diamond—presumably the instrument and bounty of some terrible crime. With mounting excitement, the narrator pursues the stranger into the "most deplorable" depths of the city, but when he finally confronts his prey, the old man fails even to register his presence. The narrator concludes that his quarry "is the type and the genius of deep crime. He refuses to be alone. *He is the man of the crowd*. It will be in vain to follow; for I shall learn no more of him, nor of his deeds."

Poe's growing fascination with deductive thinking, first expressed in his study of Maelzel's chess-player, was shown to extraordinary effect in the new story. In the early pages, as the narrator sits isolated behind the glass of the café, he turns his energy to scrutinizing the passing crowds in the "fitful and garish lustre" of the dying day: "The wild effects of the light enchained me to an examination of individual faces; and although the rapidity with which the world of light flitted before the window prevented me from casting more than a glance upon each visage, still it seemed that, in my then peculiar mental state, I could frequently read, even in that brief interval of a glance, the history of long years." In this fashion, the narrator is able to recognize a clerk by the protrusion of the right ear—"long used to pen-holding"—and a pickpocket by his "voluminousness of wristband." This seemingly magical trick of divining case histories from apparent trifles would be developed and refined by later writers ("Holmes! That's amazing!"), but in Poe's hands, the technique was focused inward, in an effort to plumb the secrets of the human soul "which do not permit themselves to be told."

"The Man of the Crowd" was followed by the innovative "The Murders in the Rue Morgue," a story Poe described almost offhandedly as "something in a new key." The story begins as Poe's narrator, another nameless young man seeking knowledge, offers a brief homily on the joys of deductive skill: "The mental features discoursed of as the analytical are, in themselves, but little susceptible to analysis. We appreciate them only in their effects. We know of them, among other things, that they are always to their possessor, when inordinately possessed, a source of the liveliest enjoyment. As the strong man exults in his physical ability, delighting in such exercises as call his muscles into action, so glories the analyst in that moral activity which *disentangles*. He derives pleasure from even the most trivial occupations bringing his talent into play. He is fond of enigmas, of conundrums, of hieroglyphics; exhibiting in his solutions of each a degree of acumen which appears to the ordinary apprehension preternatural." Poe continues in this vein for some time before concluding: "It will be found that the ingenious are always fanciful, and the *truly* imaginative never otherwise than analytic."

Having mapped out this ideal blending of the artistic temperament and the scientific turn of mind, Poe goes on to introduce its human embodiment, Monsieur C. Auguste Dupin. The narrator becomes acquainted with Dupin while studying in Paris, after a chance meeting in an obscure library, "where the accident of our both being in search of the same very rare and very remarkable volume brought us into closer communion." Dupin proves to be an intriguing figure. Born to an illustrious family, he had "by a variety of untoward events" been reduced to such poverty that "the energy of his character succumbed beneath it, and he ceased to bestir himself in the world." Left with a small income, Dupin contents himself with the basic necessities of life, apart from the sole luxury of an indulgence in books. Believing that "the society of such a man would be to me a treasure beyond price," the narrator elects to share lodgings with Dupin in a "time-eaten and grotesque mansion" not unlike the house of Usher. Cut off from the world, they devote themselves to reading and writing, emerging only to revel in the "sable divinity" of night.

During a long stroll one evening, Dupin reveals an astonishing talent. Though the pair had been walking in silence for some fifteen minutes, the Frenchman suddenly breaks into his companion's meditations with an offhand, conversational remark—as if in response to a spoken question—demonstrating that he has been following his friend's private thoughts as easily and accurately as if they had been spoken aloud. Thunderstruck, the narrator demands an explanation, with the result that Dupin easily reconstructs every link in his companion's chain of thought, ranging from the Orion nebula to a theatrically inclined cobbler. The narrator is dumbfounded: "I do not hesitate to say that I am amazed," he admits, "and can scarcely credit my senses."

Soon afterward, the narrator draws Dupin's attention to an unusual item in the newspaper. A shocking outrage has been discovered at a home in the "miserable thoroughfare" known as the Rue

Morgue. In the dead of night, the account relates, the neighborhood was roused by the sound of "terrific shrieks" issuing from a fourth-floor room. Summoning the *gendarmes*, a group of men forced their way into the room, only to find a scene of the "wildest disorder"—shattered furniture, valuables strewn about the chamber, and a blood-smeared razor resting on a chair, surrounded by clumps of human hair apparently torn out at the roots.

The two women who own the house, a Madame L'Espanaye and her daughter, are found to have been "fearfully mutilated." Madame L'Espanaye has been savagely beaten and her throat cut with such a violent, slashing stroke that it has "nearly severed her head from her body." The daughter is nowhere to be seen, until one of the investigators notices an unusual quantity of soot in the fireplace. Only then is it discovered that the body of the young woman, covered with scrapes and bruises, has been stuffed feet-first up the chimney.

The police are utterly baffled, and none of the investigators can supply a motive for the crime or a method by which it was committed. In addition, there is no clue as to how the killer got out of the room, as the doors and windows are found to have been locked from the inside, and the tapered chimney is too narrow to admit the passage of "a large cat," much less a human being. The two women are known to have led quiet and retiring lives, and although they lived comfortably, the killer has taken no interest in their valuables—four thousand francs in gold have been left untouched.

Matters grow more confused as the neighbors give their testimony. Although some eight or ten men responded to the sounds of violence, their accounts offer puzzling contradictions. All agree that the sounds of "two voices in loud and angry contention" were heard at the scene. The first was that of a gruff-sounding French-man, but the other, "much shriller" voice was that of a foreigner, though no two neighbors can seem to agree on his country of origin.

The newspaper accounts agree that no crime of such a "horri-fying character" has ever been committed in Paris, nor does there seem to be "the shadow of a clew apparent." In the absence of other suspects, the police arrest a bank clerk named Adolphe Le Bon, who brought the women their unusually large supply of cash only three days earlier.

After scouring the newspapers carefully, Dupin reveals that the imprisoned bank clerk once did him a service for which he is "not ungrateful." He determines to look into the matter for himself, telling his companion that an "inquiry will afford us amusement." After obtaining permission from the police to examine the murder scene, Dupin conducts a thorough investigation, demonstrating a "minuteness of attention" that leaves his friend bewildered. Apparently satisfied with what he has seen, Dupin returns home without another word, stopping along the way at a local news-paper office.

It is not until the following day that Dupin breaks his silence with the unexpected pronouncement that he has solved the case. In fact, he goes on to say, he expects one of the guilty parties to present himself at the door momentarily. Accordingly, he provides his companion with a pistol and advises him to use it if necessary.

As they await their caller, Dupin launches into a dreamy solilo-quy, giving his view of the events and explaining how he arrived at a solution. The problem, he insists, was not nearly so complex as the newspapers had supposed. The official investigators had "fallen into the gross but common error of confounding the unusual with the abstruse." To Dupin's way of thinking, the seemingly bizarre and inexplicable aspects of the case held a ready key to its solution, for "it is by these deviations from the plane of the ordinary that reason feels its way."

In visiting the scene of the crime, Dupin explains, he managed to observe much that had been overlooked. Although the windows of the murder chamber appeared to be locked and even nailed shut from inside, Dupin noticed that one of the nails had broken in two. He reasoned that the killer might have escaped by climbing through this window, only to have the sash fall closed behind him and held fast by a concealed spring. Because the sash appeared securely fastened—and the police had not noticed the broken nail—they had naturally assumed that the window had not been disturbed.

"The next question is that of the mode of descent," Dupin continues. This posed a considerable challenge, as the window looks out on a four-story drop. Dupin reveals that during his examination of the alley beside the house he noticed a slender lightning rod running near the window in question. He describes how it might have been possible, by means of the window's swinging shutters, to bridge the gap between the window and the lightning rod. Dupin admits that only a remarkably courageous and agile person could have done so.

A peculiar and seemingly self-contradictory portrait of the killer emerges. He possesses incredible strength, surpassing agility, and inhuman savagery. The murder is apparently unmotivated by greed, as evidenced by the fortune in gold francs left untouched. The sheer barbarity of the crime, with one victim's head severed and the other's corpse shoved up the chimney, strikes Dupin as "excessively *outré*" and perhaps literally inhuman. Having found a "most unusual" hair clutched in the hand of one of the victims,

Dupin forms a theory that the killer is not, in fact, a human being at all—a conclusion seemingly borne out by the strangely conflicting reports of the "shrill" and animal-like voice heard within the locked chamber. In addition, Dupin has noted an unusual pattern of bruises on the throat of Mlle. L'Espanaye—"the mark of no human hand"—leading him to suspect a gigantic and immensely ferocious beast: "the large fulvous Ourang-Outang of the East Indian Islands."

While his companion struggles to come to grips with this information, Dupin outlines the steps he has taken to prove his conclusions. The previous day, he explains, he called in at a newspaper office to place a notice to the effect that he had captured "a very large tawny Ourang-Outang of the Bornese species." The notice went on to say that the owner could reclaim the creature by applying at Dupin's address.

No sooner has Dupin described his actions than a "stout and muscular-looking" sailor appears at the door. When confronted about the crime in the Rue Morgue, the sailor breaks down and confesses all, confirming Dupin's remarkable hypothesis. The sailor explains that he brought the ourang-outang back from a long voyage in hopes of selling it, only to have it escape into the streets of Paris, brandishing the sailor's own razor. He followed the creature to the Rue Morgue and watched helplessly—his shouts of alarm mingling with the shrill screams of the animal—as it clambered through the window and attacked the two women inside. In shock, the sailor withdrew and left the ourang-outang to its fate. Although Dupin's newspaper notice had rekindled his hopes of profiting from the animal, the sailor now resolves to place the matter before the police: "I will make a clean breast if I die for it."

On Dupin's evidence the falsely accused bank clerk is immediately released, but the prefect of police is irritated at having been shown up, and indulges in "a sarcasm or two about the propriety of every person minding his own business." Dupin is unfazed. "Let him talk," he declares. "I am satisfied with having defeated him in his own castle."

"The Murders in the Rue Morgue" appeared in the April 1841 issue of *Graham's*. The story drew a great deal of favorable notice, with more than one critic praising the author as "a man of genius." Significantly, Poe appears to have drawn the name of his detective from a fleeting reference in a memoir entitled "Unpublished Passages in the Life of Vidocq, the French Minister of Police," portions of which had been reprinted in *Burton's*. A legendary figure, Vidocq was a one-time criminal who turned his talents to law enforcement, helping to create the Sureté, the detective bureau of the French police. The Frenchman is credited with bringing scientific rigor to the detection of crime, introducing such innovations as rudimentary ballistics, plaster-of-Paris molds of footprints, and a centralized criminal database. At the time of Poe's story Vidocq was still active in Paris, and would serve as inspiration for the character of Jean Valjean in Victor Hugo's *Les Miserables*. Vidocq's memoirs, though largely fanciful, had been a publishing phenomenon and would have provided a natural source of inspiration for Poe. In "Rue Morgue," Dupin would acknowledge the debt, describing Vidocq as a "good guesser and a persevering man." With characteristic arrogance, however, Dupin believed himself to be superior, arguing that Vidocq "erred continually by the very intensity of his investigations. He impaired his vision by holding the object too close."

For all of Dupin's bluster, Poe had a keen sense of his character's limitations. A handful of reviewers pointed out that there could be no great skill in presenting a solution to a mystery of the author's own devising. Poe himself was well aware that the effect of the story, however ingenious, had much to do with having been "written backwards," with the solution worked out in advance. A real-life detective such as Vidocq had no preordained solution to guide his investigations. "Where is the ingenuity," Poe would write, "of unraveling a web which you yourself (the author) have woven for the express purpose of unraveling? The reader is made to confound the ingenuity of the supposititious Dupin with that of the writer of the story."

The problem nagged at Poe. For several years he had cultivated an interest in real-life problems and ciphers, however abstruse, ranging from the open challenge of his cryptography series to his step-by-step elucidation of the chess-playing Turk. Now, he began to wonder if his newly defined science of ratiocination, as personified by Dupin, might be applied to some more concrete problem or mystery, perhaps even in an actual police investigation.

It was at that moment, at the Elysian Fields in Hoboken, that the body of Mary Rogers came ashore.

VIII

The Committee of Concerned Citizens

FROM THE BEGINNING, the Mary Rogers saga appeared bound up in the fortunes of James Gordon Bennett's *Herald*. Barely one year after cranking out his first issue from Wall Street, Bennett moved his operations to a new building on Nassau Street, a few hundred yards from the Rogers boardinghouse. Each day as Mary Rogers left the house, she would have felt the thunder of Bennett's double-cylinder steam presses churning out the latest edition, and seen the editor's name painted in tall block letters across the brick facade of his building.

Random chance had placed one of Bennett's reporters at Elysian Fields when Mary Rogers's body was dragged ashore, enabling the paper to provide a chilling firsthand account of the dead woman's "battered and butchered" features. "It almost made our heart sick," the reporter declared. In the days following, when city officials on both sides of the Hudson appeared to be doing nothing, the unsolved crime provided Bennett with a bludgeon to wield in the name of police and judicial reform. With Helen Jewett, Bennett had been obliged to strike an awkward balance between fatherly compassion and moral condemnation: The young woman had been "deserving of our sympathy and regard" but also "far gone in the ways of wickedness." No such ambiguities clouded the Mary Rogers case. This time, the dead woman was a "model of maidenly virtue" whose death stood as a "bitter rebuke" to all right-thinking New Yorkers.

On August 3, 1841, under the heading of "The Late Murder of a Young Girl at Hoboken," Bennett launched his first salvo. "It is now well ascertained that the unfortunate young girl, named Mary Rogers, (who three years ago lived with Anderson, the cigarman) has been cruelly murdered at Hoboken. Nothing of so horrible and brutal a nature has occurred since the murder of Miss Sands, which murder formed the basis of the story of *Norman Leslie*." This reference to the popular novel by Theodore Fay—which had drawn such a cutting review from Poe—would have given Bennett's readers an emotional benchmark. Fay had drawn inspiration from the saga of Levi Weeks, whose highly publicized trial for the murder of Gulielma Sands in 1800 saw him defended by Alexander Hamilton and Aaron Burr. The Mary Rogers case, Bennett was suggesting, would be no less momentous. He finished with a pointed call for action: "It now remains for the mayors of New York and Jersey cities to do their duties."

By the following day Bennett had fastened his impatience onto Gilbert Merritt, the Hoboken justice of the peace, whom he initially mistook for Richard Cook, the coroner. "The excitement which prevails in this city and in Hoboken relative to the bloody and mysterious murder of Mary Rogers—the crowds daily hurrying to the Sybil's Cave, to look on the scene of the deed, and the shore where her body was first discovered—are beginning to rouse the attention of the public authorities of this foul outrage upon a civilized community. The coroner at Hoboken is even waked up, and has published the following curious note:

In consequence of the great, though just excitement prevailing in this community, relative to the mysterious and desperate murder of Mary C. Rogers, at Hoboken, and in answer, once and for all, to the many inquiries addressed to me, concerning this most wretched tragedy, I must say, that it is far from my duty as a magistrate to give information, or to answer questions of idle curiosity. On the other hand, I deem it the duty of every individual that has the least regard for the well being of society, possessing any knowledge in the matter, to furnish me with all the facts (however remote they may be) relative to her absence and her murder.

In the meantime, I will assure anyone, giving me information, that their communications shall be held sacred and confidential, until after an interview, or until restriction is withdrawn.

With respect, sir, yours.

Gilbert Merritt of Hoboken"

Merritt's call for restraint would have struck most readers as perfectly reasonable, but Bennett was spoiling for a fight. "How utterly ridiculous is all this?" he asked. "It is now nearly a week since the dead body of this beautiful and unfortunate girl has been discovered, and yet no other steps have been taken by the judicial authorities, than a brief and inefficient inquest by Gilbert Merritt. One of the most heartless and atrocious murders that was ever perpetrated in New York, is allowed to sleep the sleep of death—to be buried in the deep bosom of the Hudson."

Bennett railed against Merritt and Cook for several days, blasting Merritt as an unfeeling bureaucrat and Cook as a bungling fool.

By the time Mary Rogers's body was brought to New York for its second postmortem examination, Bennett had cast such a taint on Cook's work that the New York authorities felt a need to distance themselves from the earlier findings. There is little doubt that Cook's original finding of death by strangulation was correct, but Dr. Archer, the New York coroner, recorded a verdict of death by drowning, in hopes of escaping the scorn of the press. "Dr. Archer states the fact that every dead body found in the rivers adjacent to this city appears, at first sight, to have died from violence," reported the *Atlas*. "He thinks that the post mortem examination at Hoboken was not minute or critical enough to decide the point." One can only wonder what Dr. Cook made of his colleague's observations, given the fact that his conclusions were based in large part on the strip of lace cord he had discovered wrapped around Mary Rogers's throat. It is doubtful that every dead body found in the Hudson shared this particular mark of violence.

This detail and many others were overlooked in a sudden if belated rush of coverage. Having learned their lesson from the Helen Jewett affair, New York's editors were careful not to yield the Mary Rogers story to Bennett and the *Herald*. By early August, after almost a week of silence in the press, Mary Rogers had become a newspaper sensation, and the city buzzed with outlandish and often contradictory speculation. The *New Era*, an advocate of moral rectitude, offered the peculiar hypothesis that Mary Rogers had been a suicide, driven to this extreme by the "troubling consequences" of having fallen into the ways of sin. As with the story in the *Atlas*, the fact that she had been found with a lace cord wrapped tightly around her neck—a condition rarely found in suicides—went unmentioned in the paper's columns.

Not surprisingly, the *Herald* was quick to shoot down any views that did not correspond with those of its editor. The suicide theory drew particular scorn as a "ludicrous piece of tomfoolery." Bennett's own presumption was that Mary had been assaulted by "blacklegs and ruffians," a reference to the city gangs which, he said, were "free to rob, rape and pillage with wild abandon, confident that authority presents no possible challenge." Bennett was not alone in laying the blame on the notorious gangs of New York. "We have surrendered our freedoms to these animals for far too long," declared the *Sun*. "It is now incumbent on right-thinking citizens to take action."

The murder had taken place at a pivotal moment in the evolution of New York's storied gang culture. As the city's economic slump, along with a growing influx of Irish immigrants, created an increasingly volatile climate, allegiances were forged according to neighborhood, nationality, and trade, and battles were fought on much the same lines. Gangs with colorful and distinctive names such as the Hudson Dusters and the Chichesters were reaching out to form political alliances, often serving to intimidate voters and stuff ballot boxes, and providing muscle to warring crews of volunteer firefighters, who battled each other for the rewards and spoils of their calling. "The city is infested by gangs of hardened wretches," wrote Philip Hone, the diarist and former mayor of New York. They "patrol the streets making the night hideous and insulting all who are not strong enough to defend themselves."

In Hone's view, Mary Rogers had "no doubt fallen victim to the brutal lust of some of the gang of banditti that walk unscathed and violate the laws with impunity in this moral and religious city." The *Herald* concurred, insisting that "the girl was taken by a gang of soaplocks and gamblers." In describing Mary's assailants as "soaplocks," a reference to the greased curls and long sideburns affected by some of the more dandyish thugs, Bennett was pointing his finger at gangs of men of the "Frank Rivers" type—sometimes known as "young sports"—who worked as clerks and journeymen by day and prowled the streets by night, and were known to congregate in a particular saloon on Broadway. These men, the *Herald* believed, "may perhaps have had the deed in contemplation for weeks or months. From her connection with Anderson's cigar store and the proximity of that establishment to that resort of gamblers, blacklegs, soaplocks and loafers known as 'Head Quarters,' it is highly probable that the crime was perpetrated by some of that lawless fraternity."

This marked a considerable contrast to the *Herald*'s stance during the Helen Jewett investigation, when Bennett defended the suspect Richard Robinson as a model of youthful probity. As always, a private agenda lay behind Bennett's public pronouncements. For years Bennett had been pressing for judicial reform and condemning the lawlessness of both New York and New Jersey. The Mary Rogers case presented him with an ideal platform on which to renew his campaign. It also offered an opportunity to settle old scores against two of his most bitter political enemies, Justice Henry Lynch and, especially, Justice Mordecai Noah.

A celebrated patriot, Major Mordecai Manuel Noah had enjoyed a colorful public career as a diplomat, playwright, and one-time high sheriff of New York. Over the course of his lifetime he would serve as editor of six newspapers, and had been at the helm of the New York *Enquirer* when Bennett rose to prominence as a Washington correspondent. The cordial relations between the two men faded when Bennett left the paper, and grew more strained when Bennett launched the *Herald* in direct competition. Noah had lined up against Bennett in the "Moral War," and was said to have instigated the charges of extortion against Bennett during the Helen Jewett affair.

In May of 1840, political maneuvering at City Hall created two new associate judgeships on the New York Court of Special Sessions. These were patronage appointments, and Lynch and Noah, as faithful supporters of the Whig party, suddenly found themselves elevated to the bench. A furious Bennett ridiculed the qualifications of both men and filled his paper with accounts of Noah's ineptitude. The new judge, Bennett claimed, concerned himself only with petty offenses such as the theft of pigs, so that he could collect his judicial fees more readily, while turning a blind eye to more serious offenses. "If a petty theft is effected," Bennett wrote, "the indignation of the Court of Sessions is aroused, and should it be a piece of pork or some clothes that are stolen, the poor hungry half-starved mortal is brought up to the Special Sessions, and sent to dig stone—but if a human being is suddenly and ruthlessly severed from the thread of existence, we see the ministers of Justice stand with their arms folded, waiting for a price to be bid for their exertions ere they will start on the trail of the murderers. Such a system offers an impunity to the rich ruffian, it holds a shield over the violator of female virtue, and in but too many cases, acts as a stimulant to outrages at which humanity shudders."

Noah, for his part, took his revenge from the bench, scouring Bennett's accounts of court proceedings for any factual error or discrepancy, so that he could slap him with trumped-up libel charges, bringing fines as high as five hundred dollars. On one occasion, Bennett paid a stiff penalty for misreporting a man's name: He had been off by one letter.

The Mary Rogers case appeared to offer a chance for Bennett to settle the score. When the story broke, the police and judiciary were widely seen to be mired in bureaucracy. The *Herald* launched a blistering attack:

> The recent awful violation and murder of an innocent
> young woman—the impenetrable mystery which sur-

rounds that act—the apathy of the criminal judges, sitting on their own fat for a cushion bench—and the utter inefficiency of the police, are all tending fast to reduce this large city to a savage state of society—without law—without order—and without security of any kind. Only a few days have elapsed since we saw M.M. Noah getting up in his place and gravely enumerating to the Grand Jury the serious duties they had to perform in indicting petty offenders for stealing old clothes, pork, or anything, while the blood of Mary Rogers, crying for vengeance from the depth of the Hudson, never even called forth a single remark—a solitary word—a shake of the wig, or a pointing of the finger, from this 'most venerable and upright judge.' This and such like judges exhaust their efforts and faculties—all their law and half their gospel—in procuring the indictment of a newspaper for the horrible offense of an incorrect report of a trial for stealing three pounds of pork—or pilfering a few bags of coffee—but for the taking away of the honor and the life of a virtuous, respectable, lovely young woman, the only daughter of an aged mother, Judge Noah has no time to attend to such trifles—and Judge Lynch is so much engaged in granting writs of *habeas corpus*, (fees in each case from $10 to $15) that he is equally unable to call the attention of the police or the Grand Jury to the mere violation and murder of a young woman in the lower ranks of life.

As a further example of the city's decay Bennett reached back to the Helen Jewett murder, chastising the authorities for allowing Richard Robinson, whom he now bluntly called "the murderer," to slip through their fingers. "The administration of justice in this city," he declared, "has been bringing itself into contempt every year, every week, and every day." Swept up in his indignation, Bennett managed to overlook the fact that he himself had been instrumental in securing Robinson's release.

Although his rationale may not have been straightforward, Bennett's anger struck a chord with his readership, and what began as a personal vendetta soon spread to the other newspapers. Though each journal had its own ideas of what had befallen Mary Rogers, all were united in the complaint that the police and judiciary were not doing enough. "Not a step will be taken without a reward," thundered the *Herald*, "and if they even possess a clue to the mystery, still they would keep the secret intact, like capital in trade, till public indignation has raised a sum sufficient as a reward for bringing the facts to the light of day."

By the second week of August, with no sign that either New York or New Jersey would offer a reward, Bennett resolved to force the issue. Under the heading of "A Public Meeting," Bennett called for a gathering of a "Committee of Safety" to raise private funds. "It is in vain to call upon the ministers of justice to step in and stay the plague which is at our doors and the community—at least the virtuous portion—must act for themselves," he asserted. "Let a public meeting be set afoot, a subscription raised in order to offer a reward for the murderers of Mary Rogers. We will give FIFTY DOLLARS; and we doubt not that in less than 24 hours a thousand dollars may be raised, to be paid into the hands of the Mayor of New York, for the purpose of stimulating the energetic and indefatigable police of this—the commercial and intellectual emporium of these United States. If this course is not pursued, no woman will be safe."

Bennett was playing an extraordinary game of brinksmanship. The "Moral War" had branded him a social pariah and united his

competitors in an effort to drive him out of business. Every newspaper editor in the city had cause to despise him, though not all of
them had attempted to spit down his throat in the manner of James
Watson Webb. Benjamin Day—late of the *Sun*, now editor of the
Tattler—had been branded "an infidel" by Bennett, and his
brother-in-law Moses Beach, who took over the *Sun* in 1838, was
described as having "no more brains than an oyster." Park Benjamin of the *Evening Signal*, who struggled with a physical disabil-
ity that affected his legs, was said to have been visited with a "curse
of the monster." Horace Greeley of the *Tribune*, who had once
called Bennett an "unmitigated blockhead," came in for particular
scorn: "Galvanize a large New England squash and it would make
as capable an editor as Greeley." Now, not only his rival editors but
also New York's most prominent citizens would be forced to rally
behind Bennett and the *Herald*. If they did not, they would be seen
to stand in opposition to a cause that, to all outward appearances,
was noble and selfless.

Under the flag of civic duty, the warring parties called an uneasy truce. On the evening of August 11, Greeley, Beach, and
Benjamin dutifully filed into the home of James Stoneall on Ann
Street, around the corner from the Rogers boardinghouse. It is not
known whether Benjamin Day attended, as several anonymous
"friends" were listed among some thirty-five guests, but the official roster did include Richard Adams Locke, who had boosted
Day's readership with his "Great Moon Hoax." In addition to editors and journalists, the gathering featured rising politicians such
as Caleb Woodhull, shortly to be elected mayor, and alderman
Elijah Purdy, who had authorized the second postmortem examination on behalf of the absent Mayor Morris.

Bennett knew better than to attempt to preside over the meeting himself. Instead, he kept to the background and left the

formalities to William Attree, an experienced reporter who had covered the Helen Jewett case for the *Transcript* and was now working on the Mary Rogers murder for Bennett. Attree called the meeting to order and oversaw the appointment of a chairman and secretary. Next came an open forum in which several of the men present stood and gave voice to their distress over the fate of Mary Rogers. These "learned and eloquent" addresses filled the better part of three hours. All the while Bennett sat placidly at the back of the room, nodding his head as each of the speakers passed to the front of the room.

At a few minutes before ten o'clock, as the last of the speeches appeared to be winding down, Bennett straightened and gave a nod to Attree. The young reporter stepped to the front of the room to move ahead with the principal business of the evening, the collection of funds to serve as a reward "for the arrest of any or all of those concerned in the late murder." Before proceeding with this vital matter, however, Attree paused and glanced at the faces around the room, many of them still glistening with the heat of the evening's oratory. Would it not be prudent, he wondered, to offer a written record of the noble sentiments expressed by this assemblage, to record and codify its statements of concern? A set of resolutions, perhaps? As it happened, Attree continued, he had taken the liberty of making a few notes over the course of the evening. Unfolding a sheet of paper, he cleared his throat and began to read.

Needless to say, Attree's proposed resolutions, though presented as a summary of the evening's proceedings, were in fact a note-for-note reprise of the previous week's *Herald* editorials, written by Bennett himself. Not surprisingly, they served to express "alarm and horror" over the murder and to "deprecate the apparent apathy that has characterized the Chief Magistrates of the States of

New Jersey and New York." Caught up in the heady momentum of the evening's rhetoric, the self-styled "Committee of Safety" voted unanimously to adopt the resolutions.

It was a masterful tactic from Bennett. In effect, he had contrived to put three dozen of the city's most powerful names behind his vendetta against Mordecai Noah. Although Noah and Lynch had not been mentioned by name, a specific reference to "political patronage amongst our judiciary" served the same purpose. By the end of the week, many of Bennett's rivals would reprint the resolutions in full, spreading the *Herald*'s influence across the previously insurmountable chasm between the penny press and the blanket sheets. Sitting quietly at the back of the room, Bennett allowed himself the luxury of a smile.

Having completed this business, Attree moved quickly to the collection of the contributions toward a reward. As promised, Bennett pledged fifty dollars, as opposed to five dollars from Greeley and two each from Beach and Benjamin. One of the anonymous "friends" in attendance also weighed in with a fifty-dollar contribution, suggesting that at least one of the wealthy and powerful men in the room that night was uncomfortable with the public criticism of City Hall.

John Anderson, the young owner of the cigar store where Mary Rogers had worked, was also present at the Stoneall house that evening. Anderson was known to have been deeply distraught over the murder of his former employee. By some accounts he had displayed a black-bordered sketch of Mary Rogers in the window of his shop, and would place his hand on his heart whenever her name was mentioned. He had said little throughout the evening, waving off an opportunity to address the group when it was offered, and he appeared thoughtful and withdrawn through much of the oratory. As the donations were being collected, however, he straightened in his chair and reached for his pocketbook. When his name was called, he answered with a pledge of fifty dollars. Cheers erupted at this show of generosity, but Anderson simply nodded his head to indicate that it was no more than his duty.

The gathering disbanded amid an atmosphere of "public-spirited resolve," according to the *Transcript*, with more than five hundred dollars pledged in reward money. In spite of this show of public unity, however, the newspapers resumed their skirmishing almost immediately, with Moses Beach attacking Bennett for using Mary Rogers's death as a platform for self-aggrandizement. In Beach's view, the meeting constituted a "sacrilege" in suggesting that the city's public servants were not doing their duty. Bennett lost no time in condemning Beach for his "savage attack" on the noble motives of his fellow citizens, and wondered why, if Beach found the committee's intentions so distasteful, he had been moved to make a contribution. Bennett went on to note the amount of Beach's largesse—two dollars—before asking, "Who did the fellow cheat out of that sum?"

Although a second meeting of the Committee of Safety was scheduled the following evening, there is no evidence that anything was achieved apart from a discussion of the case over port and cigars. Within days, however, the publicity surrounding the private reward money had forced the governor of New York, William Seward, to take notice. On August 31, Seward, later Abraham Lincoln's secretary of state, issued an official proclamation concerning the young woman who "was lately ravished and murdered" and acknowledged the "altogether unsuccessful" efforts of the police to bring the perpetrators to justice. That being the case, the document continued, "I do hereby enjoin upon all magistrates and other officers and ministers of justice that they be diligent in their efforts to bring the offender or offenders to condign punishment."

In a tacit admission that those efforts would likely fail, Seward added $750 in state money to the private reward, bringing the total to $1,350.

It was a pointed rebuke to the officials of New York City, and reflected Seward's awareness that police and judicial matters were likely to loom large in the coming elections. Although Seward had now effectively laid a bouquet at the feet of James Gordon Bennett, the *Herald* was unimpressed. "Governor Seward Waked Up," ran the headline over the proclamation. While admitting that "no governor ever did more," Bennett could not resist getting in a dig at the Seward administration's "appointment of such old political hacks as Noah and Lynch." The editor was more conciliatory in discussing the reward money: "If the present reward, united with that of the people's reward, can discover the murderers, we say 'God speed.'"

It is unlikely that Bennett's editorial brought much cheer to the governor's mansion. In reviewing Seward's promise to take action to restore "the peace and security of society," Bennett offered a blunt retort:

"Better late than never."

IX

A Most Notorious Scoundrel

JUST PAST TEN O'CLOCK on the night of August 5, 1841, a New York marshal led a team of constables up the gangplank of the USS *North Carolina*, a receiving ship docked in the Brooklyn Navy Yard. With the ship's duty officer leading the way, the men made their way belowdecks to the sleeping quarters and dragged twenty-two-year-old William Kiekuck from his bunk. The young sailor was placed in manacles and hustled into a dogcart waiting on the docks. Within the hour, he was at the Bowery police station being subjected to what the *Sun* would call "long and critical interrogatories by the Magistrate."

Kiekuck's arrest, one of several that took place in the week before James Gordon Bennett's "Committee of Safety" meeting, demonstrated that the police had not been quite as idle as the newspapers were reporting. At the same time, the sailor's capture established that the findings of Dr. Richard Cook, the New Jersey coroner, had not been entirely discarded. Although Cook's work had been publicly derided as amateurish and unworthy, the coroner's conclusions had led the police directly to Kiekuck in a manner that would have fit comfortably in one of Poe's tales of "ratiocination."

In "The Murders in the Rue Morgue," published just three months earlier, Poe's detective, C. Auguste Dupin, had found great significance in a piece of ribbon knotted in a manner "which few besides sailors can tie." The New York investigation had proceeded along similar lines. Dr. Cook repeatedly stressed that Mary Rogers's bonnet was fastened to her head with a unique type of knot. He insisted that this was not something a lady would have tied, but rather "a slip knot . . . a sailor's knot." Moreover, he noted that a strip of cloth torn from Mary's dress had been fashioned into a "sort of hitch at the back," presumably to serve as a handhold while dragging the body to the river. In Cook's view, these details indicated that, in all likelihood, Mary Rogers's killer had been a sailor. When the New York police learned that there had been a young sailor among the tenants of the Rogers boardinghouse, they believed they had found their man.

Kiekuck freely admitted to having an acquaintance with Mary Rogers. He had lodged at the Nassau Street boardinghouse for some two weeks during the previous year, while on leave. When questioned about the exact nature of his relationship with Mary, he denied that they were on courting terms: "far from being intimate with her," reported the *Courier and Enquirer*, "he had never walked out with her in his life." He did, however, think well enough of Mary to have called at the boardinghouse on July 3, three weeks before the murder, in order to visit with her.

In spite of Kiekuck's protests, the police had good reason to be suspicious. On Wednesday, July 28, the day Mary's body was discovered, Kiekuck was reported to have signed himself onto the *North Carolina* in a state of great agitation. "Contrary to the usual custom of sailors," noted the *Courier*, "he was apparently very anxious to get on board the ship," giving his superior the impression that he was a man on the run. "His behavior," said one of the constables, "was decidedly curious."

Although the investigators had no evidence with which to charge Kiekuck, they believed that a stretch in the Manhattan House of Detention for Men on Centre Street might be in order. Known as "the Tombs" for its white granite and Egyptian-style architecture, New York's main prison was only six years old at this time, but already it had cultivated a fearsome reputation. Overcrowded and understaffed, the prison housed "the guilty and the blameless alike," according to one source, "as it was known that even the threat of a lengthy confinement could wring a confession from an innocent man."

Apparently Kiekuck bore it stoically and resisted all pressure to confess. When it became known that the sailor was in custody without formal charges, a statement was released that he had been taken to the Tombs at his own request, "until the authorities are satisfied of his innocence." Though the language was cautious, the police clearly believed they had their man. All of their energies were now focused on establishing the sailor's guilt.

Within twenty-four hours, however, any hope of a speedy resolution to the mystery had faded. In the days before Kiekuck's arrest, a number of people had come forward claiming to have seen Mary on Broadway in the company of a young man, "someone whom she appeared to know well," according to the *Courier*. When summoned to the Tombs, however, these witnesses did not recognize Kiekuck. "Several persons were there for that purpose," reported the *Herald*, "but they failed entirely to identify him." Under close questioning, most of the witnesses admitted that they could not even be certain that the young lady they had seen was Mary Rogers.

The case against Kiekuck weakened further when the sailor provided a detailed account of his movements during the period of Mary's disappearance. He had arrived in New York the night before and passed much of his time at the home of his sister, with whom he was having breakfast on the Sunday morning when Mary was last seen at the boardinghouse. The rest of Kiekuck's time was spent with friends, swimming in the Hudson River, drinking in a public house, and enjoying the company of "a girl he knew" in the Five Points. More than a dozen witnesses, including the girl, confirmed the truth of his statement. After three days in custody, Kiekuck was released.

No explanation was offered for Kiekuck's apparent nervousness after the discovery of Mary's body, and his rush to sign back on to the ship. The police would question him several more times in the coming days, but for the moment they had no grounds to hold him. "If anything should occur which will render his presence again necessary, he can be readily found on board ship," noted the *Courier*, "but it is the opinion of a gentleman at the Halls of Justice, well versed in all the art of rogue catching, that this person is entirely innocent."

As the case against Kiekuck evaporated, the police were forced to cast their net wider in the search for suspects. This became more difficult as the news of the murder made its way onto the front pages of the newspapers, resulting in dozens of anonymous tips and letters from people claiming to have relevant information. Many of these accusations proved to be useless and even willfully misleading. "Anonymous letters speak the truth sometimes," declared one nameless informant. "E. Keyser, 43 Washington Street, knows something of the murder of M.C. Rogers. . . . You would do well to examine him." Mr. Keyser turned out to be a man in the midst of an ugly dispute with his neighbor over an unpaid debt.

Many of the city's reporters also felt the urge to offer pointers to the police. "ASK HIM," ran a headline in the *Transcript*, followed by the information that "a young man named Canter at the *Journal of Commerce* was a suitor of Mary C. Rogers and was in the constant habit of walking out with her. He was severely beaten about a year ago by three or four rivals in consequence of visiting her. He has not as yet been questioned about who the others were in the habit of visiting." The advice had merit, as Canter had played a role in Mary's disappearance from the cigar store three years earlier, and he may well have been the author of the oddly jocular account of her suicidal despair over the "gallant gay Lothario." When summoned to police headquarters, however, the newsman could add nothing to the investigation. He claimed he had not seen her in more than two years.

Another anonymous letter, addressed to the *Tattler* but reprinted in several other papers, appeared far more promising. The correspondent, who identified himself only as "T.D.W.," explained that he had "declined coming forward through motives of a perhaps criminal prudence, and even now I dare not reveal my name, because I fear that by doing so I might become the victim of a gang, who are all powerful to revenge any injury that may be done to any members of their body." In spite of these reservations, T.D.W. felt compelled to gather his courage in order to report an incident he had seen on the day of Mary's disappearance. While out "sauntering" on the shores of Hoboken that evening, he had caught sight of a rowboat gliding across the Hudson from New York. As the boat neared the shore, he "perceived that there were six men and *one young well-dressed female*, who I felt confident from description, as also from a dim recollection of my own, was the Segar Girl. Immediately as they touched the strand, the six men and the female left the boat and proceeded towards the woods." Almost at once, T.D.W. became suspicious. The men, he observed, were "of that class denominated 'rowdies'—such men for instance as hang about the doors of low gaming public houses, wear flat-brimmed hats, and affect an air of vulgar devil-may-care gentility." With mounting apprehension, he watched as the group disappeared from view. "I cannot say that the female made any opposition," he admitted. "I rather think she did not, or I would have observed it—but at all events, she was there."

Uncertain of what to do, T.D.W. watched as a second boat came sweeping over the river. "This had three men in it," he noted, "and when they landed, they jumped from the boat with great rapidity." The new arrivals spotted two other bystanders loitering nearby and rushed over to ask the whereabouts of the earlier group and the young lady. "Did you observe if they used any violence with her?" they asked. In spite of assurances that the young lady appeared unharmed, the new arrivals seemed tremendously agitated and started off toward the woods "almost at a run."

"The above is all I know about this affair," T.D.W. insisted, "but I am firmly persuaded in my own mind that the young lady brought over in the first boat was the cigar girl, who was so brutally murdered a few hours afterwards." The editors of the *Tattler* concurred, and expressed a hope that "T.D.W." would step forward to assist the police, declaring that they intended to coerce him to do so with "all the force in our office." Apparently this force was more than adequate to the task. By the following day, T.D.W. had been revealed as William Fanshaw, a local man who had been out for the day with his brother-in-law. Although Fanshaw declared himself to be "distressed and inconvenienced" by the exposure of his identity, he remained adamant that the details of his story were correct in every particular.

The city's newspapers united in calling for further information about the occupants of the rowboat, with the notable exception of the *Herald*. "There must be some mistake in this statement," insisted Bennett's paper, perhaps bristling at being scooped by the

Tattler. "On the Sunday evening in question there was a violent thunderstorm, which began before sundown and did not clear away until 10 o'clock." The *Herald* went on to conclude that the woman in the boat could not, in any case, have been the cigar girl. "Mary Rogers's face was well known to all 'young men about town' from her having been at Anderson's store. If she had been at Hoboken that day, she would have been seen by dozens of persons that would have recognized her."

Bennett's objections did not entirely discredit Fanshaw's account. If Mary Rogers had been taken directly from a boat to the remote woods, she would hardly have been recognized by dozens of people. As to the thunderstorm, the accounts of when it began and ended varied widely from place to place, as numerous correspondents were quick to point out. Before the debate could advance any further, a girl of fifteen stepped forward and identified herself as the young woman in the first rowboat. The story of her "abduction" had been greatly exaggerated, she insisted. She had been on a picnic with her parents and a "young man of her acquaintance," who took her on what was meant to be a romantic interlude on the river. Not far from shore they were overtaken by a boatload of gang thugs who roughed up her friend and rowed off with her. While the young man went for reinforcements, the "party of crass hooligans" carried her into the woods at Elysian Fields, where she was treated roughly and badly frightened, but not violated. After a short while, she said, the young men brought her safely back to New York in the boat.

By rights, this should have put an end to the story, but the notion that Mary Rogers had been murdered by gang members in a rowboat would persist in various forms for weeks to come. To judge by the number of stories that accumulated throughout August, New York's gangs were operating a vast flotilla of rowboats in their re-

lentless assault on female virtue. These numerous and often conflicting accounts culminated a few weeks later in an "exclusive" in the
pages of the *Post*, announcing that a man named James Finnegan, "a
rowdy of confirmed rascality," had been arrested under information
"amounting nearly to certainty that he is one of the wretches who
committed the outrage and murder of Mary C. Rogers." According
to the *Post,* Finnegan was the leader of a gang "whose atrocities in
various forms are familiar in the police annals." Two of the gang
members were said to be on familiar terms with Mary Rogers. On
the morning of her disappearance, it was said, they chanced to meet
her on the street and were able to persuade her to accompany them
on a boat ride across the river to Hoboken. Once there, the *Post*
continued, she "was enticed, unsuspecting, to a retired part of the
shore, and there, after the accomplishment of their hellish purposes,
brutally murdered."

By this time, all reports of progress in the investigation were
treated with due skepticism in the press. In this instance, however,
there was one detail that appeared to set the story apart from the
others. At the time of his arrest Finnegan was said to have a ring in
his possession that was a "perfect match" of one worn by Mary
Rogers on the day of her disappearance. Not even William
Kiekuck had been linked to the crime so decisively, and the press
sounded a note of cautious optimism. Perhaps, said the *Post*, the
"veil that shrouds this dark deed may be lifted for good and all."

Once again, however, the reporting of the story had been allowed to get ahead of the facts. Although Finnegan had a sinister
reputation and a police record, he also had an ironclad alibi: He
had been in church, or, rather, driving his employer to church in a
horse-drawn coach. As the *Post* backed away from its story, no further mention was made of a ring belonging to Mary Rogers, and

Finnegan now joined Kiekuck on the list of discarded suspects. "We have plenty of hooligans," noted one weary observer, "but precious little evidence."

Perhaps this explains the judicious note of caution adopted by the police and the press in mid-August, when a series of events occurred that promised at last to break the case. After two weeks of thwarted expectations, the *Courier and Enquirer* took an almost pleading tone:

> We are pleased to be able to state that at length a clue has beyond all doubt or cavil been discovered which will lead to the detection of the perpetrators of this dreadful outrage. All the affidavits and examinations heretofore taken have no bearing whatever on the case, and even the mother of the unfortunate deceased has confessed that the recent discovery is the only one that can shed light upon the fate of her daughter. The reporter is not at liberty to state all that has been told to him on the subject, but he is authorized to say that officers are now in pursuit of a man who was seen at Hoboken with Miss R. on the afternoon of the 25th of July (the day she was murdered) and that he was heard quarrelling with her. The investigation has been followed up with the most scrupulous minuteness, so as to leave scarce a shade of doubt as to his guilt, by the gentleman to whom the community owes the arrest of the most notorious scoundrel that ever escaped the gallows, and he is entirely convinced that the person now sought for is the guilty party. He has the best wishes of the whole community for his success in this outrageous affair.

The scrupulous gentleman proved to be a police constable named Hilliker, who had achieved his results through a combination of luck and dogged persistence. On Thursday, July 22, three days before Mary Rogers's disappearance, Hilliker had been on duty at the Bowery police station when a woman named Martha Morse appeared in a state of great agitation. Mrs. Morse's face and arms were covered with "angry purple bruises," and she told Hilliker that she wished to swear out a complaint against her husband, Joseph.

Joseph Morse was a well-known figure on Nassau Street, where he ran a successful engraving shop. Not yet thirty years old, he dressed in the style of a London dandy, with elaborate "mutton-chop" side-whiskers, a monocle, a long double-breasted frock coat, and, in summer, a straw hat. He was proud of his success, having worked his way up from selling newspapers on the street, and he was said to enjoy a convivial reputation among the regulars at Anderson's Tobacco Emporium. Although he had been married for several years, according to one account Morse had "not entirely ceased his addresses to the fair sex," which led to frequent confrontations with his wife. More than once police had responded to reports of spousal violence at the Morses's home on Greene Street, and the engraver often found himself turned out of the house and banished to the back room of his shop.

Mrs. Morse's formal complaint at the Bowery police station took the hostilities between the Morses to a new level. Impressed by the bruises, Officer Hilliker brought the complaint before a justice of the peace named Taylor, who issued a formal summons. Hilliker then went directly to Morse's shop on Nassau Street, only to be told by an apprentice, Edward Bookout, that the engraver had left for the day. In fact, Morse was asleep in the back room, but Bookout was accustomed to covering for his employer, who frequently hid out in the back room to dodge unpleasant confrontations with gambling companions and jilted girlfriends.

Taking the assistant at his word, Hilliker left a note asking Morse to call at the station house when he returned. Later, when Morse emerged, he was surprised to find that his wife had involved the police. Chastened, he returned home and attempted a rapprochement. The effort appears to have been successful, as Morse remained at home for three days, only to leave again on the morning of July 25 (the date of Mary Rogers's disappearance) claiming to have business in Hoboken.

Morse did not return home to Greene Street until late Monday evening. He appeared tired and more than usually short-tempered. His wife received him at the door in a state of high dudgeon, demanding to know where he had been since the previous morning. Morse replied that a sudden thunderstorm had forced him to spend Sunday night in Hoboken. Pushing his way past his wife, he announced that he was retiring for the night and went upstairs without another word. When Mrs. Morse followed a short time later, she found that her husband had changed into a fresh suit of clothes and was preparing to leave the house again. He offered no explanation, and when Mrs. Morse pressed him, she later claimed, he "hurled abuse at such volume as to be overheard by the neighbors." Pulling on his hat and coat, Morse stormed out of the house with his wife trailing close behind, still demanding to know where he was going. He had traveled less than a block when his wife overtook him, grabbed his arm, and attempted to pull him back to the house. Morse began "screaming in a rage," according to a neighbor's testimony, and then "tore part of his wife's earring out, struck her and then ran away."

The following morning, Mrs. Morse returned to the Bowery police station to swear out a fresh complaint. Officer Hilliker, annoyed that Morse had not responded to his earlier summons, brought her before Justice Taylor for a second time. Taylor now added a charge of abandonment to the earlier assault and battery complaint. When Hilliker returned to Morse's shop with the new summons, he was told by Edward Bookout that Morse had left town.

As far as Hilliker was concerned, there was nothing more he could do for the time being. Pursuing Morse out of town on a simple assault charge was out of the question; Hilliker would have had to pay his expenses out of his own pocket, and he stood to receive nothing in return apart from a small fee for serving the summons. The officer consulted with Justice Taylor, who agreed that Hilliker should simply wait. Morse would return to his wife and business soon enough.

The following day, however, Hilliker began to suspect that Morse's crimes were more serious than he had first supposed. While attending another of Justice Taylor's court sessions, Hilliker listened with mounting agitation as a pair of witnesses came forward with information that they believed might shed light on the Mary Rogers investigation. The two men had been walking along the river at the Elysian Fields when they saw a young couple sitting on a bench by the water. Their attention was drawn by the fact that the two were arguing, and that the young lady appeared to be particularly upset. The woman, they said, was dark-haired and very attractive, and wore a light-colored dress and a flowered bonnet. The man had prominent black muttonchops, and wore a frock coat and a straw hat. Although the two witnesses thought little of it at the time—"Looks like a lovers' quarrel," one of them said—they later became convinced that the young woman had been Mary Rogers. "The description matched in every particular," they insisted.

Hilliker felt certain that Joseph Morse, with his muttonchop whiskers and dandyish mode of dress, was the man seen with Mary

Rogers. After the mistakes made in the pursuit of William Kiekuck, however, he felt a need to proceed cautiously. Hoping to build a more convincing case, he set out to question anyone who might provide independent confirmation of his suspicions. From Mrs. Morse he learned that the engraver had been in Hoboken at the time of the murder. From a neighbor he heard additional examples of Morse's violent behavior. A local shopkeeper told him that Morse's luggage had been shipped out of town, suggesting that the engraver intended to lie low for some time. On further inquiry, Hilliker learned that the bags had been sent to Boston. Hilliker speculated that the luggage might have been forwarded on to the home of Morse's mother in nearby Nantucket.

At the Rogers boardinghouse, Hilliker took down a more complete description of the murdered girl from her cousin, Mrs. Hayes, noting that it matched every detail of the account of the girl seen at Hoboken. Convinced now, Hilliker went to the Dead House for a sample of fabric from the dress Mary Rogers had been wearing at the time of her death, which he then showed to one of the witnesses who had appeared before Justice Taylor earlier in the day. The witness recognized the fabric at once: The girl he had seen at Elysian Fields, he said, had been wearing a dress made of the same material.

For Hilliker, this completed the chain of evidence. Returning to the police station, he laid out his findings for Justice Taylor, along with some conclusions he had drawn. As a native of Nantucket, a prominent whaling town, Morse had spent time at sea as a young man, and would have been familiar with sailor's knots of the type found during the postmortem examination. Moreover, Morse would have had any number of opportunities to strike up an acquaintance with the murdered girl. His shop on Nassau Street was just a few doors down from the Rogers boardinghouse, and his home on Greene Street was only a few steps farther away. Morse was also known to have been a patron of Anderson's Tobacco Emporium. Although neighbors had heard him declare his intention of going to Hoboken on the fatal Sunday, no one could account for his whereabouts that evening. In Hilliker's mind there was no room for doubt: Joseph Morse was the prime suspect in the Mary Rogers murder.

Justice Taylor immediately issued a warrant for Morse's arrest. In light of this new information, Taylor no longer felt content to wait for Morse to return to New York of his own accord. If at all possible, he said, Hilliker should go to Boston and bring the suspect back in chains. Hilliker shrugged his shoulders. He literally could not afford to chase Morse to Boston, and the police force had no budget to allow for such contingencies. Taylor considered the problem. He had confidence in Hilliker, and had been stung by the relentless criticism of the "stagnant judiciary" coming from Bennett's *Herald*. Taylor decided to take the matter into his own hands. Reaching into his pocket, the justice pulled out his purse and handed over eighty dollars of his own money. "Bring me Mary Rogers's killer," he said. Hilliker nodded and tucked the money into his shirt.

Leaving the judicial chambers, Hilliker went straight to Nassau Street. Taylor's show of confidence had charged him with a grim sense of purpose. His instincts told him that Morse was probably lying low at his boyhood home in Nantucket. Determined not to waste Taylor's money, Hilliker resolved to confirm his suspicions with an interrogation of Edward Bookout, Morse's apprentice, before making the long trip. He hauled Bookout back to the police station and subjected him to a harsh interrogation, telling him that Morse was now a suspect in the Mary Rogers murder. Bookout appeared genuinely shocked and told Hilliker all he knew. Morse had originally planned to go to Nantucket but then thought better of it, the apprentice said. Instead, he went to Worcester and left instructions for Bookout to send word when it was safe to return to New York.

Hilliker listened attentively. How, he asked, was Bookout supposed to get word to Morse? A post office box had been rented for this purpose. Had there been any communication thus far? Bookout winced. Yes, he admitted, he had just sent a letter telling Morse that the police were tracking his luggage. Furthermore, he had suggested that if his employer wished to escape detection he would have to change his appearance, perhaps by switching to more somber clothing and shaving off his distinctive muttonchops.

Hilliker left the police station with a growing sense of urgency. Although Bookout's letter had made no mention of the Mary Rogers investigation, Hilliker believed that he was now racing the clock: He could not afford to let the apprentice's information put Morse on guard. So long as Morse assumed that he was simply dodging spousal assault charges, he would probably remain where he was in hopes that the matter would blow over. If he realized that the police were actively pursuing him—and tracking his luggage— he would likely conclude that they suspected him of the more serious crime. In that case, he might well flee before Hilliker could reach Worcester. If Morse managed to slip out of the country, it was unlikely that he would ever be brought to justice.

Hilliker boarded the first available boat for Boston, determined to intercept Bookout's letter before Morse could collect it. His next priority would be to make a positive identification of Morse. Toward that end he had arranged to bring along the witness who had not only seen Mary Rogers arguing with the well-dressed man at Elysian Fields but also recognized the strip of fabric from Mary's dress. If the witness could identify Joseph Morse as the man he had seen with Mary Rogers, Hilliker's case would be made.

Traveling by carriage from Boston, the two men arrived in Worcester at three o'clock on the afternoon of Saturday, August 14. Hilliker went straight to the town post office and found to his relief that no mail had yet arrived for Joseph Morse. The constable and his witness began making the rounds of the local taverns, eventually tracing Morse to a small rooming house in the town of Holden, some seven miles away.

In Holden, Hilliker left his witness to wait in a nearby saloon while he took up a vigil outside the rooming house. At nine-thirty that evening, a man with black muttonchop whiskers wearing a frock coat emerged from the house. Assuming the man to be Morse, Hilliker fell into step beside him and asked if he would care to join him for a drink, explaining that he was a stranger in town. The man readily assented, giving no sign of suspicion or alarm. At the saloon, Hilliker took a seat near the table where he had left his witness. After buying a round of drinks, Hilliker gave his witness time to study the suspect's face and listen to the sound of his voice. After a few moments, the witness gave a nod.

Hilliker was satisfied. He cleared his throat: "Your name, sir, is Joseph Morse, I believe, and you are under arrest."

As Hilliker later recounted the scene, Morse half-rose from the table and demanded to know the charges against him. "On the complaint of your wife," answered Hilliker. At this, Morse appeared "strangely satisfied" and took his seat again. "Oh," he said. "Is that all?"

Hilliker glanced again at his witness seated at the next table. "Yes," he said, "and for the murder of Mary Rogers."

X

The Lost Hour

FOR SEVERAL MOMENTS Hilliker's accusation hung in the air as Morse wavered between outrage and disbelief. Hilliker calmly repeated the charge, and formally served Morse with Justice Taylor's arrest warrant. Growing indignant, Morse attempted to argue his way out of the situation, claiming that a mistake had been made. Finally, when Hilliker threatened him with extradition, Morse bowed to the inevitable and allowed himself to be placed under arrest.

The following day, a steamship carrying Hilliker and his prisoner arrived in New York, along with Hilliker's obliging witness. Morse was taken to the Tombs, where the second of the two witnesses—who had not accompanied Hilliker to Massachusetts—easily picked Morse out of a group of a dozen men. In Hilliker's view, the noose was tightening around Morse's neck.

Justice Taylor was summoned to take charge of the situation and a lengthy round of interrogations began. As the gravity of the situation sank in, Morse began to plead his innocence in terms that only served to bolster the case against him. He insisted that he had not been at Hoboken on the day in question; he had gone to Staten Island instead. When Justice Taylor produced the testimony of several friends and neighbors, all of whom recalled hearing Morse declare his intention of going to Hoboken, the suspect allowed as how he had spent the day in "solitary reflection," during which he lost track of his whereabouts. In response to this, Taylor confronted Morse with the statements of witnesses who had seen him in the company of a young woman. Morse admitted that he may have exchanged a pleasantry or two, but he could not recall any particulars.

As Morse's evasions and contradictory statements accumulated, Justice Taylor grew even more convinced of his guilt. The newspapers, too, quickly set aside their earlier caution and declared that the murderer of Mary Rogers had at last been captured. While the *Herald* noted that "all examinations of the suspect were strictly private, and the Mayor has forbidden any publication of what transpired on the subject," the paper nonetheless felt comfortable in stating that the evidence gathered tended to "foster guilt upon Morse." The other papers were less circumspect. "The guilty party is at last in custody," wrote the *Courier and Enquirer*, while the *Sun* declared that "Morse will surely pay the penalty for his crime."

Apparently there were some in New York who were not willing to await the verdict of the criminal justice system. On the night of August 17, according to one account, a lynch mob formed outside the Tombs calling for Morse's blood. While the story does not appear in any firsthand news account, it might, if true, help to explain why Morse decided on the following day that he was now prepared to tell Justice Taylor the "full truth" of the matter.

Morse's statement, later reprinted in many of the daily newspapers, acknowledged that he had, in fact, enjoyed the company of a young woman on the Sunday in question. "I met a young lady about noon," he testified. "I had met her before, and persuaded her to go with me to Staten Island. We went there, to the Pavilion, and had some refreshments and I kept her mind employed till after the last boat departed." The method by which Morse kept his companion's mind employed would require some elaboration. It later emerged that Morse contrived to miss the ferry by the "devious expedient" of setting the hands of his pocket watch back by one hour, so that the young lady would not realize that they were in danger of becoming stranded. With no other means of getting back to New York, he and the young lady were then obliged to check into a rooming house. There, Morse admitted, "I tried to have connexion with her but did not succeed." After the young lady had spent the remainder of the night repelling his advances, Morse said, he brought her back to New York and "left her in good friendship" at the corner of Greenwich and Barclay streets.

Apparently such episodes were not unusual for Morse, as he could not recall the name of the young lady in this particular instance. Only later, when he heard about the murder of Mary Rogers, did it occur to him that his unwilling companion might have been the cigar girl. "If it was," he insisted, "I had no hand in murdering her, as I left her in good feeling." His flight from New York, he explained, had nothing to do with what occurred on Staten Island; he simply wished to withdraw to a safe distance while his wife recovered her better nature after the unpleasantness of Monday evening. Had he remained in town, he feared she might have had him arrested.

If the young woman with whom he passed the night in Staten Island had indeed been Mary Rogers, Morse maintained, he could offer no clue as to her final fate. In Massachusetts, when he read the newspaper accounts of her death, he wondered if perhaps she had done away with herself in despair over the damage that their dalliance might do to her reputation. Later, he claimed, when it became clear that she had been murdered, he reproached himself "most earnestly" for allowing her to fall victim to a gang. It seemed to him now, however, that his companion could not have been Mary

Rogers, as the girl he took to Staten Island had been wearing a black dress, and the cigar girl was known to have worn white.

If Justice Taylor hoped to find clarity in Morse's statement, he came away more bewildered than ever. Even before the suspect had finished speaking, Taylor began chipping away at various elements that did not ring true. If, as Morse claimed, he took the young lady to Staten Island, why had he been seen arguing with her in Hoboken? Was it truly plausible that a man could spend an entire night attempting to seduce an unwilling young woman and fail to learn her name? Why, if Morse was innocent of her murder, had he not immediately given a full and candid statement to the police, even after two days of incarceration?

Through it all, Morse remained consistent on one point: his companion, whoever she was, had been alive and well when he left her. After all of the suspect's previous vacillations, however, Taylor felt little inclination to believe this or any other detail of the account. As Morse's story churned through the press, the entire city seemed to come to an agreement on the matter of his guilt. It was felt that any man who would set his watch back in the hope of seducing a young woman might well resort to murder when his advances were spurned. Not even Morse's wife could be persuaded to speak in his defense.

From his cell on the interior quadrangle of the Tombs, Morse would have been able to see the rough planks of the gallows platform in the center courtyard. The looming presence of the scaffold and gibbet was meant to instill fear, and Morse had more reason than most to shudder at the sight. In all likelihood, he would be next in line. Morse's execution, the newspapers agreed, would be a proud moment for the city of New York.

Then, astonishingly, salvation arrived from an unexpected quarter. On August 20, as Justice Taylor prepared to file a formal murder indictment, a group of four men came forward to testify that they had seen Morse on Sunday, July 25, in the company of a young woman dressed in black. The four men, who were acquaintances of the engraver, had read his statement in the previous day's newspapers and recalled meeting him on the street that morning. If this sudden revelation seemed suspicious or overly convenient, it would not remain so for long. Unlike Morse himself, this new group of witnesses was able to supply the name of the girl in black. She was Mary Haviland, the daughter of a "highly respectable widow lady" living on Morton Street. Incredulous, Justice Taylor dispatched Officer Hilliker to bring Miss Haviland to the police station. He returned within the hour escorting the young woman, who was said to be "a rather handsome girl, not yet seventeen years of age, who appeared terribly effected in giving her statement."

Miss Haviland's testimony, elicited amid "frequent sobs and expressions of despair," confirmed Morse's story to the last detail. She had traveled with him to Staten Island on the Sunday afternoon in question, she said, where he "kept my attention off the time until the last boat started for New York." After trying unsuccessfully to hire a rowboat, the young woman resigned herself to the situation and agreed to pass the night in a hotel, but only after extracting a "solemn promise" from Morse that they would occupy separate rooms, and that a "female of the house" would remain with her to insure the propriety of the arrangements. Arriving at the hotel, Miss Haviland found that no female chaperone was available, so she attempted to keep Morse out by wedging a chair and her parasol against the door. These safeguards proved ineffective; no sooner had she retired for the evening than Morse managed to push his way into the room.

Justice Taylor listened to this account with sympathetic concern, and asked if Morse had taken any liberties. Miss Haviland responded that he "kissed me and hugged me a good deal, and he tried to persuade me to yield to his wishes, but I resisted all night." Taylor then asked if Morse had used force or violence. "I can't say that he tried to use force," she responded. Unconvinced, Taylor asked a second time if Morse had resorted to violence. Miss Haviland admitted that Morse's threats frightened her to such an extent that she agreed to lie down on the bed and partially undress, whereupon he "tried to persuade me to consent to his wishes in every way, but I refused." A later account would claim that he attempted to get his way "by dint of threats that he would expose and hold her name up to odium, and by other means such as might be expected from a man like himself."

At length, Miss Haviland managed to cool Morse's ardor by threatening to raise a shout of "murder" at the window. She then passed the remainder of the night seated in a chair with a sheet wrapped tightly about her. In the morning, Morse brought her back to the city. If their parting had not been quite in the spirit of "good friendship" that Morse had claimed, at least he left her alive and well.

Even now, Justice Taylor could not bring himself to take the story at face value. He ordered that Morse be returned to his cell, then he took the unusual step of traveling to Staten Island personally, where he interviewed several employees of the hotel where Morse and Miss Haviland passed their restive night. The hotel staff readily confirmed every detail. Incredulous, Taylor boarded the ferry back to New York and called a meeting of his colleagues. There could be no doubt, he told them: Morse was innocent.

Officer Hilliker, in particular, was devastated by this news. For several days he had been exhilarated in the belief that he had cracked the case single-handedly, and would likely be rewarded with fame and promotion. Instead, he now learned that he had succeeded only in tracking down a fugitive wife-beater—a crime which, at the time, was held to be on a par with pig-stealing.

As word of Morse's eleventh-hour reprieve spread through the city, the *Herald* captured the public's sense of incredulity. "This is one of the most extraordinary cases that ever came before a criminal court in any country. At the very moment that some scoundrels were ravishing and murdering Mary Rogers at Hoboken or New York, Morse was trying to seduce a girl at the Pavilion at Staten Island. All our readers remember the statement we gave yesterday, from Morse's own lips, as to where he was on the fatal Sunday. Every word he said, and we published, was true. As there is an abundance of evidence to show that he was with this girl on Sunday 25th July, of course the accusation as to having participated in the murder of Miss Rogers falls to the ground. He will undoubtedly, however, have to stand a trial for the attempt to commit a rape upon this girl."

Even this prediction failed to come to pass. Although the press initially withheld her name, Miss Haviland's identity was easily discerned from the many other details supplied—including her address—and the unwelcome notoriety kept her "half deluged in tears" for many weeks. Fearful of prolonging the ordeal, she declined to press charges, and grew so distraught over her public humiliation that she was reported to be suicidal.

Although Miss Haviland's testimony had resolved the matter of Morse's guilt, several perplexing questions remained. "One thing we should like to know," wrote the *Herald*, "who are the two men who swore at the police office that they saw Morse sitting with Mary Rogers at Hoboken on the fatal evening? Who are they? Ought they not to be examined at once before they attempt to swear away the life of another man?" It was a fair question; the testimony of the two men, and their subsequent positive identification of Morse, had very nearly seen the engraver tried for the murder of Mary Rogers. The curious precision and unwavering conviction of their testimony—even going so far as to identify a strip of fabric from the dead woman's dress—suggests a misguided eagerness on the part of the two men, or perhaps a line of leading questions from an overenthusiastic Officer Hilliker. Whatever the case, the names of the two witnesses never appeared in the newspapers or court records, and their puzzling testimony had no further impact on the investigation.

Morse remained in jail for another day on the original charges of assault and abandonment until his lawyer could arrange for bail. Morse's wife, in the meantime, had acquired a lawyer of her own, with whom she had initiated divorce proceedings. Upon his release from jail, however, Morse went straight home to Greene Street, where he somehow persuaded his wife to forgive his trespasses. In days to come, the newspapers would be filled with letters from his friends attesting to his unblemished character and the excellence of his work as an engraver. Even the most innocuous of the charges against him—that he used tobacco and had been a patron of Anderson's Tobacco Emporium—were hotly denied. "Morse has a reputation for industriousness and is a fine artist," declared the *Sun*, "and we leave him with those kind words which our Savior spoke to fallen man—Go, and sin no more."

The *Herald* was far more pointed: "We regret to state that the outrage upon this unfortunate girl remains as much a mystery as ever, evidence having been yesterday adduced, proving unquestionably that Morse had no hand in the murder of Miss Rogers, although it was satisfactorily proved that he is a most consummate scoundrel. Morse is to keep clear of Staten Island, and of young ladies in black especially, for the future. Thus ends that nine days wonder."

XI

Crackpots and Gossipists

WITHIN FORTY-EIGHT HOURS of Joseph Morse's release from the Tombs, New Yorkers were greeted with the surprising news that Mary Rogers was alive and well and living in Pittsburgh. According to a letter published in the New York *Planet*, the body pulled from the water at Elysian Fields had been that of some other unfortunate young woman. The "much discussed young seegar vendor," the letter continued, had fled New York after a vicious quarrel with her mother. Mrs. Rogers, it seems, had insisted that her daughter honor her pledge to marry Daniel Payne, the cork cutter, but Mary refused on the grounds that her "heart was possessed by another." Unwilling to submit, the distraught young woman was said to have written a note filled with "bitter reproaches" and quit her home forever, hastening instead to Pittsburgh, where her true love awaited her.

There is no evidence that anyone took this letter seriously, as the *Planet* operated on the lowest tier of the penny press, but the story it purported to tell was fairly typical of the wild rumors and surmises that came into play in the wake of the Joseph Morse episode. Having reached a misplaced consensus on Morse's guilt, the newspapers now once again parted company and resumed their earlier postures, seeking to fill the vacuum created by the departure of the "devious engraver." The names of earlier suspects now returned to prominence, including those of Daniel Payne, Mary's fiancé, and Alfred Crommelin, her would-be suitor. Crommelin was now rumored to have abandoned the city, and Payne was said to be imprisoned in the Tombs. Both men were also accused of having written the notorious warning letter to Joseph Morse in Worcester, advising him to alter his appearance and flee. None of these stories was true. "This affair seems to furnish a great deal of twaddle to the penny papers," wrote James Gordon Bennett, who had lately raised the price of the *Herald* to two cents and considered himself to have ascended to a more rarified plane.

Amid the swirling rumors and hearsay, city and state officials stepped up their efforts once again. New York's board of aldermen weighed the possibility of adding another five hundred dollars to the reward money, while Governor Seward let it be known that he would issue a pardon to any accomplice to the crime who came forward with details. The New York police, meanwhile, had learned from the example of Joseph Morse and were playing their cards closer to the vest. As a result, the arrest of Archibald Padley on August 27, three days after the official release of the engraver, was conducted under conditions of near total secrecy.

Padley, Alfred Crommelin's loyal friend, appears to have been a suspect of last resort. As a former resident of the Rogers boardinghouse he had known Mary Rogers reasonably well, having described her at Gilbert Merritt's Hoboken inquest as a "worthy girl of the very highest character." Following Crommelin's falling out with Payne, the steadfast Padley had left Nassau Street with his friend, and he had been with Crommelin at Hoboken when Mary's body was discovered. It is not known what evidence, if any, came to light to connect Padley to the crime. What is clear is that he was taken to the Tombs in the dead of night and subjected to a three-day interrogation by a justice named Milne Parker. During this period Padley was refused the services of a lawyer, and denied all information concerning the charges against him or the identity of his accuser. Apparently these tactics were not unusual for Justice Parker, who was already under indictment for a similar breach of ethics.

After three days the situation came to the attention of Justice Taylor, who was known to have exercised better judgment in his interrogation of Joseph Morse. In the absence of any compelling evidence against Padley, Taylor issued a release order on the morning of August 31, only to learn that Padley had been set free a few hours earlier—without the knowledge of George Hyde, the keeper of the prison. Both Hyde and Taylor were outraged, and made angry statements to the press. Padley, they said, had been arrested and interrogated "without respect to procedure" and "without the shadow of evidence" linking him to the crime. "The liberty of the citizen cannot thus be outrageously violated," Taylor insisted. Not surprisingly, Bennett's *Herald* was quick to seize on this latest example of judicial malfeasance. "Everything in relation to this lamentable affair seems to be clothed not merely with some impenetrable mystery, but to be conducted by the authorities with a greater degree of secrecy, and consequently of injustice, than most other judicial investigations," Bennett wrote. "It may be law, but it is not justice."

If Padley's interrogation had been shrouded in secrecy, the police were even more circumspect in their questioning of John Anderson, the owner of the cigar store. It was natural enough that the police should have taken an interest in Anderson, who at the very least would have been able to provide information about the background of his former employee. As with all wealthy and prominent citizens of the time, however, the police would have had to show extraordinary discretion, under the threat of possible legal recriminations.

This would have been especially true in the case of Anderson, who had powerful allies at City Hall. It is all the more remarkable, then, that shortly after the Morse affair Anderson was taken into police custody, though perhaps not officially placed under arrest, and subjected to close questioning by the authorities. The information did not appear in any of the newspapers, suggesting that Anderson was able to use his influence to suppress it, and it is not known whether there were any legitimate grounds for suspicion. Even so, the episode placed the young businessman in an exceedingly delicate position. Anderson knew that the mere fact of his interrogation would foster a suspicion of his complicity, whether warranted or not. For a man with political ambitions, this might well prove ruinous. Anderson's fears were justified. In spite of his efforts to hold back the information, it later emerged that the story of Anderson's interrogation at police headquarters had circulated among the city's leading citizens, creating an impression of the tobacconist as a man with a skeleton in his closet. Although he had taken an active role in stimulating the murder investigation, even pledging fifty dollars at the Committee of Safety meeting, Anderson would find himself shadowed by association with the crime for many years to come.

Alfred Crommelin, meanwhile, found himself under attack in Benjamin Day's *Tattler*. Though the editor had high praise for Crommelin's "self-denying perseverance" in the days following Mary Rogers's disappearance, he insisted that Crommelin's identification of the dead woman's body was entirely without merit. From the beginning, Day had been an advocate of the theory that Mary Rogers was still alive. Although he attempted to distance himself from the *Planet* and other "crackpots and gossipists," Day claimed to have a "myriad of provoking reasons" to believe that the body pulled from the Hudson had not been that of the cigar girl. Over the course of several days he and the *Tattler* staff elaborated on these reasons, often in stomach-churning detail. It was well known, Day claimed, that a corpse submerged in water remained below the surface for some while. After a period of six to ten days, as the body decomposed and natural gases were produced, the body would eventually rise to the surface. Since Mary Rogers had been missing only three days, the *Tattler* insisted, her body would not have had sufficient time to rise from the bottom of the river.

Furthermore, the *Tattler* claimed, since the process of decomposition was known to be greatly slowed by immersion in water, it did not seem likely the victim's features would be unrecognizable. Yet Crommelin had stated that the face was "entirely ruined," which it should not have been after only three days in the river. Adding to the confusion, the state of the victim's features had obliged Crommelin to resort to other means of making his identification. These alternate forms of recognition, the *Tattler* claimed, were entirely baseless. Crommelin had torn open the young woman's sleeve and claimed to make out "distinctive markings" on the bare arm. When pressed, however, he admitted that these markings were simply a pattern of hair, which could hardly be counted as an ironclad means of identification. Similarly, Crommelin had laid a particular emphasis on the "delicate shape" of the victim's feet, a characteristic which, in the cold light of day, could not be counted as unique or even noteworthy.

In the opinion of the *Tattler*, the true flaw in Crommelin's testimony lay in his fixed idea of what he would find in Hoboken. He had gone there in search of Mary Rogers, so when he happened upon the recovery of an unidentified corpse, he examined it "not for appearances to show who the drowned person was, but for facts to strengthen his own preconceived opinion that he had found the murdered body of Mary C. Rogers." Crommelin's identification, therefore, amounted *"to nothing at all."*

Crommelin, at least, was said to have been well-intentioned in his efforts. By contrast, Dr. Richard Cook, the New Jersey coroner, was dismissed in the pages of the *Tattler* as "the subject of contemptuous sneers by nearly all the physicians in the city." Chief among his blunders, the paper declared, was his willingness to accept Crommelin's statement as gospel instead of waiting for a proper identification by a member of the family. Moreover, the paper continued, Cook had conducted the postmortem examination with unforgivable haste, committing so many errors that if his evidence were to be published, its very "absurdity would make him a byword at once."

Several other points troubled the *Tattler*. Because of Mary Rogers's fame as the "beautiful seegar girl," she could scarcely have gone to Hoboken or even "passed the length of three blocks in Broadway" without being recognized by a host of witnesses. Then there was the odd fact that both Phoebe Rogers and Daniel Payne had appeared strangely apathetic when told of the body found at Elysian Fields. The two had seemed so unperturbed by this report that it appeared to H. G. Luther, who delivered the unhappy tidings, that "the news was not unexpected." Perhaps this reaction could be better understood if, as the *Tattler* assumed, Payne and Mrs. Rogers were certain that Mary was still alive. What Luther had mistaken for apathy might instead have been confusion over an appropriate response.

All of these facts, and many more besides, brought the *Tattler* to the "inescapable certitude" that Mary Rogers was not the unfortunate girl found dead in Hoboken. How else to explain the fact that Payne and Mrs. Rogers had allowed the city to arrange for the burial, which neither of them had troubled to attend, at the Varick Street church rather than in the Rogers family plot?

The *Tattler*'s theories, though provocative, overlooked a great deal of contradictory information. Benjamin Day's rivals were quick to seize upon his omissions. "Many people now begin to be-lieve that Mary has not been murdered after all," the *Herald* noted. "Still, it [does] seem incredible that the clothes of Mary should be found on the body of a stranger."

Other flaws soon emerged. Setting aside the uncertain merits of the *Tattler's* conclusions concerning "natural gases," there was one obvious defect. Day had repeatedly stated that a three-day immer-sion in the river would have slowed the body's decomposition, rendering it probable that Crommelin would have been able to recognize the dead woman's features. Since he did not, the reason-ing went, the body had probably been submerged for a longer period, and therefore could not have been Mary Rogers. In all likelihood, however, the face was already horribly disfigured when the body went into the water. An eyewitness at Hoboken spoke of a face that was "butchered to a mummy" when the body came out of the water, and Dr. Cook testified to heavy bruising and swollen tissues. Added to this is the uncertainty as to when Crommelin ar-rived on the scene. It is possible that the corpse had been lying on the bank for some time before Crommelin saw it, suffering further ravages from the 90-degree heat. In these circumstances, it is un-likely that the face would have been easily recognized.

Similarly, the *Tattler* had claimed that Mary Rogers would have been recognized if she had been out in public on the day in ques-tion, but in fact there had been numerous sightings to place her on Broadway and at Hoboken at various times on that Sunday. Al-though many of these reports, like the one that led to the arrest of Joseph Morse, were of dubious merit, it was not accurate to say that Mary Rogers had passed unnoticed through the Sunday crowds.

As to the charge of indifference on the part of Phoebe Rogers and Daniel Payne, the Rogers family itself raised a strenuous objection, On August 25, a cousin of Mary's by the name of Edward B. Hayes (the son of Mrs. Hayes, Phoebe's sister), appeared at the editorial offices of the *Tattler* to complain about the paper's portrayal of his relations. As soon as he got word of the tragedy, Hayes claimed, he had gone to Hoboken himself with the intention of viewing the body, although his fragile nerves prevented him from actually doing so. With respect to the actions of Payne and Phoebe Rogers, they had allowed themselves to be guided—"perhaps ill-advisedly"—by the counsel of Alfred Crommelin. According to Hayes, Crommelin had come to him after the New Jersey inquest and stated in blunt terms that Payne must be prevented from going to Hoboken at all costs. Payne, in Crommelin's view, was "a madman" whose interference would only derail the investigation. Accordingly, Hayes said, he went to Payne's brother, John, and convinced him to take the cork cutter out of the city for a few days, presumably to recover from the shock of his fiancée's death. At the same time, Crommelin advised Mrs. Rogers and the other members of the family to remain at home and keep quiet about the murder, so as not to distract from "the detection of the perpetrators of the deed." According to Hayes, Crommelin even went so far as to advise them not to speak with the police, insisting that he himself would serve as the family's liaison.

Mr. Hayes professed a particular irritation at the suggestion that no member of the family had troubled over Mary's funeral arrangements. He insisted that Mr. Downing, one of the cousins Mary was supposed to have been visiting on the fatal Sunday, had not only arranged for the funeral but also paid the expenses. Furthermore, Downing had been present along with Payne as Mary was laid to rest in the family plot—not in the Varick Street church, as several newspapers had reported.

Having delivered himself of these complaints, Hayes withdrew from the offices of the *Tattler* demanding that a formal apology be published. This was not done, but the substance of his remarks was reported at great length, including the detail of Mary's burial in the family plot, which was rather at odds with the paper's fierce insistence that the young woman was, in fact, still alive. The *Tattler* also printed a letter from Payne that arrived shortly afterward, declaring that the story Hayes had told was "strictly true in every particular."

By this time Alfred Crommelin had grown accustomed to seeing his actions and his testimony attacked in print. One paper had dismissed him as a "meddler" and another as a "fretful busybody," prompting him to complain to Justice Gilbert Merritt about the manner in which "the lower order of the press" had seen fit to "heap odium" upon him. Merritt, who himself had recently been characterized as "a model of judicial incompetence," advised Crommelin to ignore the barbs. "Admitting all this, what of it?" he asked. Instead, he urged Crommelin to "enjoy the proud satisfaction of having performed your duty, as you have faithfully and diligently done so far, day and night, in endeavoring to ferret out, and bring to justice, the concealed though wretched murderer of Miss Rogers."

In the wake of this latest attack in the *Tattler*, however, Crommelin could no longer stay quiet. While he might have held his tongue out of respect for Edward Hayes, the letter of affirmation from Daniel Payne, his old rival, struck him at his most sensitive point. Indignant and spoiling for a fight, Crommelin went to the offices of the *Courier and Enquirer* to present his side of the story. Buttonholing a reporter, he spent the better part of an hour giving a loud and blustering justification of his actions. He said that he resented "most earnestly" the suggestion that his identification of Mary's body had been in error. For verification, one needed only to recall that Phoebe Rogers herself had confirmed Crommelin's statement based on the clothing found on the body, even down to the detail of "some particular repairs done on the Saturday evening previous to her leaving home." Surely, Crommelin insisted, the matter of the clothing was decisive?

The following day, the substance of Crommelin's remarks crossed Benjamin Day's desk at the *Tattler*. Even now, the editor refused to yield. He printed a forceful reaffirmation of his earlier position that Mary Rogers was alive, conveniently glossing over the family's claims to have buried her. He went on to point out that Crommelin had not seen Mary in some time, having declined to answer the overtures she made in the days prior to her disappearance. His identification of the girl's clothing, then, could not be counted as reliable. The fact that Phoebe Rogers and at least two other relatives had also recognized the clothing went unmentioned.

This was a shrewd gambit on Day's part. Although the *Tattler* once again offered backhanded praise for Crommelin's "selfless efforts" in the matter, the article served as a reminder that he had ignored a plea for help from Mary Rogers at the moment of her greatest need, reinforcing the notion of him as a man attempting to ease a guilty conscience. The testimony of such a man, Day implied, could hardly be accepted uncritically.

Outraged, Crommelin bypassed the *Courier and Enquirer* and sent a blistering letter directly to Day's *Tattler*. Although several friends and city officials had advised him to hold his tongue, he resolved that he could not allow "a certain class of the penny press to go on from day to day to calumniate me." It was a matter of public record, he declared, that Mary Rogers had been buried by the city at a cost of $29.50, and that both Mr. Callender, the clerk of police, and Mr. McCadden, the undertaker, were prepared to affirm this fact under oath. As to the other charges against his truthfulness, Crommelin called for "an open investigation of all and every part of my conduct in relation to the inquiries respecting the murder of Miss Rogers," as opposed to the "secret inquisitorial proceedings" to which his friend Archibald Padley had been subjected. He went on to insist that the same rigorous standard be applied to the other principal figures of the investigation, including Phoebe Rogers, Daniel Payne, Edward Hayes, and several of the journalists and police officers who had besmirched his good name. "I fear no questions," Crommelin declared, "and wear no mask."

By this time Crommelin had become a figure of fun in most of the city's newspapers. His demand wasn't taken seriously, although a public inquiry of the sort he suggested, however unorthodox or contentious, might have helped to burn away some of the fabrications and half-truths. Five weeks had now passed since the murder, and in that time much had been said and written—some of it true, some of it false, and quite a bit falling somewhere in between. Each day brought some dramatic but unproven assertion that swept through the city's saloons and oyster houses, only to be supplanted the following day by something even more sensational. One rumor claimed that Mary had been spotted boarding a ship bound for France, on the arm of a mysterious older gentleman. Another story, printed in the *Herald*, told readers that "old Mrs. Rogers burned up a bundle of letters belonging to Mary on the day of the inquest. This ought to be explained." Crommelin would have been particularly interested in clarifying a widely circulated claim as to the reason for Mary's visit to his office in the days before the murder. It was said that Phoebe Rogers had sent her daughter to try to sell a due bill in the amount of fifty-two dollars (an I.O.U. from a former tenant) so that Mary would have the use of the money while Crommelin took on the job of collecting the debt. If true, this would have confirmed that Mary had something more than a simple family visit in mind when she left Nassau Street that morning. In the climate of journalistic one-upmanship that persisted in the weeks following the murder, however, it is difficult to separate truth from rumor. "There is yet a mystery in this business," wrote Bennett at the end of August, "which time alone can unravel."

Two days later, the unraveling began.

XII

The Murder Thicket

ON THE AFTERNOON OF AUGUST 25, 1841, a widow named Frederica Loss sent her two younger sons—Charles, age 16, and Ossian, age 12—to collect sassafras bark from a nearby grove. Mrs. Loss was the proprietor of an establishment called Nick Moore's Tavern, a roadhouse near the shore of Weehawken, New Jersey, a short distance north of Elysian Fields. In addition to a small number of guest rooms, the Loss inn offered light refreshments, cakes, and liquor for sale to visitors whose wanderings took them beyond Castle Point and Sybil's Cave.

The two boys, named Kellenbarack after their father, who no longer lived with the family, took a path that led some four hundred yards from the house along an unused carriage route. The trail ran down toward a river dock known as Bull's Ferry, winding past a dense thicket where the boys often played games of hide-and-seek. It was an unsightly tangle of beech trees and briar shrubs entwined along a stone wall, forming a thick canopy over a cramped interior space. Inside, four craggy boulders served as a crude grouping of stools and benches.

As Mrs. Loss's sons neared the thicket that afternoon, a flash of white caught the eye of Ossian, the younger boy. Pushing his head through an opening, he saw a piece of cloth lying on one of the rocks. He scrambled through the tangle of branches, closely followed by his brother, Charles, and snatched up an unfamiliar garment. "Hello," he called, "there's somebody has left their shirt." As the older boy examined the fabric, he realized that he was holding a woman's petticoat. Looking around, he noticed several other items of female clothing. A silk scarf was draped across another of the boulders, and hanging across the interior branches were strips of fabric that appeared to have been torn from a white dress. As he gathered up the garments and handed them to his brother, Charles made another discovery: A ladies' parasol and handkerchief were wedged into a gap between one of the boulders and a tree trunk. Carrying the two items back through the opening of the thicket, he examined them in the sunlight. The delicate silk of the parasol was partly rotted from lying on the damp ground, and the handkerchief was badly stained. Even so, Charles could make out a pair of initials delicately embroidered along the hem: "M.R."

The two boys bundled up their discoveries and carried them back to their mother. Mrs. Loss examined each article carefully, then folded up the torn and discolored pieces of clothing and placed them in a drawer. Seven days would pass before she took them out again. No convincing explanation for this delay was ever offered. Perhaps at first Mrs. Loss failed to draw a connection between the items and the missing cigar girl. Possibly she hoped that the reward money would continue to increase as the authorities grew more desperate. When pressed, she would only say, according to later newspaper accounts, that she had hesitated to come forward in the belief that "something might turn up to make them more useful than if she handed them over at once."

Whatever the reason for the delay, Mrs. Loss had clearly acquainted herself with the Mary Rogers saga by early September, when she made an appointment to see Justice Gilbert Merritt at the Hoboken police station. Merritt listened attentively as Mrs. Loss told her story, but one imagines, after the Joseph Morse episode, that he approached the matter with caution. He would later say that there was something about Mrs. Loss's manner that put him on guard, and it seemed odd to him that she had declined to bring any of the articles of clothing with her to the interview. On hearing the details, however, Merritt realized that this new discovery, if genuine, marked a major breakthrough in the case.

Merritt dispatched Dr. Cook, the coroner, to Mrs. Loss's tavern to examine the evidence. Cook, too, had reason to be wary of leaping to conclusions, but in his mind there could be no doubt. The items belonged to Mary Rogers, and the strips of fabric had been torn from the dress she wore at the time of her death. In all likelihood, then, the thicket at Nick Moore's Tavern was the spot where Mary Rogers had been murdered.

As officials from both sides of the Hudson converged on the scene, the New York police issued a formal request to the city's newspapers to suspend all mention of the case until this new development could be properly explored. The editors complied for the most part, but not without teasing hints of a coming revelation. "When we are permitted," promised the *Herald*, "we will lift the veil, and show scenes of blood and brutality that will make the hair stand on end."

For Gilbert Merritt, the discovery held out the promise of vindication. Having weathered four weeks of hostility in the press, he lost no time in making his way to Nick Moore's Tavern to examine the grounds for himself. This type of spadework was normally left to constables, but Merritt was taking no chances. After studying the thicket where the clothes had been found, he settled himself in the front parlor of the inn to interview each member of the family. Although his manner was open and cordial, the magistrate had unmistakable suspicions about Mrs. Loss and her sons.

Under Merritt's steady gaze, Mrs. Loss began to draw together the scattered threads of a story that would go through several changes and embellishments in the coming days. The initial version was fairly straightforward: On Sunday, July 25, a young woman had entered the tavern in the company of a young man with a "swarthy" complexion. The young lady was perhaps twenty years of age, dark-haired and very attractive. She wore a white linen dress and carried a parasol. Mrs. Loss recalled the dress in particular because it was similar to one owned by her sister, a coincidence that she had remarked upon at the time. The young woman's manner, Mrs. Loss recalled, was "very affable and modest." She realized now that the young woman must have been Mary Rogers.

Five or six young couples were gathered in the parlor at the time, and Mrs. Loss could not be certain whether Mary Rogers and her companion had arrived separately or with the larger group. When a tray of liquor was circulated, the swarthy man offered a glass to Mary. She declined, asking for lemonade instead. After a short time, the pair rose to leave. Mary took her escort by the arm and bowed her thanks to Mrs. Loss as the couple strolled off down the path leading toward the water.

As dusk fell, Mrs. Loss sent her eldest son, Oscar, to drive away a bull that had wandered down the path from a neighbor's property. A short time later, she heard a cry from the woods near the tavern. She recalled it as "a frightful screaming as if of a young girl in great distress, partly choked, and calling for assistance, and sounded like 'Oh! Oh! God!' etc., uttered in great agony." In spite of the extraordinary precision of this description—she stated repeatedly that the shout was that of a young girl or a woman—Mrs. Loss concluded that it had come from Oscar. Fearing that her son had been gored by the escaped bull, she rushed from the house calling the boy's name. "As soon as she called out," the *Herald* later reported, "there was a noise as of struggling, and a stifled suffering scream, and then all was still."

Mrs. Loss soon learned that her son was safe, having successfully driven off the neighbor's bull. She gave no further thought to the agonized, choking female screams she had heard. "All sorts of riotous miscreants" were prowling and sparring in the area that day, she said. She assumed the sounds had signified nothing more ominous than spirited horseplay. Indeed, it was known that a number of gangs had rowed over from New York and gathered at a "rum hole on the mud bank" not far from the Loss inn, and several fights had disturbed the peace of the afternoon. In days to come there would be a great deal of speculation as to whether one of these gangs might have attacked Mary Rogers and her companion. At the time, however, only one crime was known to have been committed: A group of gang members had "seized all the cakes" laid out on a refreshment table and refused to pay for them.

Upon close examination by the police, the "murder thicket," as it soon came to be called, yielded up several important clues. "It is between two roads and the distance across is from thirty to forty feet," ran a description in the *Sun*. "It can only be entered on all fours, or on the hands and knees. It requires a man with young limbs to get into the place at all. No girl under any circumstances could be persuaded to go voluntarily in such a place among the stones, sharp rocks and dirt—particularly after a rain, when the leaves and earth would be so wet and filthy. Arriving at the inside, there is not a flat rock there—not a platform or even surface, a foot in diameter. There is hardly a place to sit down—and no place upon which a person could lie down with any more ease than he could in a barrel with nail points inward through its sides."

Inside the thicket, signs of violence were evident in the soft dirt, along with the imprints of a man's high-heeled boot. One of the torn strips of fabric hanging from the branches was found to have been pierced three times by a thorn, apparently indicating a prolonged ordeal. "The place around was stamped about, and the branches were broken, and roots bruised and mashed, all betokening that it had been the scene of a very violent struggle," noted one account. "And it appeared from the position of the articles as if the unfortunate girl had been placed upon the middle broad stone, her head held forcibly back, and then and there horribly violated by several rowdies, and ultimately strangled."

Tracks leading away from the thicket toward the river were also visible, along with a long, shallow furrow of dirt, as though someone had dragged a heavy weight in that direction. Two fences stood between the thicket and the river. At the points where the fences crossed the trail of footprints, several railings had been knocked out to allow easier passage. The discarded rails were still lying in the nearby grass. The railings and the tracks in the dirt appeared to confirm one of Dr. Cook's conclusions; during the initial inquest, the coroner had noted a long strip of fabric wound three times around the body and tied in "a sort of hitch." Cook had speculated that the fabric served as a kind of handle, allowing the murderer to drag the body away for disposal in the river.

For some, the evidence of the murder thicket raised troubling questions. How could these clues have passed unnoticed for so many weeks? Was it really plausible that the clothing and the marks in the soil could have remained undisturbed for more than a month? A suspicion arose that the scene had been staged by Mrs.

Loss or her sons, possibly with an eye toward collecting the reward. Or perhaps, if the articles of clothing were found to be genuine, Mary Rogers's murderer might have planted the evidence in an effort to distract attention from the actual murder site.

As the rumors and hearsay gathered force, Mayor Morris issued another plea for the newspapers to refrain from comment, insisting that idle speculation would inhibit the progress of the investigation. After more than a week of silence, however, the press could no longer restrain itself. On September 17, James Gordon Bennett openly flouted the wishes of City Hall with a lengthy comment on the discoveries at Weehawken, complete with an engraving of Nick Moore's Tavern, with a caption identifying it as "The House Where Mary Rogers Was Last Seen Alive."

True to form, the *Herald* presented the new evidence as an ironclad confirmation of the view it had embraced from the beginning, that Mary Rogers had fallen victim to one or more members of a gang of "soaplocks and rowdies." The paper painted a vivid portrait of the crime and its aftermath, with the villain cowering "by the dead and mangled body of his victim in that dark thicket, with no eye but that of God upon the murderer and the murdered maid, until all was still—perhaps 'til midnight. Then, tying the frock around her to form a handle, he carried her to the river, and hurled her in, and fled, too horror-stricken to think of returning to the scene of the murder to remove the articles found by the boys."

Bennett and William Attree, his crime reporter, quickly dismissed the notion of contrivance or falsehood about the recovered articles of clothing: "In order that it may not be supposed that these things were placed there recently, it is proper to state that from their appearance this could not have been the case. The things had all evidently been there at least three or four weeks. They were all mildewed down hard from the action of the rain, and stuck together from the mildew. The grass had grown around and over some of them." As if this weren't compelling enough, the *Herald* noted, the petticoat and shawl were found to have been infested with small bugs identified as "cellar jackass, an insect that always gets into clothing lying in wet places." To bolster its argument, the *Herald* published a sketch of the thicket over a caption reading: "The Actual Spot Where the Shocking Murder and Violation of Mary Rogers Took Place." Owing to the limited printing techniques of the day, the engraving left a great deal to the imagination. As a later commentator would remark, "The sketch could pass equally for a simoom in the Arabian desert, or twilight in a drunkard's stomach."

As the Weehawken discoveries became public, a new witness stepped forward whose testimony appeared to support the notion that Mary Rogers had been murdered at the thicket. Adam Wall, a Hoboken coach driver, reported that he had been waiting for fares at the river dock on the Sunday in question when a friend pointed out a strikingly attractive young woman in the company of a "swarthy man." The woman, Wall now realized, must have been Mary Rogers. The couple declined to accept a ride, Wall said. Instead, they set off on foot down the path leading to Weehawken. Wall also claimed to have caught a glimpse of the corpse that came ashore at Castle Point three days later. On reflection, he felt positive it was the same person.

Wall, like Mrs. Loss, could give no good reason for his delay in coming forward. On further questioning, he claimed that he had not drawn a connection between the pretty girl he had seen and the missing cigar girl until his friend jogged his memory some time afterward: "So," Wall was told, "that pretty cigar girl was killed that day I pointed her out to you." Wall's evidence, as numerous papers pointed out, did not inspire confidence. Like Mrs. Loss, he soon fell under suspicion of having concocted his story with an eye toward collecting the reward money.

As the debate grew, curiosity-seekers once again flocked to New Jersey, and Mrs. Loss began to do a brisk business in liquor and lemonade. Boatloads of visitors arrived daily to wander over the grounds of the infamous thicket, and all but a few of them called in afterward at Nick Moore's Tavern to enjoy the thrill of sitting at the very spot where Mary Rogers was last seen alive.

Not all of these visitors were thrill-seekers. At three o'clock on the afternoon of October 7, Daniel Payne, Mary Rogers's beleaguered fiancé, crossed the Hudson and made his way to Weehawken. He wore a brown frock coat over a black suit, and his high silk hat was wound with a black band of mourning crepe.

Grim-faced and haggard, Payne made his way to the Loss inn, where twelve-year-old Ossian Kellenbarack was tending bar. Payne ordered a brandy and water, knocked it back in a single gulp, and asked for directions to the spot where Mary Rogers was said to have met her death. By this time Ossian had devised a profitable sideline in conducting tours of the murder thicket, but Payne did not want an escort. Instead, after fortifying himself with another brandy and water, Payne set off alone down the carriage road.

At ten o'clock that evening, Payne stumbled through the doors of a tavern in Hoboken and asked for a brandy and water. His clothing was askew and he appeared highly agitated over the loss of his hat. "I suppose you know me," he said. "I'm the man that was promised to Mary Rogers." He paused over his drink. When he spoke again his voice had gone thick: "I'm a man in a great deal of trouble."

The following morning, a local farmer named James McShane came across Payne sprawled facedown, sobbing in the wet grass. The smell of alcohol hung in the air. To McShane, this could mean only one thing. "My dear man," he said, "are you a Frenchman?" On receiving assurances to the contrary, McShane helped the fallen man to his feet. Payne made a half-hearted attempt to brush his clothing, then stumbled off in the direction of Castle Point, still mumbling about his missing hat.

A short time later, Payne's hat was found lying on the soft ground of the murder thicket. Nearby were glass shards from a vial of laudanum, an alcoholic tincture of opium sweetened with sugar. At the time laudanum was in wide use as a pain reliever and "nerve tonic," but the drug was reviled by temperance advocates for its addictive and potentially toxic qualities. Payne had purchased his supply at an apothecary on Ann Street, a few steps away from the Rogers boardinghouse. Apparently he uncorked the vial upon reaching the murder thicket, and drained the contents as he surveyed the scene of his fiancée's final struggles. Turning away, he smashed the empty glass vial against a rock and wandered off toward the river.

He did not get far. Within a few hours, Payne was found lying prone on a bench near Sybil's Cave, his head hanging a few inches off the ground. By chance, the first man to reach him was a doctor, who rolled him over and loosened his collar. Payne's eyes were glassy, and a soft moan rose from his lips. The doctor rushed away to get help, but by the time he returned, Daniel Payne was dead.

In his pocket was a penciled note: "To the World—Here I am on the spot; God forgive me for my misfortune in my misspent time."

PART THREE

The Fatal Sabbath

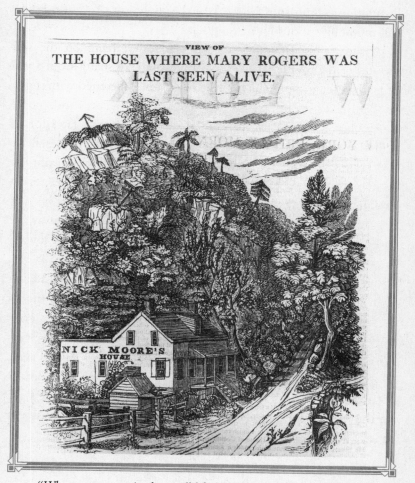

VIEW OF

THE HOUSE WHERE MARY ROGERS WAS
LAST SEEN ALIVE.

NICK MOORE'S
HOUSE

*"When we are permitted we will lift the veil, and show scenes of blood
and brutality that will make the hair stand on end."*
—*Herald* (New York), September 17, 1841
Courtesy of American Antiquarian Society

Circumstances, and a certain bias of mind, have led me to take interest in such riddles, and it may well be doubted whether human ingenuity can construct an enigma of the kind which human ingenuity may not, by proper application, resolve.

—Edgar Allan Poe, "The Gold-Bug"

There are ideal series of events which run parallel with the real ones. They rarely coincide. Men and circumstances generally modify the ideal train of events, so that it seems imperfect, and its consequences are equally imperfect.

—Friedrich von Hardenburg, "Moralische Anisichten"
(Epigraph of "The Mystery of Marie Rogêt")

XIII

A Somewhat Wasted Heart

GILBERT MERRITT REACHED Castle Point before Daniel Payne's body had a chance to cool. Crouching over the lifeless form, Justice Merritt resolved to conduct as thorough and irreproachable an investigation as could be imagined. This time, there would be no charges of mismanagement.

As a pair of doctors arrived to examine the corpse, Merritt proceeded to round up witnesses. Next he sent word to Robert Morris, the mayor of New York, along with the New York coroner, Dr. Archer, and Justice Taylor, who had presided over the Joseph Morse affair. Finally, Merritt requested a positive identification from Payne's brother.

In contrast to the Mary Rogers inquest, Daniel Payne's death had occurred on a relatively mild October afternoon. Most of Merritt's woes in the earlier case arose from his eagerness to finish before the remains "consumed themselves." Payne's corpse, by comparison, showed few signs of decay. Merritt decided to convene the official inquest the following morning in order to allow time to marshal his evidence and notify the family members. The body would pass the night cooling on blocks of ice.

By nightfall, as the newspapers learned of Payne's death, speculation ran rampant. When it became known that Payne had died with a bundle of papers in his pocket, a rumor sprang up that he had left a written confession to the murder of Mary Rogers. One story had it that he had not only admitted killing his fiancée but three other women as well.

The inquest convened at eleven o'clock on the morning of October 9 in a private room in a hotel opposite one of the Hoboken ferry landings. The site was probably selected as a courtesy to Mayor Morris and Justice Taylor, who had chartered a private boat and braved a heavy storm in order to attend. While extra chairs were brought in to accommodate the distinguished visitors from New York, the body of Daniel Payne was laid out on a table at the front of the room. The dead man's hat, which had caused him so much anxiety in his final hours, rested on his chest.

The first witness to be sworn in was Dr. Samuel Griswold of New York, who had been walking with his friend Dr. Clements when they came upon Payne in his final moments, sprawled out in a "state of stupefaction" on a bench by the river. The "peculiar position" in which he lay, with his head lolling off the edge of the bench, might well have hastened his death, Griswold testified. Possibly the man had fallen and struck his head. In any case, it became evident to Griswold within moments that Payne was dying. Nothing remained to be done but to summon help and to try to make the dying man comfortable.

As Dr. Griswold left the witness stand, his friend Dr. Clements took his place and confirmed Griswold's testimony. The unfortunate man had been beyond the reach of medical help when they happened upon him, Clements said, and showed no awareness of their presence. Clements added that he had put his nose to the dying man's mouth and noted that the breath smelled sour.

After a great deal of irrelevant testimony from a pair of cork cutters who had read of the death in the morning papers, Payne's brother John stepped forward to be examined. Under prompting from Merritt, he stated for the record that the body at the front of the room was that of Daniel Payne. "He was habitually a drinking man," John Payne said, adding that his brother had been "out of his mind since the affair of Mary Rogers."

John Payne's testimony was followed by that of Alfred Crommelin. He had not seen or spoken to the dead man since their brief and frosty encounter in the parlor of the Rogers boardinghouse while both men were searching for the missing woman. Crommelin's value as a witness is highly suspect; he offered no testimony as to the deceased's habits and background that had not already been elicited from others, and he could throw no light on Payne's actions in his final days. By this time, however, Crommelin had become the public face of the Mary Rogers saga, and it was well known that he wanted a public hearing in relation to the murder. Although Payne's inquest could hardly have been said to fill that function, Crommelin's appearance provides a measure of Gilbert Merritt's desire to be thorough. If Crommelin hoped at last to give his definitive account of the Mary Rogers investigation, however, he was to be disappointed. Merritt limited Crommelin's statement to facts related directly to Payne's death. Crommelin could offer little more than an additional identification of the body and a half-hearted statement of reconciliation toward the dead man: "there was no coolness between us."

Several tavern keepers and other witnesses offered a patchwork account of Payne's drunken wanderings during the final two days of his life. Justice Merritt had taken great care to conduct the inquest according to established protocol. As a result, the woman whose testimony was the most potentially explosive had been shuffled in with this group of otherwise inconsequential witnesses. Mrs. Frederica Loss, the proprietor of Nick Moore's Tavern, now stood to testify on behalf of her twelve-year-old son, who had served Daniel Payne one of his last drinks.

A great deal hinged on Mrs. Loss's statement. Although Daniel Payne had been questioned repeatedly and cleared of all suspicion in the murder of Mary Rogers, there were many on both sides of the Hudson who doubted his innocence. Although his alibi had appeared unshakable, questions remained about his conduct and his apparent lack of concern following the report of her murder. Now, in the aftermath of Payne's dramatic death, these doubts returned to the fore. An unspoken agenda lay behind Merritt's methodical adherence to procedure: Could Payne have been with Mary Rogers on the day of her death? Was he the mysterious "Swarthy Man"?

The room fell silent as Mrs. Loss made her way forward. Dressed in a Sunday frock, the innkeeper seemed well aware of the gravity of the situation, and not at all displeased by the attention focused upon her. She nodded companionably at Justice Merritt as he came forward to question her, as though he might be offering a cup of tea. Merritt, for his part, appeared stone-faced. His tone was brisk and businesslike as he asked his first question: Did Mrs. Loss recognize the man whose body lay at the front of the room, the late Daniel Payne? Mrs. Loss hesitated, apparently taking the measure of the room. Yes, she said after a moment. She knew the dead man's face.

A low murmur went through the gallery of witnesses. Merritt's face tightened as he took a step forward. How, he asked, did she know him? She had not been present when her son Ossian served Payne his brandy on the day before his death (Ossian had already been questioned privately). Was Daniel Payne the man who had accompanied Mary Rogers to the Loss inn on the day of her disappearance? Again Mrs. Loss hesitated. She looked up at Justice

Merritt with a cool and steady gaze. No, she said. That man had been "younger, thinner and not so tall." Daniel Payne did not resemble him at all.

Merritt stepped back, a scowl pulling at his features. Clearly, his feelings toward Mrs. Loss had not warmed since their first encounter in his chambers, when he concluded that she knew more than she was saying. A note of anger crept into his voice as he repeated his earlier question: How, then, did Mrs. Loss come to recognize the dead man? Had Payne visited the tavern on some other occasion? Yes, Mrs. Loss answered airily, Payne had once gone hunting in the vicinity, she believed. Perhaps he stopped in for a drink. The answer did not satisfy Merritt. He continued his questioning, asking in various ways if Mrs. Loss might perhaps be mistaken on this point. Perhaps Payne might have been the stranger who accompanied Mary Rogers after all? Mrs. Loss would not be swayed: Daniel Payne, she insisted, was not the Swarthy Man. Although she recognized his face, and could not be quite certain where she had seen him before, she was adamant that he had not accompanied Mary Rogers to the tavern. Frustrated, Merritt brought his interrogation to a close.

Merritt's shoulders slumped as Mrs. Loss returned to her seat. All hopes of a decisive breakthrough in the Mary Rogers murder were now dashed. As Dr. Cook, the Hoboken coroner, was sworn in to report on the findings from Payne's autopsy, the proceedings reverted to a routine inquest.

Payne's stomach had been opened, Dr. Cook reported, but the contents revealed nothing unusual apart from the remains of a last meal that appeared to have been potatoes. The brain was found to be congested with blood, possibly the result of the lowered position of the head at the time of death. Cook also thought that he detected the smell of laudanum in the brain, though this "might have been imagination" sparked by the discovery of the empty vial at the murder thicket. Payne's other organs, Cook testified, appeared to be normal, although the heart appeared "somewhat wasted, which might account for his melancholy."

Cook stopped short of declaring an exact cause of death, and the vagueness of his conclusions suggests that he was attempting to cover all contingencies. Payne's death was widely reported as a suicide, the result of despair—or perhaps a guilty conscience—over the death of Mary Rogers. Payne's actions in his final days, together with the note found in his pocket, strongly supported the notion that he had come to Weehawken to take his own life. For the purposes of the inquest, however, the evidence was by no means decisive. Many of the accounts of Payne's death—both at the time and subsequently—referred to the vial of laudanum he had purchased as "vile poison," but this was largely rhetorical bluster at a time when the drug was both legal and widely prescribed. Certainly the drug was capable of a toxic effect if taken in large or prolonged doses, but it was not generally perceived to be poisonous. When abused, however, laudanum could easily cause a fatal overdose—"the eternal sleep of melancholia," as a writer of the day phrased it. Painless and readily obtained, laudanum was popular with those who wished to end their own lives, and accidental overdoses were frequent among those with a weakness for the drug.

In Payne's case, the coroner could not make a categorical statement of intent. The quantity of laudanum Payne consumed was unknown: He had smashed the vial against a rock at the murder thicket, and apparently no one inquired at the Ann Street apothecary where he had purchased it. In the absence of other evidence, Cook concluded vaguely that Payne's "manner of passing the previous twenty-four hours of his life must have tended to his death," and added that the "peculiar position" of the head during his final stupor on the bench had "probably hastened" his death. The jury deliberated briefly and returned a verdict that death had occurred owing to "congestions of the brain, supposed to be brought about by exposure and irregularity of living, incident to aberration of mind."

It was a maddeningly inconclusive set of findings, in spite of Merritt's determined efforts. Once again, the press scented blood. Justice Merritt was accused of being "utterly ignorant of the rules of evidence," and it was suggested that no right-thinking person would be caught dead in New Jersey. Much comment focused on the documents Payne had with him at the time of his death. Although the contents of his supposed suicide note had been released, the other papers remained under wraps, giving rise to speculation about incriminating letters and an anguished confession. Hoping to quiet the rumors, Merritt announced that there was nothing to be gained in the release of the dead man's papers, as they shed no light on the death of Payne or the murder of Mary Rogers. This did not satisfy everyone. "What has the Learned Justice to hide?" asked the *Sun*, but Benjamin Day's *Tattler* took a more diplomatic view: "Except in melodramas, villains are not in the habit of leaving tell-tale bits of paper about, or committing themselves with paper and ink."

For the most part, however, the *Tattler* took a very dim view of Merritt and the Weehawken findings. Incredibly, Benjamin Day was still clinging manfully to his theory that Mary Rogers was alive, and he appeared determined to shoot down any contradictory fact or supposition that appeared in the pages of James Gordon Bennett's *Herald*. A few days before Payne's death, Day had sent one of his best men to examine the murder thicket and to interview Mrs. Loss, hoping to poke holes in the new evidence. After a day in Weehawken, Day's reporter returned and filed a lengthy report in the pages of *Brother Jonathan*, the sister publication of the *Tattler*. The new findings, as Day was quick to point out, cast serious doubt on the testimony of Mrs. Loss with respect to the final hours of Mary Rogers: "If the narrative throws a little discredit on a portion of the chain of circumstantial evidence which has been paraded in the newspapers, we cannot help it."

According to *Brother Jonathan*, Mrs. Loss had given a new statement that "destroyed a great part of the unity of the Weehawken murder narrative," and even reversed many of the conclusions that had been drawn by the police. Previous reports had stressed that Mary and the so-called Swarthy Man had arrived and departed separately from the other couples taking refreshment in Mrs. Loss's parlor that afternoon. In her statement to *Brother Jonathan*, however, Mrs. Loss no longer appeared certain of this point. It was possible, she now admitted, that Mary and her companion might have departed with the larger group. If so, there would have been perhaps a dozen people who were aware of Mary's presence at Weehawken that day. It seemed incredible that not one of them had come forward—whether they had a hand in her murder or not—especially in light of Governor Seward's promise of immunity from prosecution for any accomplice who came forward.

Mrs. Loss also appeared to waver on her earlier account of the screams she had heard outside her home that evening. Her previous statements had been extraordinarily precise, employing terms such as "choked" and "stifled." Now, under close questioning from the *Brother Jonathan* reporter, she backpedaled. There had been a scream, certainly, but perhaps only one, and the sound was rather indistinct. Adding to the confusion, Mrs. Loss claimed that upon hearing this scream she hurried from the house and passed within ten feet of the thicket, but she had not heard or seen anything amiss.

Brother Jonathan also cast doubt on the *Herald*'s claim that the evidence could have passed unnoticed for so many weeks. Unwilling to take Mrs. Loss and her sons at their word, Day's reporter tracked down another neighbor, who happened to be the tenant of the property where the thicket sat. When questioned, this gentleman merely "shook his head incredulously at the circumstance of the clothes having lain so long in the thicket undisturbed." He had seen no signs of anything unusual, and knew nothing of any of the so-called evidence, such as the missing fence railings, until he read the newspaper reports. "The fence is in perfect order now, at any rate," he insisted.

Brother Jonathan also tracked down Adam Wall, the coach driver who reported seeing Mary heading toward Weehawken. Wall's testimony, the paper believed, was entirely worthless. "He did not remember having seen the girl on that Sunday until a month afterward," the reporter protested, "and is not very clear upon it now." Furthermore, Wall's friend, who had supposedly jogged the coach driver's memory on the subject, had not been produced. "Why," asked *Brother Jonathan*, "has he never come forward amid all the outcry that has been made?"

The questions raised in the pages of *Brother Jonathan* cast serious doubt on the prevailing theories concerning the murder thicket. Benjamin Day's motives were far from pure—even when discussing the coroner's report, his reporters dutifully preserved the fantasy that the cigar girl was still alive, making tortured references to "the supposed body of Mary Rogers"—but the results sparked a fresh round of debate over what had transpired in Weehawken. Even in the description of Mrs. Loss as "a very clever intelligent little woman of about forty," the paper managed to convey a sense of cunning and deceit. "We left the ground far from satisfied that 'the thicket' had been anything more than the depository of the garments, etc., by interested hands," noted the reporter, "long after the disappearance of Mary C. Rogers."

Inevitably, Mrs. Loss and the Weehawken murder theory soon found a champion in James Gordon Bennett. The *Herald* lost no time in heaping scorn on Benjamin Day and his newspaper's claims: "It is worse than idle on the part of many persons who ought to know better to attempt to throw a doubt over the locality of the murder of this poor girl. It was undoubtedly done at Weehawken." Bennett also offered a gallant defense of Mrs. Loss, who was described as "a fine, intelligent good-looking lady" of presumably laudable German descent. For good measure, he also shaved ten years off the *Sun's* estimate of her age, placing her at "about thirty years."

The *Herald* brought out its heavy artillery to defend the thicket itself. A detailed illustration of the Weehawken shoreline appeared at the end of September, with labels showing the location of the thicket, the abandoned road that ran alongside, and other points of interest. To Bennett's way of thinking, the sketch provided inarguable proof that the thicket was so remote and isolated that a "thousand persons may pass the spot even now and not notice it." For these reasons, he insisted, it was entirely probable that the crime could have been committed without drawing notice, and that the evidence could have lain undisturbed for several weeks. "So much then," the *Herald* sniffed, "for the silly statement that the articles must have been recently put there or they would have been discovered before."

Doubts persisted, however. In the pages of the *Herald* and elsewhere, speculation ranged from a single murderer to a gang of rowdies. The continuing mystery surrounding Mary's companion, the "Swarthy Man," also attracted a great deal of comment. Perhaps he, too, had been murdered by the gang that set upon Mary. If so, his body had not yet been discovered, and might well be lying at the bottom of the Hudson. Or perhaps he himself was the killer, having flown into a murderous rage when Mary rebuffed his advances. If that were the case, observed the *Journal of Commerce*, it was surprising that Mary should have tolerated his company at all, as he could only have been a very coarse and ill-bred sort of man. "A piece of one of the unfortunate girl's petticoats was torn out and tied under her chin, and around the back of her head, probably to prevent screams," the paper noted. "This was done by fellows who had no pocket handkerchiefs." In other words, no proper gentleman could have had a hand in the matter, since a man of breeding would have used his own linen.

As the contradictions and inconsistencies mounted, it became clear that the discoveries at Weehawken, along with the inconclusive results of Daniel Payne's inquest, raised more questions than they answered. Several accounts of the items found in the thicket listed a pair of ladies' gloves among the articles of clothing recovered, with the *Herald* going so far as to say that the gloves had been turned inside out, as if "forcibly drawn from her hands in a hurry." This presented a troubling discrepancy with the reports of Mary's corpse as it was pulled from the water at Castle Point. Several of these accounts reported that Mary's gloves were found on her dead hands, with the *Herald* going so far as to remark on the "light gloves . . . with the long watery fingers peering out." Although this attracted little notice at the time, it marked a substantial incongruity. Perhaps one or the other of the accounts had been in error, and the mistaken detail had simply been repeated in the other newspapers, but for the time being, the contradiction was difficult to reconcile. Meanwhile, the crowds continued to swarm over the grounds of the murder thicket, which no longer seemed quite as remote and isolated as Bennett had claimed. If, as

Benjamin Day implied, Mrs. Loss had sought this notoriety to some degree as a means of increasing her business, the plan had succeeded brilliantly.

Daniel Payne was laid to rest in New York on Monday, October 11, two days after the conclusion of the Weehawken inquest. When it became clear that his dramatic death would yield no solution to the Mary Rogers mystery, public interest in the drama slowly began to fade. Soon enough, the newspapers had a new sensation: the grisly ax murder of local printer Samuel Adams, whose mutilated corpse had been discovered neatly concealed in a packing crate, awaiting shipment to New Orleans. The trial and subsequent suicide of the killer, John C. Colt—brother of the famous firearms manufacturer—would hold New York spellbound for months to come.

For the moment, Mary Rogers was yesterday's news.

XIV

A Wave of Crimson

IN PHILADELPHIA, where the newspaper reports from New York were widely reprinted, Edgar Allan Poe followed the Weehawken developments with keen interest. He remained intrigued with all forms of news from New York, though the struggles of his life there now seemed safely behind him. In contrast to the utter poverty and desperation of his household on Carmine Street, Poe now had cause for satisfaction. His salary of eight hundred dollars from *Graham's Magazine*, though far from munificent, afforded him a sense of stability he had not known before in his adult life. By the end of 1841 he had moved with his wife and mother-in-law to a small townhouse on Coates Street at the northern edge of the city. As he had promised long ago in Richmond, he sought to provide Virginia with the comforts of privilege. The new house was furnished with a small piano, a harp, and a pair of songbirds in a gilded cage.

On January 20, 1842, the day after Poe's thirty-third birthday, a small group of friends gathered in the parlor of the house on Coates Street to hear Virginia sing and play upon the harp. "There was something peculiarly angelic and ethereal about this sight of Virginia playing the harp in the parlor by her own fireside, that almost transported Poe," wrote an early admirer of the writer.

"Dressed in white, singing in the glow of the lamplight, she became the personification of the Victorian heroine. The notes mounted higher, very true and clear—suddenly she stopped, clutched her throat, and a wave of crimson rushed down over her breast."

Ashen-faced, Poe carried his wife upstairs and laid her on the bed, then turned and ran for a doctor. Poe must have known, even before the doctor's grim confirmation, that his wife's hemorrhage signaled the onset of what was often described as "death-in-life," or tuberculosis. He would also have realized that her prospects for survival were slim. Tuberculosis accounted for nearly one-quarter of all deaths in nineteenth-century America, and the limited treatments available—such as lengthy removals to healthful climates and sanatoriums—were beyond the resources of an editor making eight hundred dollars a year.

Virginia would spend two weeks in precarious health, scarcely able to breathe except when fanned with fresh air. At times her coughing grew so severe that it seemed she would choke to death, and more than once the bleeding resumed. Heartsick, Poe remained at her side, brooding over the hand-to-mouth existence that had left his wife weakened and vulnerable. More than one visitor observed that the cramped and musty house in which they lived— luxurious by their usual standards—could only have made Virginia's condition worse. The room in which the patient lay was so tiny that the sloping roof all but pressed down on her head.

George Graham, Poe's employer, observed that Poe's "love for his wife was a sort of rapturous worship of the spirit of beauty which he felt was fading before his eyes. I have seen him hovering around her when she was ill, with all the fond fear and tender anxiety of a mother for her first-born, her slightest cough causing in him a shudder, a heart-chill that was visible."

Soon enough, Virginia's illness would throw its shadow across Poe's work. In "The Masque of the Red Death," published just a few months after Virginia's first attack, Poe dwelled on themes of plague and contagion, along with the "horror of blood," and concluded with a grisly affirmation of death's "illimitable dominion over all." In "Eleonora," also written during the early stages of the illness, Poe returned to the theme and meditated on the grim new circumstances of his life. The story featured a young man living an idyllic life with his young cousin, Eleonora, and her mother in a paradise known as "the Valley of Many-Colored Grass." All too soon, however, Eleonora tearfully exclaims that "she had seen that the finger of Death was upon her bosom—that, like the ephemeron, she had been made in perfect loveliness only to die."

In the months to follow, Poe wavered between cautious optimism and absolute despair. "My dear little wife has been dangerously ill," he told one friend in February, "but to-day the prospect brightens, and I trust that this bitter cup of misery will not be my portion." By the summer, however, he was referring to Virginia's "renewed and hopeless illness," and declaring that "I have scarcely a faint hope of her recovery."

For a time Poe threw himself into his work, contributing reviews, poems, and stories to *Graham's Magazine*, and finding advantage in his growing reputation. When he learned that Charles Dickens would be touring Philadelphia in March of 1842, Poe wrote to request an interview, sending along a copy of *Tales of the Grotesque and Arabesque*. Poe also included copies of his past reviews of Dickens's work, attesting to the sincerity of his admiration for the writer he once called "the greatest British novelist." Among these was an article offering comment on the murder intrigue of *Barnaby Rudge*, written shortly after the early chapters began to appear in serial form. Although the book's conclusion would not be published for several months, Poe had been able to predict, correctly, that "Barnaby, the idiot, is the murderer's own son."

Poe made a powerful impression on Dickens. The visiting author gave two lengthy interviews to Poe at Philadelphia's United States Hotel on March 7, 1842. Dickens took particular note of Poe's reviews, and would later describe the young critic as a man "who taketh all of us English men of letters to task in print, roundly and uncompromisingly." Although the meeting took place under the auspices of *Graham's*, Poe was not bashful about turning it to his personal advantage: By the end of the interview, Dickens had agreed to help Poe find a publisher in Britain. The work of Dickens would continue to make itself felt in Poe's work, not least in the case of a loquacious raven that figures in the pages of *Barnaby Rudge*. In his review of the novel, Poe mused at length on the manner in which this detail might have been used to greater effect: "Its croakings might have been *prophetically* heard in the course of the drama."

In spite of the advantages of his position at *Graham's*, Poe quickly fell into the same resentful frame of mind that had led to his difficulties at *Burton's* and the *Southern Literary Messenger*. He confided, shortly after joining the magazine, that "notwithstanding Graham's unceasing civility, and real kindness, I feel more & more disgusted with my situation." Poe had cause for indignation. The magazine's extraordinary success was reaping a fortune for Graham, but Poe's earnings remained fixed at their original level, which he now considered meager to the point of insult. As the gloom of Virginia's illness took hold, Poe's bitterness deepened. On the morning after the initial hemorrhage, Poe asked Graham to advance him two months' salary to help ease the expected burden. Graham refused, and the family soon fell back into a state of penury.

At the same time, the success of *Graham's* rekindled Poe's hopes for a magazine of his own. His friend Thomas Holley Chivers, a Georgia poet who took a keen interest in Poe's welfare, went out of his way to flatter these ambitions. "It is not my opinion that you have ever been, or ever will be, paid for your intellectual labours," Chivers declared. "You need never expect it, until you establish a Magazine of your own." Here, too, Poe nursed a personal grievance against his employer. Graham had promised, when Poe joined his magazine, that he would help to launch Poe's own *Penn Magazine* within a year. As *Graham's* grew in circulation and profitability, however, the promise was forgotten. Poe recognized that he had been a victim of his own success. "Every exertion made by myself," he wrote, served to make *Graham's* a "greater source of profit" and left its owner "less willing to keep his word with me."

Matters reached a crisis in April of 1842. Following a brief illness, Poe returned to his desk to find that his duties had been assumed by Charles Peterson, an associate editor. It may well be that Peterson had simply acted to cover for Poe in his absence, but Poe found cause for offense. Always sensitive about his status as an editor, he believed he had been slighted and perhaps passed over for promotion. Soon, he took his leave of the magazine. As with Poe's earlier editorial positions, there would be a difference of opinion as to whether he left voluntarily or was fired. "Either Peterson or Poe would have to go," Graham said at one stage, "the two could not get along together." Poe insisted that he had resigned to pursue his own interests, citing disgust with the "namby-pamby" character of the magazine and the "insulting" salary. In contrast to his earlier hostility toward Thomas Willis White and William Burton, however, Poe felt no great animosity for the "very gentlemanly" Graham, with whom he claimed to have "no misunderstanding."

Whatever the reasons, Poe's departure from *Graham's* marked a return to abject poverty. With Virginia's illness adding to his burdens, one can only wonder why he took such an ill-advised step. "Probably the whole truth as to Poe's resignation of this editorship will never be known," wrote one of Poe's early admirers. "Doubtless it was due to a combination of causes. There was the constitutional restlessness—the 'nervous restlessness which,' as he acknowledges, 'haunted me as a fiend,' and which at times overpowered him, and drove him from place to place in a vain search for the El Dorado of his hopes; there was the ever-lingering desire to found a magazine of his own, and, what must be confessed, the beginning of those 'irregularities' which, during the remainder of his life, at certain more or less lengthy intervals, destroyed his hopes and placed his reputation in the power of implacable foes."

These "irregularities" took hold almost at once. For the most part Poe had abstained from drinking during his tenure at *Graham's*, but now he returned to the bottle and suffered devastating consequences. All accounts agree that Poe had a dramatically low tolerance for alcohol. At a time when dram shops and rum holes lined the streets, and the phrase "Let's liquor" was a common greeting, Poe's constitution left him uniquely vulnerable. He was unable to stop at a single drink, and the first glass was sufficient to transform him from a personable gentleman to a coarse and staggering "good fornaught." His friend Frederick Thomas observed that "if he took but one glass of weak wine or beer or cider, the Rubicon of the cup was passed with him, and it always ended in excess and sickness." The French poet Charles Baudelaire, himself no stranger to stimulants, would note that Poe "did not drink like an ordinary toper, but like a savage, with an altogether American energy and fear of wasting a minute, as though he was accomplishing an act of murder, as though there was *something* inside him that he had to kill."

Poe's reasons for drinking were plain enough—Virginia's illness, his return to poverty, his literary disappointments—but his recourse to alcohol served in turn to make each of these problems significantly worse. Over the course of fourteen months at *Graham's*, Poe had earned roughly a thousand dollars in salary and contributor's fees. His literary income over the course of the next three years would amount to only $121. Once again Poe considered abandoning his writing, or at least supplementing it with some presumably less taxing form of employment. Although he remained hopeful of launching his own magazine, now recast as *The Stylus*, he also pursued the possibility of a government sinecure with the Philadelphia Customs House. After failing to win an appointment locally, he traveled to Washington in hopes of pleading his case directly to President Tyler, whose son Robert had expressed admiration for Poe's criticism. Anxious at the prospect of the important interview, Poe attempted to quiet his nerves with a glass of port. Not long afterward, he was spotted stumbling around the capital with a greenish pallor, and his coat turned inside out. Poe did not meet the president, and failed to make a favorable impression on anyone else who might have helped him find employment.

As circumstances pushed him back to the writing desk, Poe sought new publishers for some of his magazine stories. Earlier, from the offices of *Graham's*, he had written to Lea & Blanchard, the publishers of *Tales of the Grotesque and Arabesque*, to offer a revised collection of his work, expanded to include newer stories such as "The Murders in the Rue Morgue." The publisher declined, explaining that they had not yet "got through" the earlier edition. In spite of the refusal, Poe had hopes for future dealings with Lea & Blanchard. "I am anxious that your firm should continue to be my publishers," he told them. That being the case, Poe is likely to have kept an eye on the types of books that found favor with the firm. It is perhaps significant, then, that in early 1842, as Poe made his exit from *Graham's*, Lea & Blanchard published a book by William Gilmore Simms entitled *Beauchampe*. Simms was a prominent editor and novelist of the day, and the author of numerous volumes of poetry. Although Poe would have occasion to denigrate his "inaccurate English" and "proneness to revolting images," he nevertheless considered Simms to be "immeasurably the best writer of fiction in America." *Beauchampe* would have been especially likely to engage Poe's attention. Like *Norman Leslie*, the book took inspiration from a real-life murder case, and the source of *Beauchampe* was especially close to Poe's heart. Simms had based his story on the 1825 Beauchamp-Sharp murder case, the so-called Kentucky tragedy that had also been the inspiration for Poe's blank-verse drama "Politan." Poe was clearly aware of the book, and even offered a brief comment in *Graham's*, published after his departure: "The events upon which this novel is based are but too real. No more thrilling, no more romantic tragedy did ever the brain of poet conceive than was the tragedy of Sharpe and Beauchamp."

Poe undoubtedly took note of the manner in which Simms crafted the material into a popular novel, in contrast to his own seventeenth-century Italian intrigue. At the same time, he must have found it galling that Lea & Blanchard had accepted the Simms book—and made a success of it—while declining Poe's own collection of stories. It seems entirely possible, in the uncertain days following the loss of his editorial post, that the popularity of the Simms book turned Poe's mind in the direction of writing a story based on a celebrated crime.

Poe had every reason to feel that his credentials in this arena were as good or better than those of Simms. Beginning with "Maelzel's Chess-Player" he had made a particular specialty of solving puzzles and posing conundrums to his readers, ranging from the coded messages of his popular cryptography series through the "insoluble mystery" of his most recent success, "The Murders in the Rue Morgue." He remained sensitive, however, to the charge that "Rue Morgue," though undeniably clever, suffered from the artificial contrivance of its solution—a puzzle, as he would later write, created "for the express purpose of unraveling." In a sense, *Beauchampe* also suffered from a preordained solution, since the grisly outcome of the Kentucky tragedy was well known and would not come as a surprise to the reader. It is possible that this defect suggested a new possibility, a means by which the artistry of "Rue Morgue" might be combined with the analytical rigor of "Maelzel's Chess-Player." If Poe fixed his attention on a crime that had not, as yet, been solved, all of these objections would be answered. He could not be accused of constructing his own puzzle, nor would the reader know the solution until Poe himself supplied it. This would not only make the story dramatically satisfying, but it would also provide a striking and altogether unique example of ratiocination, or the power of analytical reasoning.

There is no record of how Poe fastened on the Mary Rogers murder as a source of inspiration. Although he would have remembered the celebrated cigar girl from his days in New York, he had been obliged to follow the details of the murder investigation at a distance. The story had attracted wide attention in Philadelphia, however, with the city's *Saturday Evening Post* reprinting nearly all of James Gordon Bennett's coverage from the *Herald*. The editor of the *Post* was Charles Peterson, who also worked as an associate at *Graham's* and had helped to spark Poe's departure by assuming his duties. In August of 1841, during the first wave of press attention in New York, Peterson had called for an "analysis" of the crime in the pages of the *Post*. This was hardly a novel idea during the frantic early days of the coverage, but the fact that Poe knew Peterson personally may have planted a seed in his mind. The death of Daniel Payne later in the year would have brought the case back to Poe's attention at a time when he was closely studying *Barnaby Rudge*, with a particular emphasis on the mechanics of the mystery. In the pages of *Graham's* Poe had offered his readers a short tutorial on "the design of *mystery*," and invited them to peruse the Dickens novel "with a pre-comprehension of the mystery," so that "these points of which we speak break out in all directions like stars, and throw quadruple brilliance over the narrative."

Possibly the Daniel Payne suicide happened to cross Poe's horizon at a time when he was especially susceptible to the idea of writing another crime story, having studied the works of Dickens and Simms so carefully. Or perhaps, as has often been suggested, the "pecuniary embarrassments" to which he was prone had forced him to make an attempt to repeat the success of "Rue Morgue." Whatever the case, it is clear that the Mary Rogers saga came to occupy his full attention within days of his departure from *Graham's* in April of 1842.

Two months later, on June 4, Poe sent a letter to Joseph Evans Snodgrass, the Baltimore editor, with whom he maintained a friendly correspondence. Snodgrass had recently become the editor of the Baltimore *Sunday Visiter*, the journal that had awarded a fifty-dollar prize to "MS. Found in a Bottle" nearly ten years earlier. Poe now hoped to revive the association. He wrote:

> I have a proposition to make. You may remember a tale of mine published about a year ago in "Graham" and entitled the "Murders in the Rue Morgue." Its *theme* was the exercise of ingenuity in detecting a murderer. I am just now putting the concluding touch to a similar article, which I shall entitle "The Mystery of Marie

Rogêt—a Sequel to 'The Murders in the Rue Morgue.' " The story is based upon that of the real murder of Mary Cecilia Rogers, which created so vast an excitement some months ago in New-York. I have handled the entire design in a very singular and entirely *novel* manner. I imagine a series of nearly exact *coincidences* occurring in Paris. A young grisette, one Marie Rogêt, has been murdered under precisely similar circumstances with Mary Rogers. Thus under pretense of showing how Dupin (the hero of the Rue Morgue) unraveled the mystery of Marie's assassination, I, in fact, enter into a very rigorous analysis of the *real* tragedy in New-York. *No point* is omitted. I examine, each by each, the opinions and arguments of our press on the subject, and show (I think satisfactorily) that this subject has never yet been *approached*. The press has been entirely on a wrong scent. In fact, I really believe, not only that I have demonstrated the falsity of the idea that the girl was the victim of a gang of ruffians, but have *indicated the assassin*. My main object, however, as you will readily understand, is the analysis of the *principles of investigation* in cases of like character. Dupin *reasons* the matter throughout.

For all of Poe's enthusiasm, the decision to revive Auguste Dupin for the new story probably had more to do with business than the principles of investigation. Because "Rue Morgue" had been widely praised on its publication the previous year, he undoubtedly hoped that presenting the new story as a sequel, rather than an original composition, would enhance its value and perhaps serve as a further enticement for a future collection of stories. At the same time, transferring the events of the Mary Rogers case to Dupin's Paris afforded a safe remove from the rigid facts of the case, in spite of Poe's insistence on the "nearly exact *coincidences*" of his story. If some of the details did not precisely match those of the New York drama, Poe could put it down to the change of venue.

Poe's letter to Snodgrass, however, showed no sign of a man hedging his bets. Poe clearly implied that he had not only examined the case but solved it—"*indicated the assassin*," as he wrote, "in a manner which will give renewed impetus to investigation." Having set out this tantalizing précis, Poe turned to the matter of finances, treading delicately so as to avoid revealing the extent of his desperation. "The article, I feel convinced, will be one of general interest, from the nature of its subject. For reasons which I may mention to you hereafter, I am desirous of publishing it *in Baltimore*, and there would be no channel so proper as the paper under your control. Now the tale is a long one—it would occupy twenty-five pages of *Graham's* Magazine—and is worth to me a hundred dollars at the usual Magazine price. Of course I could not afford to make you an absolute present of it—but if you are willing to take it, I will say $40. Will you please write me upon this point?—by return mail, if possible."

By raising the specter of *Graham's*, Poe meant to suggest that he could easily place the story elsewhere at a higher price. Snodgrass, he implied, would be foolish not to snatch up this bargain, taking advantage of the author's curious whim to have the story published in Baltimore. For all of that, Poe's unstated reasons for wishing to publish in the *Visiter* cannot have been inviolate. That same day, he sent a nearly identical letter to George Roberts, editor of the Boston *Notion*, stating that he was desirous of having the story published in Boston, and raising the price to fifty dollars.

Neither Roberts nor Snodgrass rose to the bait, possibly because the price, modest as it was, appeared excessive compared to the alternatives available to them. At the time, magazine editors could take advantage of the total absence of international copyright restrictions to publish foreign authors—such as Dickens—without payment of any kind. Although many editors, like George Graham, made an effort to give preference to American authors, there were always less expensive options to be had. Poe's bargain price for "Marie Rogêt," reasonable as it was, could not compete with the flood of free material from abroad.

In despair, Poe turned to William Snowden of the *Ladies' Companion* of New York. It was not a particularly good match. Earlier that year, Poe had complained about the "contemptible pictures, fashion-plates, music and love tales" crowding the pages of *Graham's*. The *Ladies' Companion* offered these same features in abundance, but, as the title clearly indicated, with the sensibilities of the female reader foremost in mind. Snowden sought to attract women of "exquisite refinement and taste," though Poe would later deride the magazine as "the *ne plus ultra* of ill-taste and humbuggery." A typical issue from 1842 featured poems and stories with titles such as "The Smile of Love" and "Birth-Night Reveries," along with comment on the latest "quietly appointed" walking dresses and the sheet music for an "original ditty" entitled "When Time Hath Bereft Thee." In this context, Poe's story, with its lengthy descriptions of the gases produced by decaying corpses, would likely have seemed out of place.

Behind the scenes, however, William Snowden had good reasons for wanting to publish Poe's story. Snowden had been a member of the Committee of Safety, the group of concerned New Yorkers who met at the home of James Stoneall in days following the murder. Snowden had subscribed five dollars to the reward money, making him one of the more generous contributors, ahead of Horace Greeley and Park Benjamin. Like many others at that meeting, Snowden had been disappointed that the efforts of the committee had produced no appreciable results. Nearly a year had passed, and in spite of the flurry of activity surrounding the discovery of the murder thicket and the death of Daniel Payne, Mary Rogers's killer remained at large. In accepting Poe's story for publication, Snowden may have hoped to revive interest in the case and provide, as Poe had suggested, "renewed impetus to investigation."

Having completed the sale to the *Ladies' Companion*, Poe sank into a creative lethargy, hastened by a further deterioration of the conditions at home. "The state of my mind has, in fact, forced me to abandon all mental exertion," he confessed to a friend. "The renewed and hopeless illness of my wife, ill health on my own part, and pecuniary embarrassments have nearly driven me to distraction."

There were greater embarrassments to come.

XV

A Series of Coincidences

THE NOVEMBER 1842 ISSUE of Snowden's *Ladies' Companion*, featuring "The Mystery of Marie Rogêt," rolled off the presses slightly ahead of schedule, appearing in the third week of October. Nearly 20,000 words in length, Poe's story was far too long to be published in a single issue, so editor William Snowden divided it into three installments for publication in three successive issues. Billed as "A Sequel to 'The Murders in the Rue Morgue,'" the opening pages were tucked between an article entitled "The Bible: Its Description of the Character and Attributes of God" and a story entitled "The Old Oak Chest," by Mrs. Caroline Orne.

Snowden's readers were accustomed to a sedate and morally uplifting tone in the pages of the magazine—"healthful and improving," in the phrase of the time—and the editor likely hesitated before unleashing Poe's graphic, blood-drenched tale. Still, though more than a year had passed since the death of Mary Rogers, Snowden knew that the cigar girl still cast a powerful spell. All but a handful of readers of the *Ladies' Companion*, even those of the most "exquisite refinement and taste," would have been familiar with the saga, and perhaps even walked the grounds at Elysian Fields where the body had come to rest. Many would also have been acquainted with the various conflicting theories of the case, especially those of James Gordon Bennett and Benjamin Day. Poe's story, however unseemly in its details, would have been a return to familiar ground, in spite of the transfer of the action from New York to Paris.

Lest there be any doubt as to the inspiration of the story, Poe's unnamed narrator, the companion of C. Auguste Dupin, offered a clear statement of intent in the opening pages of the story, echoing the words Poe had used in his letters to prospective publishers: "The extraordinary details which I am now called upon to make public, will be found to form, as regards sequence of time, the primary branch of a series of scarcely intelligible *coincidences*, whose secondary or concluding branch will be recognized by all readers in the late murder of MARY CECILIA ROGERS, at New York."

In reading the story, these coincidences (a term Poe uses to indicate a calculated design, rather than happenstance) soon become readily apparent. Poe introduces a beautiful grisette, or young working-class woman, named Marie Rogêt, the daughter of Mme. Estelle Rogêt, who keeps a pension in the Rue Pavée St. Andrée. Marie, the readers are told, had worked in the shop of a parfumier, Monsieur Le Blanc, whose establishment "became notorious through the charms" of the lovely young woman. Readers soon learn that the courtly Monsieur Beauvais wished to marry her, but Marie instead had become engaged to the dissipated Monsieur St. Eustache.

After Marie has spent roughly a year behind the counter of the perfume shop, her admirers are "thrown into confusion by her sudden disappearance from the shop." Monsieur Le Blanc is unable to account for her absence, and Mme. Rogêt is "distracted with anxiety and terror." With the newspapers calling for action, the police are preparing to launch an investigation when suddenly Marie reappears—"in good health, but with a somewhat saddened air." No explanation of her absence is offered, and all inquiry, "except that of a private character, was of course immediately hushed."

Five months later, on a sunny morning in June, Marie leaves home to visit an aunt on the Rue des Drômes, but she never arrives. After four days, her battered corpse is found floating in the Seine. "The atrocity of this murder," Poe writes, together with "the youth and beauty of the victim, and, above all, her previous notoriety, conspired to produce intense excitement in the minds of the sensitive Parisians." Poe is careful to insert a number of details culled from the official accounts of the Mary Rogers investigation, drawing in particular on the statements of Daniel Payne and Alfred Crommelin, who are represented as St. Eustache and Beauvais. Poe relates a conversation between Marie and St. Eustache, her "accepted suitor," in which she declares her intention to visit her aunt, but he takes pains to say that the information was conveyed "to him only," implying that it may not be trustworthy. Similarly, Poe describes the manner in which St. Eustache "was to have gone for his betrothed at dusk," only to break his promise at the prospect of a heavy rain. Monsieur Beauvais, too, comes in for "some color" of suspicion, in spite of his heroic efforts to locate the missing woman: "A visiter at his office, a few days prior to the disappearance, and during the absence of its occupant, had observed *a rose* in the keyhole of the door, and the name 'Marie' inscribed upon a slate which hung near at hand."

The behavior of Marie's mother is also scrutinized. In the early hours of Marie's disappearance, Mme. Rogêt is heard to express a fear that "she should never see Marie again," and when the unhappy news is received at the pension, an "impression of apathy" is noted. Although Mme. Rogêt's behavior is considered odd, allowances are made for her "age and grief."

In describing the condition of Marie Rogêt's corpse, Poe employs language and details that would not have been customary in the pages of the *Ladies' Companion*:

> The face was suffused with dark blood, some of which issued from the mouth. No foam was seen, as in the case of the merely drowned. There was no discoloration of the cellular tissue. About the throat were bruises and impressions of fingers. The arms were bent over on the chest and were rigid. The right hand was clenched; the left partially open. On the left wrist were two circular excoriations, apparently the effect of ropes, or of a rope in more than one volution. A part of the right wrist, also, was much chafed, as well as the back throughout its extent, but more especially at the shoulder-blades. . . . The flesh of the neck was much swollen. There were no cuts apparent, or bruises which appeared the effect of blows. A piece of lace was found tied so tightly round the neck as to be hidden from sight; it was completely buried in the flesh, and was fastened by a knot which lay just under the left ear. This alone would have sufficed to produce death. The medical testimony spoke confidently of the virtuous character of the deceased. She had been subjected, it said, to brutal violence.

Clearly Poe had availed himself of the testimony of Dr. Cook, the Hoboken coroner, indicating the degree to which he intended his story to mirror the actual murder. Several other crucial details follow, such as the strip of fabric wound at the waist and tied in a "sort of hitch" at the back, and the loop of "fine muslin" found hanging at the neck. Readers are also told that the strings of Marie's bonnet had been fastened in a knot that "was not a lady's, but a slip or sailor's knot."

As the story progresses, the details continue to run in close parallel with the events of the New York investigation. Although a speedy solution to the murder is expected, the police soon founder. False arrests are made, and rumors fly. A committee of concerned citizens gathers to tender a reward for the capture of the killers. A full pardon is offered to any accomplice who might come forward to inform on the murderer or murderers. The corpse is disinterred and subjected to a second postmortem examination. The scene of the murder is discovered in the woods of the Barrière du Roule, near the public house of a Mme. Deluc, who claims to have seen the victim in the company of a "young man of dark complexion." Finally, Monsieur St. Eustache is found dead with a vial of laudanum close at hand. In spite of all this, the French police make no progress in solving the case. At the end of several weeks, a mood of grim frustration has settled over the city.

In desperation, and with "the eyes of the public upon him," Prefect G—— of the police resolves to consult with Auguste Dupin, whose earlier conduct in the drama of the Rue Morgue had made a considerable "impression upon the fancies of the Parisian police." As it happens, Dupin and his unnamed companion have heard nothing of the murder of the young grisette. After the excitement of the Rue Morgue, they have once again withdrawn into their monastic habits. "Engaged in researches which had absorbed our whole attention, it had been nearly a month since either of us had gone abroad, or received a visiter, or more than glanced at the leading political articles in one of the daily papers," writes the narrator. "The first intelligence of the murder was brought us by G——, in person."

The prefect arrives at Dupin's lodgings in a state of high agitation, believing that both his reputation and honor are at stake—"so he said with a peculiarly Parisian air." The prefect pleads with Dupin to turn his mind to the mystery, offering him a "liberal proposition" if he will undertake its solution. At length Dupin gives his assent and the prefect settles in to give a lengthy discourse on the case and its many challenges. "Dupin, sitting steadily in his accustomed armchair, was the embodiment of respectful attention," the narrator records. "He wore spectacles during the whole interview, and an occasional glance beneath their green glasses sufficed to convince me that he slept not the less soundly, because silently, throughout the seven or eight leaden-footed hours which immediately preceded the departure of the Prefect."

The following morning, the well-rested Dupin launches his investigation in earnest. With only police reports and newspaper accounts to guide him, he pledges to solve the mystery from the solitary comfort of his armchair. Dupin observes, in commencing his study of the public accounts, that he must "bear in mind that, in general, it is the object of our newspapers rather to create a sensation—to make a point—than to further the cause of truth." Therefore it would be a mistake, he suggests, to take these accounts at face value. With that in mind, he begins to search for the truth behind the rhetoric.

The chief difficulty of the Marie Rogêt investigation, Dupin says, will be the "commonplace" nature of the crime, in contrast with the extraordinary circumstances of the Rue Morgue murder. In the earlier case, the seemingly inexplicable details—the locked room; the inhuman strength and agility of the murderer—were the ones that hastened its solution. By contrast, the comparatively routine aspects of Marie Rogêt's death will make it far more difficult to solve. "This is an *ordinary*, although an atrocious instance of crime," Dupin insists. "There is nothing peculiarly *outré* about it. You will observe that, for this reason, the mystery has been considered easy, when, for this reason, it should have been considered difficult of solution." It has been all too simple, Dupin goes on to say, for the police to imagine various modes and motives for the murder. As a result, they have fallen into the trap of assuming that one of these many theories must be correct. "But the ease with which these variable fancies were entertained," he explains, "and the very plausibility which each assumed, should have been understood as indicative rather of the difficulties than of the facilities which must attend elucidation."

In Dupin's view, the real solution will be found in the details which do not at first appear to fit: "I have before observed that it is by prominences above the plane of the ordinary that reason feels her way, if at all, in her search for the true." The essential question, Dupin contends, is not "what has occurred?" but rather "What has occurred that has never occurred before?"

Searching for these "prominences," Dupin gives his attention to the prevalent theories of the French newspapers and the police, effectively deflating each one as he holds it up to scrutiny. By extension, Poe undertakes to shoot down the efforts of the New York investigators, and the pet theories of the major newspaper editors. Poe appears to take particular relish in dissecting the work of James Gordon Bennett and the "gang of ruffians" theory. It is impossible, Dupin states, that the crime could have been committed by a gang. For proof, he points to the evidence of a violent struggle at the murder thicket, and the signs that the body had been dragged along the ground after death. These traces, he notes, had been interpreted as clear evidence of a group of attackers. "But do they not rather demonstrate the absence of a gang?" Dupin asks. "What struggle could have taken place—what struggle so violent and enduring as to have left its traces in all directions—between a weak and defenseless girl and the gang of ruffians imagined? The silent grasp of a few rough arms and all would have been over."

Moreover, Dupin continues, at the conclusion of the crime a gang would simply have carried the body away to the river, rather than take the time to fashion a cloth hitch and drag the corpse along the ground. By the same token, a gang would not have left articles of clothing behind; there would have been extra hands available to gather up the incriminating evidence. The crime scene can only be understood, Dupin observes, "if we imagine but *one* violator." A single man would have had a struggle to overpower his victim, and would have had to resort to a hitch to dispose of the body, leaving himself too burdened to gather up the stray articles of clothing that were strewn on the ground. If any final evidence is needed, Dupin says, it can be found in the "altogether irresistible" weight of the large reward offered for information about the crime. "It is not to be imagined for a moment," he declares, "that some member of a gang of low ruffians, or of any body of men would not long ago have betrayed his accomplices. Each one of a gang, so placed, is not so much greedy of reward, or anxious for escape, as fearful of betrayal. He betrays eagerly and early that he may not himself be betrayed. That the secret has not been divulged is the very best of proof that it is, in fact, a secret. The horrors of this dark deed are known only to one living human being, and to God."

Before abandoning the subject, Dupin even takes time to address the memorable remark about the deed having been carried out by "fellows without pocket handkerchiefs." The comment, he explains, was intended to establish that the crime had been carried out by "the lowest class of ruffians," but in the detective's view, it serves exactly the opposite purpose. "You must have had occasion to observe," Dupin remarks, "how absolutely indispensable, of late years, to the thorough blackguard, has become the pocket-handkerchief." Indeed, Dupin insists, such men will be found to have a handkerchief "even when destitute of shirts."

Dupin shows a similar verve in refuting a "persistent rumor" that Marie Rogêt is still alive, allowing Poe to take aim at Benjamin Day and his newspapers. Under the pretense of allowing Dupin to muse over a lengthy article in a French paper called *L'Etoile*, Poe quotes and paraphrases the theories originally found in the pages of the *Tattler* and *Brother Jonathan*. In Dupin's retelling of the events, the editor of *L'Etoile* is found to be indignant over the manner in which the police have accepted the identification of the corpse provided by Monsieur Beauvais: "What, then, are the facts on which M. Beauvais says that he has no doubt the body was that of Marie Rogêt? He ripped up the gown sleeve, and says he found marks which satisfied him of the identity. The public generally supposed those marks to have consisted of some description of scars. He rubbed the arm and found *hair* upon it—something as indefinite, we think, as can readily be imagined—as little conclusive as finding an arm in the sleeve."

Poe demonstrates a great deal of craft in advancing the newspaper editor's point of view, as it appears at first glance to be unanswerable. But Dupin is given equal fluency in refuting the claim: "M. Beauvais, not being an idiot, could never have urged, in identification of the corpse, simply *hair upon its arm*. No arm is *without* hair." The newspaper, Dupin claims, has resorted to a "perversion" of the testimony. "He must have spoken of some *peculiarity* in this hair. It must have been a peculiarity of color, of quantity, of length, or of situation." Moreover, Dupin contends that this peculiarity is just one of several points upon which the identification rests. Taken together with the recognition of the clothing, hat, and shoes found on the corpse, the testimony of Beauvais gathers undeniable force. His statement,

Dupin contends, does not rely on any one single point, but on a succession of telling points. "Each successive one is multiple evidence," Dupin says, "proof not added to proof, but multiplied by hundreds or thousands."

As for Beauvais himself, Dupin dismisses him as "a busy-body, with much of romance and little of wit." He brushes aside the various factors that might seem to indicate guilt or a guilty conscience—the business of the rose in the keyhole; the "elbowing the male relatives out of the way" in the wake of the discovery; and the apparent determination that "nobody should have anything to do with the proceedings except himself." In Dupin's view, there is a "charitable interpretation" for these actions: "It seems to me unquestionable that Beauvais was a suitor of Marie's; that she coquetted with him; and that he was ambitious of being thought to enjoy her fullest intimacy and confidence. I shall say nothing more upon this point." Dupin, unlike the New York press, leaves the disappointed suitor with a shred of dignity.

Putting aside the identification of the corpse, Dupin turns to *L'Etoile*'s forensic pronouncements. According to the newspaper, the body found in the Seine could not be Marie's because it had not been in the water for a sufficient period of time to rise to the surface: "All experience has shown that drowned bodies, or bodies thrown into the water immediately after death by violence, require from six to ten days for sufficient decomposition to take place to bring them to the top of the water." The statement is imported nearly verbatim from the pages of the *Tattler*, and it sets Dupin off on a lengthy and rather startlingly graphic discussion of the buoyancy of dead bodies. One wonders how many readers of the *Ladies' Companion* were edified by Dupin's thoughts on the stomach gases produced by the "acetous fermentation of vegetable matter," or the manner in which a person with "an abnormal quantity of flaccid or fatty matter" might be expected to remain afloat long after drowning.

Dupin even quotes one of *L'Etoile*'s more abstruse contentions, again echoing a statement from Benjamin Day's newspapers: "Even where a cannon is fired over a [submerged] corpse, and it rises before at least five or six days' immersion, it sinks again, if left alone." Dupin's answer to this has the ring of authority, although one doubts that either he or his author could have had any practical experience in this area. "The effect produced by the firing of a cannon is that of simple vibration," Dupin states. "This may either loosen the corpse from the soft mud or ooze in which it is imbedded, thus permitting it to rise when other agencies have already prepared it for so doing, or it may overcome the tenacity of some putrescent portions of the cellular tissue, allowing the cavities to distend under the influence of the gas." In either case, he asserts, the body will not sink again, as *L'Etoile* has claimed, at least not "until decomposition has so far progressed as to permit the escape of the generated gas."

To Dupin's way of thinking, the premise raised in the pages of *L'Etoile*—that the body found floating in the Seine was not that of Marie Rogêt—serves to demonstrate "little beyond the zeal of its inditer." It is sheer folly, he concludes, to suggest that Marie Rogêt might still be alive.

Having dispensed with two of the most prominent theories of the case, Dupin takes a wildly unorthodox approach to solving the crime. He explains that he intends to divert his attention from "the event itself" and instead direct his energies to "the contemporary circumstances which surround it." In other words, he intends to widen his focus dramatically, even at the risk of becoming mired in seemingly irrelevant details. "In the analysis which I now propose," Dupin says, "we will discard the *interior* points of this tragedy, and concentrate our attention upon its *outskirts*. Not the least usual error, in investigations such as this, is the limiting of inquiry to the immediate, with the total disregard of the collateral or *circumstantial* events. It is the mal-practice of the courts to confine evidence and discussion to the bounds of apparent relevancy. Yet experience has shown, and a true philosophy will always show, that a vast, perhaps the larger portion of the truth arises from the seemingly irrelevant." In other words, as a later writer would state more succinctly, Dupin was proposing a method "founded upon the observation of trifles."

Toward this end, Dupin proposes to spend a week in solitary contemplation of the various accounts of the case. "I will examine the newspapers more generally than you have as yet done," he tells his companion. "It will be strange indeed if a comprehensive survey, such as I propose, of the public prints, will not afford us some minute points which will establish a *direction* for inquiry."

At length Dupin emerges with six "extracts," or snippets of information, from various newspapers that, he claims, will combine to suggest a solution. At first glance, these six clippings appear to have little to do with the murder. The first recounts Marie's brief disappearance from the parfumerie three years earlier. The second extract amplifies the first: "An evening journal of yesterday refers to a former mysterious disappearance of Madamoiselle Rogêt," it reads. "It is well known that, during the week of her absence from Le Blanc's *parfumerie*, she was in the company of a young naval officer much noted for his debaucheries. A quarrel, as it is supposed, providentially led to her return home."

The third extract reports an "outrage of the most atrocious character," the abduction and mistreatment of a young girl at the hands of a boatload of gang members. Apparently based on William Fanshaw's fretful account of devil-may-care rowdies in flat-brimmed hats, the clipping describes the manner in which the girl was "brutally treated" and then returned to her parents. Though the newspaper draws no connection to the Marie Rogêt affair, Dupin has seen fit to include it.

The fourth extract makes oblique reference to the saga of Joseph Morse, the hapless engraver who nearly found himself convicted of the murder: "We have received one or two communications, the object of which is to fasten the crime of the late atrocity upon Mennais; but as this gentleman has been fully exonerated by a legal inquiry, and as the arguments of our several correspondents appear to be more zealous than profound, we do not think it advisable to make them public."

The fifth snippet concerns the prevailing tide of opinion, expressed through several "forcibly written communications," that "the unfortunate Marie Rogêt has become a victim of one of the numerous bands of blackguards which infest the vicinity of the city upon Sunday."

The sixth and final of Dupin's clippings concerns an empty boat spotted floating down the Seine: "Sails were lying in the bottom of the boat," it reads. "The bargeman towed it under the barge office. The next morning it was taken from thence without the knowledge of any of the officers."

Dupin's companion is nonplussed. "Upon reading these various extracts, they not only seemed to me irrelevant, but I could perceive no mode in which any one of them could be brought to bear upon the matter in hand," he admits. "I waited for some explanation from Dupin."

Dupin's friend, like the reader, would have to wait some time for that explanation. Because Poe's original manuscript had weighed in at nearly 20,000 words, William Snowden had been obliged to divide the story into three installments for publication in three successive issues of the *Ladies' Companion*. As with the serial publication of

Dickens's novels, Poe may have hoped that spacing out the story would help to generate suspense, and afford a greater span of time in which to turn the publicity to his advantage. It must be said, however, that Snowden carved up the manuscript as if he were grinding out sausage links, without any regard for the ebb and flow of the story. The first section broke off almost in midsentence during the discussion of floating bodies, and the second ended abruptly in the midst of Dupin's contemplation of the murder thicket. The two interruptions were awkward and deflating, and did nothing to encourage the reader's continued interest.

Even so, Poe felt encouraged by the warm response of his friends and colleagues when the first installment of "Marie Rogêt" appeared. His spirits continued to lift as conditions at home began to improve. "I am happy to say that Virginia's health has slightly improved," he had written in September of 1842. "Perhaps all will yet go well."

Although he remained in serious financial straits, he hoped that "Marie Rogêt" would restore some of the status he had lost with his departure from *Graham's*, and help to secure his dream of launching his own literary journal. The second installment was due to appear during the third week of November. The third and final section, containing what Poe hoped would be a dramatic and highly provocative solution to the murder, would be published at the height of the December holidays.

In his manuscript, as he prepared to "indicate the assassin" of Marie Rogêt, Poe made reference to a mode of thinking he described as the "Calculus of Probabilities," which he defined as a means of applying the most "rigidly exact" aspects of science to the intangible "shadow and spirituality" of speculation. In its purest form, he implied, the Calculus of Probabilities would allow his conclusions in the case of the fictional Marie Rogêt to be applied to the mystery surrounding the real-life Mary Rogers. With that in mind, the conclusion of "The Mystery of Marie Rogêt" promised to be the talk of New York.

AT THAT PRECISE MOMENT, however, came a very surprising development, as though the Calculus of Probabilities had risen up to deal a crushing blow. For the past year the official inquiry into the death of Mary Rogers had been all but dormant, leaving a clear field for Poe and his literary detective work. Suddenly, on November 18, just as the second installment of "Marie Rogêt" was due to appear, the name of Mary Rogers found its way back onto the front pages of the newspapers. The stark headline in the New York *Tribune* left no room for equivocation. It read simply:

THE MARY ROGERS MYSTERY EXPLAINED.

XVI

A Mansion Built on Baby Skulls

ON NOVEMBER 1, 1842, a woman's screams were heard once again at Nick Moore's Tavern in Weehawken. The police arrived to find that a tragic accident had befallen Frederica Loss, the tavern's proprietor. One of her sons had been cleaning a shotgun when he lost his grip and the weapon accidentally discharged. The blast caught Mrs. Loss in the knee and knocked her to the floor, where she lay howling in agony as she clutched her mangled leg.

The Kellenbarack boys carried their mother to her bed and summoned a physician, but the wound soon became septic. For ten days Mrs. Loss lay in a state of delirium, babbling incoherently in both English and German. As her condition worsened, the feverish woman was troubled by hallucinations, and began to see the spirit of a young woman hovering at the bedside. "Take her away!" Mrs. Loss cried, waving a trembling hand at the vision. "Shoo away!"

The family physician, Dr. Gautier, treated the injury with ointments and poultices, but the patient continued to decline. When the last of his remedies failed to produce any benefit, Gautier informed the Kellenbarack boys that their mother was not likely to recover. As they absorbed this news, the boys were overheard to remark that upon their mother's death there would be a terrible reckoning: "The great secret," they said, "will come out."

Justice Gilbert Merritt hurried to the tavern as soon as he heard of the accident. More than a year had passed since the revelation of the murder thicket and the death of Daniel Payne, and in that time Merritt had never entirely let go of his suspicions of Mrs. Loss. Her story of the discovery of Mary Rogers's effects sounded improbable and incomplete to the magistrate's ears, as was her confused and inconsistent account of the screams she heard on the fatal evening. Merritt's suspicions deepened during Mrs. Loss's unconvincing testimony at the inquest after Payne's death. Now, with Mrs. Loss on her deathbed, Merritt hoped that she would feel compelled to unburden her conscience.

Dr. Gautier had already attempted to question Mrs. Loss about the Mary Rogers mystery, though his methods left much to be desired. Finding his patient deep in the throes of her delirium, the doctor leaned in close and shouted the name of the murdered woman "suddenly and loudly" into her ear. When "no effect was elicited," Dr. Gautier concluded that Mrs. Loss knew no more of the unhappy affair than she had revealed in court.

Justice Merritt was not content to let the matter rest there. He spent several hours at the dying woman's bedside, hoping that she would shake off the effects of her fever, and he held a series of pointed interviews with her sons. When he emerged from the sickroom, Merritt would say little of his findings, but rumors circulated that, at long last, a solution to the Mary Rogers mystery was close at hand.

On November 10, Mrs. Loss died of her injury. The following day, Justice Merritt held an inquest that promptly returned a verdict of accidental death. The brevity of the proceeding and the spare language of the court record gave no hint of Merritt's suspicions. Behind the scenes, however, the magistrate was in close contact with the mayors of New York and New Jersey, preparing to put his conclusions before the public.

Under the headline of "Murder of Mary C. Rogers," the *Morning Courier* gave a hint of coming revelations: "Reports have been in circulation for some days past that discoveries have been made as to the manner in which this unfortunate female came to her death." The paper went on to say that prior to her death Mrs. Loss "charged her two sons to make known the circumstances attending the death of Mary Rogers, which she had before concealed."

Three days after the death of Mrs. Loss, Gilbert Merritt filed an affidavit accusing her and her sons of complicity in the death of Mary Rogers. For the first time, Merritt made an open declaration of what he had long suspected. He charged that:

> in the month of July 1841, he (this deponent) as a magistrate held an inquest on the body of Mary C. Rogers, at Hoboken, in said County of Hudson, who this deponent believes was murdered; and this deponent further saith that from information he has obtained and facts in his possession, he verily believes that the murder of the said Mary C. Rogers was perpetrated in a house at Weehawken, called 'The Nick Moore House,' then kept by one Frederica Loss, alias Kellenbarack (now deceased) and her three sons, to wit: Oscar Kellenbarack, Charles Kellenbarack, and Ossian Kellenbarack, all three of whom the deponent has reason to believe are profligate and worthless characters; and this deponent further saith, that he has just reason to believe that the said sons and their mother kept one of the most depraved and debauched houses in New Jersey, and that all of them had a

knowledge of and were accessory to, and became partic-
ipators in the murder of said Mary C. Rogers, and the
concealment of her body.

Merritt's language was uncommonly blunt for a legal document
of the time, but he stopped short of stating what he believed to have
been the exact cause of Mary Rogers's death. That information, he
believed, was far too explicit for the public record. Frederica Loss, in
Merritt's opinion, had been a notorious abortionist. Mary Rogers,
he believed, had died while undergoing an abortion under Mrs.
Loss's roof.

In a sense, it was a notion that had been in plain view throughout
the entire drama. Virtually every issue of the *Herald* and many other
newspapers of the day carried a large advertisement on its back page
for the services of Madame Restell, a "female physician and professor of midwifery," whose long career as an abortionist had earned her
a reputation as "the wickedest woman in New York." Madame
Restell, whose real name was Ann Trow Lohman, had come to New
York from England in 1831 and set off on a professional path that
would earn her an estimated one million dollars and a lavish Fifth Avenue brownstone known as "The Mansion Built on Baby Skulls."

At the time of Mary Rogers's death, Madame Restell was very
much in the public eye. In July of 1841—just a few days before
Mary Rogers's body was discovered—Madame Restell was tried in
New York's Court of Special Sessions for administering "certain
noxious medicine" and procuring a miscarriage "by the use of in-
struments, the same not being necessary" for the preservation of
life. Although abortion was held to be a misdemeanor offense at
the time, a recent provision stated that if the procedure was performed after the quickening of the fetus—the point at which

movement could be detected—the act would be prosecuted as manslaughter. Since the case for which Madame Restell was being tried had resulted in the death of the patient, the charge against her was elevated to murder. In spite of the severity of the charge, the proceeding was widely viewed as a show trial; a sop to the city's clerics and moral reformers who were outraged by the manner in which the police turned a blind eye to Madame Restell's practices. Although "Madame Killer" was convicted and sentenced to a year in prison, she never served the term.

At the time Madame Restell ran her business from a house on Chambers Street, not far from Phoebe Rogers's boardinghouse and within view of City Hall. The fashionable address allowed her to draw customers from all walks of life, and her services were tailored accordingly. "In the heart of this Metropolis she holds her bloody empire," observed the *Police Gazette*. "Her patients are of three classes, and her treatment has an equal scope." In an early pamphlet detailing Restell's "Life and Horrible Practice," these three categories of treatment were described in detail: "First, there were her powders as a preventative; if these failed, as without the greatest care they might, there were the monthly pills to overcome obstructions; and if these were unsuccessful there, as a last resort, was an asylum in the house of Madame Restell." There, the account continued, the patient would be subjected to "powerful drugs to produce an abortion, or the use of mechanical means to bring about a premature delivery."

In addition to her establishment on Chambers Street, Madame Restell also ran a network of abortion parlors that stretched across the river to Hoboken. "It is well known that Madame Restell keeps a large number of apartments . . . for the accommodation of females in accouchement," the *Police Gazette* continued, and the number that avail themselves of such facilities in a city where licentiousness stalks abroad at midday may be guessed at, but not counted. It is well known that females frequently die in ordinary childbirth. How many, then, who enter her halls of death may be supposed to expire under her execrable butchery? Females are daily, nay, hourly, missing from our midst who never return. Where do they go? What becomes of them? Does funeral bell ever peal a note for their passage? Does funeral train ever leave her door? Do friends ever gather round the melancholy grave? No! An obscure hole in the earth; a consignment to the savage skill of the dissecting knife, or a splash in the cold wave, with the scream of the night blast for a requiem, is the only death service bestowed upon her victims. Witness this, ye shores of Hudson! Witness this, Hoboken beach!

With this reference to the alarming number of bodies washing up on the banks of New York's rivers—and the pointed mention of the spot where Mary Rogers's corpse came ashore—the *Police Gazette* sought to draw a link between the abortionist and the cigar girl. Given the fact that the trial of Madame Restell occurred at the very moment of Mary Rogers's death, it is not surprising that there should have been an attempt to make a connection, even before the discoveries in Weehawken came to light. Many of the key figures in the Restell trial were also involved in the Mary Rogers drama, most notably Judge Mordecai Noah, who presided over the Restell proceedings, and Justice Gilbert Merritt, who took the initial affidavits. James Gordon Bennett, who was served with three counts of libel by Judge Noah during the Restell trial, hinted at the possibility of a "wicked disgrace" while theorizing that Mary Rogers had been imprisoned in a house of assignation. "These dens of iniquity form a society among themselves—governed by their own rules, and marauding upon all decency and respectability," the *Herald* charged. "They are even protected by the police—and who ever heard those abominable haunts made the subject of a charge by their Honors of the Sessions?"

The *Police Gazette* was far less circumspect. "We speak of the unfortunate Mary Rogers," the journal declared. "Experience and futile effort have proved that we have heretofore followed a wrong trail."

With Merritt's accusation of Mrs. Loss, the rumors and suppositions quickly assumed the tone of established fact. Although no official connection between Madame Restell and Frederica Loss could be established, it was assumed that Nick Moore's Tavern was one of Restell's outposts, or that Mrs. Loss was one of dozens of enterprising "widow ladies" who had followed in Restell's footsteps. Some accused Mrs. Loss of having performed the procedure personally, while others assumed that she simply provided facilities for an anonymous roster of physicians. Despite the lack of evidence connecting Madame Restell to the Nick Moore House, she continued to be vilified as the personification of abortion, preying on young women who presumably would otherwise have chosen a more righteous path. One magazine would portray her as a grim-faced harpy, cradling a bat-winged monster with a dead infant in its jaws.

Horace Greeley's *Tribune* was the first to go on record with the claim that Mary Rogers had died as a result of an abortion. On November 18, one week after the death of Mrs. Loss, the paper ran a story claiming that the dying woman had sent for Justice Merritt so that she might confess her sins. According to the *Tribune* account, Mrs. Loss revealed that Mary Rogers had come to her establishment "in company with a young physician who undertook to procure for her a premature delivery." This procedure, risky enough under the best of circumstances, went disastrously wrong. "While in the hands of her physician she died," the *Tribune* continued, "and a consultation was then held as to the disposal of her body. It was finally taken at night by the son of Mrs. Loss and sunk in the river where it was found."

The *Tribune* also attempted to explain why the dead woman's effects were later discovered at the murder thicket. "Her clothes were first tied up in a bundle and sunk in a pond," the paper reported, "but it was afterwards thought they were not safe there, and they were accordingly taken and scattered through the woods as they were found." The *Tribune* did not elaborate on why this course of action would have been thought safer than leaving the clothes in a pond.

On the strength of these new developments, the two elder sons of Mrs. Loss were placed under arrest. As they awaited a formal hearing, Merritt worked to build his case against them. According to the *Tribune*, Mrs. Loss's confession left no doubt that her sons had been willing participants in the crime. That being the case, Merritt intended to prosecute them as accessories to murder. "No doubt we can apprehend can be entertained of the truth of this confession," insisted the *Tribune*. "Thus has this fearful mystery, which has struck fear and terror to so many hearts, been at last explained away by circumstances in which no one can fail to perceive a Providential agency." Although the identity of the so-called Swarthy Man—now thought to be Mary Rogers's physician, rather than her escort—remained unknown, Merritt expressed confidence that he would soon be identified and arrested.

These shocking revelations promised to set off a fresh wave of outrage in the newspapers. Before Greeley's rivals could fire up their presses, however, Gilbert Merritt stepped forward to smother the new disclosures. The *Tribune*, he insisted, had gone too far in its reporting. In an attempt to contain the growing speculation about the case, he sent a carefully worded retraction to James Watson Webb, the editor of the rival *Courier*: "I noticed a statement in the *Tribune* of this morning relative to a confession said to have been made before me by the late Mrs. Loss, which is entirely incorrect, as no such examination took place, nor could it, from the deranged state of Mrs. Loss' mind."

The *Tribune* refused to back down. Although Greeley now admitted that he had erred in stating that a confession had been made directly to Merritt, he continued to insist that a confession had been made. "We gave the facts as they were told to us by two Magistrates of this City," the paper proclaimed, "and as we understood them on the authority of a statement made by Mr. Merritt himself to Mayor Morris." Privately, it was assumed that Merritt's denial had been made to avoid charges of impropriety in his proceedings against the Kellenbarack boys.

James Gordon Bennett and the staff of the *Herald* were overjoyed to think that Horace Greeley's *Tribune* had botched the story. To underscore his competitor's gaffe, Bennett reprinted the *Tribune's* original story alongside Merritt's letter of denial. Greeley, whom Bennett had compared unfavorably to a "galvanized squash," lost no time in striking back: "Our envious neighbors who cannot endure the knowledge that we gave the first development of the Mary Rogers mystery may as well forbear their snarling. They only set the public laughing at their ludicrous misery." When Greeley repeated his claim that two magistrates had corroborated the story, Bennett demanded their names. The *Tribune* declined to respond.

Justice Merritt, meanwhile, did his best to stay above the fray. In spite of the denials of his letter to the *Courier*, he firmly believed that events had transpired exactly as the *Tribune* had reported, and that the Kellenbarack boys were guilty accomplices. According to some accounts, he had even gone so far as to scour a blueprint of the tavern, seeking to discover a secret chamber in which he believed the abortion had been performed.

If Merritt's theory was correct, a great many unexplained details of the Mary Rogers saga would now fall into place. One of the more troubling aspects of the investigation had been the frequently reported "apathy" of Phoebe Rogers and Daniel Payne when they were informed of Mary's death. Mrs. Rogers, in particular, had been visibly distraught on the Sunday of the disappearance, but by Wednesday she appeared stoic to the point of indifference. H. G. Luther, the man who conveyed the unhappy news from Hoboken, was reported to have said, "I distinctly felt that the news was not unexpected." If, in fact, Payne and Mrs. Rogers had been aware that Mary intended to undergo a risky abortion, their response may be better understood. If the news had come not as a shock but as a confirmation of their worst fears, following several days of anxious worry, they might well have registered a sense of grim resignation rather than the surprise Luther had expected. It would also have been possible that Payne and Mrs. Rogers had already learned of the death through other channels, so that Luther's report of the recovery of the body came not as news but only as a sad corroboration. In either case, the visitor might well have mistaken their response for an inappropriate lack of emotion.

By the same token, Mrs. Rogers's anxiety in the early hours of her daughter's disappearance is more readily understood as concern over a dangerous medical procedure. Several newspapers reported Phoebe Rogers as saying, shortly after her daughter left home on the fatal Sunday, that "in all probability" she would "never see Mary alive again." At the time, this statement seemed wildly overwrought, as Mary was believed to have gone no farther than Jane

Street to visit her aunt, a journey not thought to be especially perilous. Though Mary had not returned in the evening as expected, this was readily explained as the consequence of a heavy thunderstorm. If Phoebe Rogers had genuinely believed that her daughter was simply passing the night with her relative, she would have had no reason for alarm. If, however, she knew that her daughter had gone to an abortionist, she would have had good reason to fear for Mary's life.

The actions of Alfred Crommelin, too, take on a different shading if considered in this light. Mary's two visits to Crommelin's office just before her disappearance, and the rose she placed through the keyhole of his door, had formed an especially puzzling element of the drama. When Crommelin quarreled with Daniel Payne and made his dramatic exit from the Nassau Street boardinghouse, he pledged to Mary that he would always stand by her in times of need. Very likely her visits to his office indicate that she wished to take him up on the offer. It had been reported in some quarters that Mary went to Crommelin to try to sell him a due bill in the amount of fifty-two dollars, so that she would have the use of the money while Crommelin took on the job of collecting the debt. If Mary intended to undergo an abortion, her need for this money becomes clear: The fee at that time ranged widely between twenty and one hundred dollars. At the same time, Crommelin's apparent sense of guilt over his failure to act takes on a new significance, as does his rather vehement insistence on acting as the guardian of Mary's reputation. At the Hoboken inquest, Crommelin maintained that he had "never heard her virtue questioned in the least" and that she had "borne an irreproachable character for chastity and veracity." The fact that Crommelin felt obliged to offer such assurances might be seen as an example of a man protesting too much. If he was aware that an abortion took place, he may have hoped to shield Mary's reputation by attesting to her sterling character. If so, his display of chivalry, however well-intentioned, had serious consequences. At one stage Crommelin took it upon himself to discourage the Rogers family from speaking directly with the police or the press, claiming that it would be best if he alone served as the family's representative. This might have helped to safeguard Mary's good name, but it could only have impeded the investigation. It is also possible that Crommelin's agitation on this point had an influence on Dr. Cook, the coroner, when he pronounced that the dead woman had "evidently been a person of chastity and correct habits." The statement did no favors for Cook's reputation, and may have discouraged investigators from pursuing a more useful line of inquiry.

In the days following Mary's death, a number of newspapers had reported on a quarrel overheard by Phoebe Rogers's housemaid. A few days before Mary's disappearance, it was said, she and her mother had a heated exchange that ended with a promise from Mary that she would not marry Daniel Payne. Phoebe Rogers offered no confirmation of the rumor, but the possibility of an unwanted pregnancy affords a different interpretation to the story. If Mary had been carrying Payne's child, she may have agreed to marry him with the expectation of having the baby. If she later thought better of the situation—perhaps owing to her mother's objections—and determined to end the pregnancy, some of her subsequent behavior falls into place. On the morning of her disappearance, Mary deliberately lied to Payne about her plans for the day. Possibly she did not wish him to know that she planned to end the pregnancy, an action she might well have seen as a means of freeing herself from the obligation to marry him. Or perhaps Payne had expressed reservations about the engagement, driving Mary to extreme measures.

Whatever the truth of the situation, it clearly left Payne with a tortured conscience, as evidenced by his alcoholic decline, his agonized death, and the guilt-ridden message he left behind.

On November 19, a week after the death of Frederica Loss, a contentious hearing convened in the court of Justice Stephen Lutkins in Jersey City. Lutkins, Merritt, and several other magistrates subjected the two older Kellenbarack boys to a grueling round of questions, attempting to expose the "nefarious nature" of their late mother's clandestine business at the Nick Moore House, and her role in the fate of Mary Rogers. By all accounts, the proceeding was a confused and disappointing affair. A team of three lawyers appeared to represent the interests of the Loss family, with the result that even the most pointed of the magistrates' questions were deflected into a tangle of legal prevarication. With their lawyers guiding their testimony, the Kellenbarack brothers easily turned aside the accusations against them, and dismissed the most grave of the charges as harmless hearsay. Even the "great secret" alluded to in an earlier statement was now explained away in mundane terms; it was, they explained, merely a reference to a private cure for rheumatism.

The hearing closed on a disappointingly inconclusive note, with no formal charges filed. Merritt and Lutkins went directly into a closed-door session with Mayor Morris, leading observers to conclude that further action would be taken. "It is understood there is something more of deep and overwhelming interest yet in the wind," wrote Bennett in the *Herald*. "The magistrates are on the scent and these investigations will not end here." The *Courier*, having backed away from its report of Mrs. Loss's confession to Merritt, continued to insist that some admission of guilt had been made: "That it was made to *someone* we have little doubt; and we firmly believe that the statement we give embraces the true explanation of the manner of this unfortunate woman's death."

ALTHOUGH JUSTICE LUTKINS'S HEARING had been inconclusive, the city's newspapers appeared to unite behind the notion that Mary Rogers had died during an abortion. "The case of Mary Rogers remains, it seems, legally unexplained," wrote the Newark *Daily Advertiser.* "But we understand the investigation will be pursued, as it is believed that the recent statement of the manner of her death is true."

Neither of the two coroners who examined Mary Rogers's body, Dr. Cook of Hoboken or Dr. Archer of New York, offered any comment. For Dr. Cook, in particular, the Weehawken scenario promised a fresh wave of public ridicule. At the initial inquest, Cook's testimony concerning Mary Rogers's sexual violation had been strangely ambiguous. While he had stated confidently that the victim had been "brutally violated by no fewer than three assailants," he also asserted that prior to that time Mary Rogers had evidently been a properly virginal young woman. Now, in light of Justice Merritt's theory concerning the Nick Moore House, it seemed likely that Dr. Cook had mistaken the evidence of a horribly botched abortion for signs of sexual violation.

If this were the case, however, several crucial questions remained unanswered. Mary Rogers had been found with a lace cord tied "fast around her neck" and deep finger-mark bruises at her throat. Whatever ambiguities may have clouded Dr. Cook's conclusions about the "feminine region," he had been perfectly clear about the evidence for strangulation. He offered concise and unequivocal descriptions of "echymose" prints in the shape of a man's fingers, and a "crease round the neck" caused by the lace garrote. A bungled abortion procedure, no matter how horrific, could not account for these clear signs of strangulation.

By the same token, Merritt's theory failed to account for much of the behavior of Mrs. Loss and her sons. The scattering of Mary Rogers's clothing in the so-called murder thicket had been discovered by the Kellenbarack boys, and brought to the attention of Gilbert Merritt by Mrs. Loss herself. If, in fact, Mrs. Loss had been running an abortion parlor in a secret room of her tavern, it is difficult to understand why she should have called attention to herself in this manner. Up to the point she came forward with Mary Rogers's effects, there had been no connection between the Nick Moore House and the murder. Although the tavern enjoyed increased business as "the place where Mary Rogers was last seen alive," this could hardly have been worth the risk of drawing suspicion where none had existed before.

Even so, for all of the doubts and contradictions, the notion that Mary Rogers had perished during an abortion took a firm hold. The *Courier* joined several other newspapers in declaring that "the mystery has at last been solved." This eagerness to accept an unproven verdict had more to do with a sense of public outrage than with evidence. Once again, the death of the beautiful young cigar girl had become entwined in a thread of civic concern, as with the earlier assumption that she had fallen victim to a gang. With clergymen decrying Madame Restell from the pulpit, and newspapers such as the *Advocate of Moral Reform* producing hand-wringing editorials, the Mary Rogers saga took on a new and even darker currency. At the same time, Mary Rogers herself came to be seen in a different and not altogether flattering light. If the accusations against Mrs. Loss were true, it would no longer be possible to view the cigar girl as an innocent "specimen of maidenhood," as one newspaper had described her. She now came to be seen as an unfortunate, if not entirely blameless, victim of a barbaric practice—a sacrifice to the horrors of Madame Restell. "O mothers! Save your innocent daughters from a fate like this," wrote a popular novelist of the day, "and O daughters! Behold one of your sisters treading the black path to the tomb. Pity her! Save her!"

Amid this building tide of public indignation, it was easy to overlook the fact that it had not been clearly established that an abortion had actually taken place. By the end of November, the furor in the press subsided, though further developments were expected at any moment. Gilbert Merritt continued trying to build a case against the Loss family, though the Kellenbarack boys had long since been released for lack of evidence. The *Courier* expressed a hope that a final resolution would not be long in coming. For now, the paper admitted, nothing further could be learned: "This mysterious matter sleeps for the present."

For Edgar Allan Poe, the drama in Weehawken could not have come at a worse moment. The third and final installment of "Marie Rogêt," containing his fictionalized solution to the case, was only days away from publication. Up to this point, Poe believed that he had crafted an elegant and entirely plausible hypothesis. Now, however, as the notion of Mary Rogers's death at the hands of an abortionist took hold, Poe's conclusions would be proved false, laying him open to a potentially devastating public humiliation at the very moment that he was seeking to restore his beleaguered fortunes. In "The Fall of the House of Usher," Poe had created a chilling scene in which the "lofty and enshrouded" figure of Madeline Usher rises from her coffin and drags her brother to his death, while their Gothic mansion collapses around them. Poe might have seen the specter of Mary Rogers in much the same light, emerging from her grave to preside over his ruin.

The critics, Poe knew, would be ruthless. There were many in New York who had not forgotten the savagery of his reviews in the *Southern Literary Messenger*, and most especially his evisceration of Theodore Fay's *Norman Leslie*. That novel, like "Marie Rogêt," had been based on a sensational New York murder case, and Poe had gone out of his way to sneer at its "poetical licenses." Now that Poe had availed himself of the same licenses, he could well imagine the sound of knives being sharpened.

If the critics poured scorn on "Marie Rogêt," Poe knew that his hopes for launching his own literary magazine might well be dashed. "Touching 'The Stylus,': —this is the one great purpose of my literary life," he wrote. "I wish to establish a journal in which the men of genius may fight their battles; upon some terms of equality, with those dunces the men of talent." In the final months of 1842, as the first of the *Ladies' Companion* installments appeared, Poe began discussions with Thomas C. Clarke, an influential Philadelphia editor, about financing the magazine. When Clarke agreed to enter into a partnership, Poe had reason to believe that his dream would soon be realized. He told a friend that George Graham had made "a good offer" to have him return as editor of *Graham's*, but he felt sufficient confidence in the prospects of his own magazine to decline. "It is my firm determination to commence . . . on the first of January next," he wrote in early October of 1842. "The difficulties which impeded me last year have vanished, and there will be now nothing to prevent success."

Poe was in desperate need of that success. His financial distress, according to his friend Frederick Thomas, had sent him to new depths of poverty. Worse yet, according to Thomas, Poe had slipped back into a pattern of drinking to disastrous excess, leaving his household and ailing wife in a state of agitation and disarray. An acquaintance who met him during this period described how Poe begged him for fifty cents so that he might get a meal: "Though he looked the used-up man all over—still he showed the gentleman. I gave him the money—and I never saw him afterwards."

In November, Poe's plans for *The Stylus* received a serious blow. The financing of the magazine was contingent on Poe's ability to obtain a comfortable sinecure at the Philadelphia Customs House, a prospect he had sabotaged with his renewed drinking. "I would write more," he complained in a letter to a friend, "but my heart is too heavy. You have felt the misery of hope deferred and will feel for me."

Poe wrote those words on November 19. The following day, news of the developments in Weehawken appeared in a Philadelphia newspaper under the headline of "New York Mystery Solved." Poe realized at once that he would have to take action. The first two installments of his story had already appeared. The third and final section, containing his solution, was scheduled for the following month, and may already have been set in type. If that final installment appeared as originally written, all of Dupin's theories and conclusions would appear misguided and even naïve in light of the happenings in Weehawken. Even more embarrassing, all of Poe's brash pronouncements about "scarcely intelligible coincidences" and the Calculus of Probabilities, already published in the initial installment, would be exposed as empty boasts.

With the publication date looming, Poe proceeded much as Auguste Dupin had done in the first installment of "Marie Rogêt": He locked himself away with the newspapers, studied the problem "more generally" than he had done before, and plotted a way forward.

XVII

The Vanishing Rowboat

AS HE STRUGGLED to salvage his story, Poe took a close look at what he had already written. His original solution to "The Mystery of Marie Rogêt" had been a marvel of ingenuity. Although the late-breaking developments in Weehawken now forced him to reexamine it, Poe's initial version offered a compelling and altogether unique approach to the affair. As he returned to the narrative in the light of the new information, Poe saw how difficult the task before him would be.

Dupin had already laid the groundwork for his solution in the early stages of the story, through his careful reading of the six newspaper extracts. Dupin was particularly intrigued by the extract concerning the "atrocious" assault on a young woman at the hands of a gang of ruffians. According to the newspaper account, the victim had been out rowing with her family when a gang seized her and subjected her to "brutal" treatment, only to release her unharmed some moments later.

To Dupin's mind, there seemed to be a remarkable coincidence at work. It struck him as improbable that this outrage should have occurred in a manner so precisely similar to the one that was supposed to have been perpetrated on Marie Rogêt—and at almost exactly the same time and place. The two events had so much in common, Dupin believed, that the coincidence had served to influence the tide of public opinion—leading people to believe that both assaults must surely have been the work of gang members. In fact, Dupin insisted, the strange concurrence of the two attacks should have had the opposite effect. If anything, the fact that a gang assault was known to have taken place in the one instance, involving the girl and her family, stood as a powerful argument against an identical assault being carried out against Marie. "It would have been a miracle indeed," Dupin said, "if, while a gang of ruffians were perpetrating, at a given locality, a most unheard-of wrong, there should have been another similar gang, in a similar locality, in the same city, under the same circumstances, with the same means and appliances, engaged in a wrong of precisely the same aspect, at precisely the same period of time!"

Dupin applied a similar piece of reasoning to his contemplation of the murder thicket. "Notwithstanding the acclamation with which the discovery of this thicket was received by the press, and the unanimity with which it was supposed to indicate the precise scene of the outrage, it must be admitted that there was some very good reason for doubt," Dupin allowed. "That it was the scene, I believe—but there was excellent reason for doubt." Under the guise of examining these doubts, Poe undertook a rigorous examination of the clash between Benjamin Day and James Gordon Bennett over the questions surrounding the thicket. Dupin began by raising the possibility that the murder may actually have occurred elsewhere, possibly even at Marie's doorstep. If this were the case, he reasoned, it might follow that the murderer or murderers had cause to fear that the true scene of the crime would be discovered. "In certain classes of minds," Dupin stated, "there would have arisen, at once, a sense of the necessity of some exertion to redivert this attention." What better way could be imagined, Dupin suggested, than to plant articles of clothing in this obscure thicket, so as to put the investigators onto a false scent?

In order to present this theory as plausible, however, Dupin must first deflate the arguments advanced in a newspaper called *Le Soleil*—which closely parallel those of Bennett's *Herald*—concerning the rotting and mildewed state of the articles of clothing, and the manner in which grass had sprung up over some of the items. Dupin began his discussion by observing that grass grows rapidly in warm weather, "as much as two or three inches in a single day." (This cannot be counted as one of Dupin's more compelling remarks—at that rate, the grass inside the thicket would have reached a height of more than seven feet by the time the articles were found.)

Dupin's discussion of the mildew discovered on some of the dead woman's effects must also be treated with caution. "Is he really unaware of the nature of this mildew?" he says, scoffing at the editor of *Le Soleil*. "Is he to be told that it is one of the many classes of fungus, of which the most ordinary feature is its upspringing and decadence within twenty-four hours?"

However misleading Dupin's scientific data may be, his tone of conviction lends a persuasive veneer. In fact, he claims, "it is exceedingly difficult to believe that these articles could have remained in the thicket specified for a longer period than a single week." Dupin gives several additional reasons for this conclusion. First, he remarks, experience has shown that it is extremely difficult for a "lover of nature" to "slake his thirst for solitude" amid the wooded regions on the outskirts of a major city. This is especially so on a Sunday, he continues, when all manner of "town blackguards" find themselves released from the bonds of labor, and free to seek "escape from the restraints and conventionalities of society." In such circumstances, the idea that the murder thicket could have remained isolated during the crime and undisturbed for weeks afterward must be looked upon "as little less than miraculous."

In addition to town blackguards, in Dupin's view, the thicket would also have been a magnet to the sons of Mme. Deluc, who lived in the nearby tavern. With its dense foliage and splendid arrangement of stones it formed a natural hiding place and play area. Its proximity to their house (*"within a few rods,"* Dupin points out) would have made it a daily destination, along with the fact that the boys were frequently sent out looking for sassafras bark in the vicinity. "Would it be," Dupin asks, "a rash wager—a wager of one thousand to one—that *a day* never passed over the heads of these boys without finding at least one of them ensconced in the umbrageous hall, and enthroned upon its natural throne? Those who would hesitate at such a wager, have either never been boys themselves, or have forgotten the boyish nature. I repeat—it is exceedingly hard to comprehend how the articles could have remained in this thicket undiscovered, for a longer period than one or two days."

That being the case, it strikes Dupin as far more likely that the items found within the thicket had been placed there within a day or so of their discovery. In support of this contention, he points out the strangely artificial arrangement of the clothing, which has been placed "as if upon shelves" by a careful hand: "On the *upper* stone lay a white petticoat; on the *second*, a silk scarf; scattered around, were a parasol, gloves, and a pocket-handkerchief." To Dupin's way of thinking, this suggests careful staging, rather than the signs of a genuine struggle. "Here is just such an arrangement as would *naturally* be made by a not over-acute person wishing to dispose the articles *naturally*," Dupin insists. "But it is by no means a *really* natural arrangement. I should rather have looked to see the things *all* lying on the ground and trampled under foot. In the narrow limits of that bower, it would have been scarcely possible that the petticoat and scarf should have retained a position upon the stones, when subjected to the brushing to and fro of many struggling persons."

Dupin is also suspicious of the fragments of clothing found hanging from the interior branches of the thicket, which had been repeatedly described as "torn strips" of cloth. It would be nearly impossible, Dupin claims, for the thorns of the thicket to tear the fabric in such a fashion. "I never so knew it," he tells his companion, "nor did you." If the dress had truly been snagged by thorns, he continues, the cloth would have torn in ragged, irregular patches, rather than tidy strips. Here again, Dupin sees evidence of careful staging, rather than the natural effects of a struggle.

Dupin cuts to the heart of the matter when he declares that the true particulars of the scene "could only have been ascertained from the words, and thus from the recollections, of two small boys; for these boys removed the articles and took them home before they had been seen by a third party." It was a vital observation: Long before the police had been notified, the two boys in Poe's story, like Charles and Ossian Kellenbarack, had snatched up all of the items from inside the thicket and carried them home to their mother. No one ever saw the arrangement of the clothing and other articles at the scene except the boys themselves. Any discussion of the thicket as the scene of the crime, therefore, must stand or fall on the accuracy of their description. It should be remembered that the younger boy, Ossian, was twelve years old at the time. His brother Charles was sixteen.

Dupin does not dwell on the point. For the moment he is more interested in exploring the implications of his theory about the staging of the murder scene. Having established to his own satisfaction that the clothing and other articles could not have gone unnoticed for an entire month, he speculates as to why the evidence should have been planted in the murder thicket at a later date. The answer, he believes, lies in the fifth of the extracts he has culled from the newspapers, which reads: "We have received several forcibly written communications, apparently from various sources, and which go far to render it a matter of certainty that the unfortunate Marie Rogêt has become a victim of one of the numerous bands of blackguards which infest the vicinity of the city upon Sunday. Our own opinion is decidedly in favor of this supposition. We shall endeavor to make room for some of these arguments hereafter."

The timing of these "forcibly written communications," or letters to the editors, strikes Dupin as highly suspicious, as their appearance coincides almost exactly with the discovery of the clothing at the murder thicket. He suggests that the "guilty authors" of the letters are none other than the criminals themselves, who had become fearful that authorities were on the point of discovering the true scene of the crime. In arranging a plausible alternative at the murder thicket, and then drawing attention to it in the newspapers, the murderer or murderers were acting with "the view of diverting attention from the real scene of the outrage."

Having said all of this, Dupin goes on to suggest that discovering the actual scene of the crime holds no real importance. "You will not have apprehended me rightly," he says, "if you suppose it my design to *deny* this thicket as the scene of the outrage." In spite of all that he has said on the matter, he considers it to be "a point of minor importance" when weighed against the other questions in the case. "We are not engaged in an attempt to discover the scene," he says, "but to produce the perpetrators of the crime." In this, he insists, the critical question remains whether Marie fell victim to a gang or a single murderer. Seen in this light, the clothing in the thicket assumes a new and very different importance. The arrangement of the items is clearly intended to suggest the work of a gang, but Dupin looks beyond this artifice to confront an even stranger conundrum. He cannot understand, he says, the "startling circumstance of the articles' having been left in this thicket at all, by any *murderers* who had enough precaution to think of removing the corpse." To Dupin, it seems impossible that these evidences of guilt should have been left by accident, especially the embroidered handkerchief that pointed so clearly to the identity of the victim. "If this was an accident, it was not the accident *of a gang*," Dupin concludes. "We can imagine it only the accident of an individual."

Though the official investigators have embraced the evidence at the murder thicket as proof of more than one attacker, the scene only makes sense, Dupin claims, if "we imagine but *one* violator." In language that clearly recalls Bennett's poetics in the *Herald*, Poe paints a vivid scene of the solitary murderer cowering beside the corpse of his victim. "He is alone with the ghost of the departed," Dupin begins. "He is appalled by what lies motionless before him. The fury of his passion is over, and there is abundant room in his heart for the natural awe of the deed. His is none of that confidence which the presence of numbers inevitably inspires. He is *alone* with the dead. He trembles and is bewildered." Only now, Dupin says, does it occur to the panicked murderer that he must find a means of disposing of the corpse. With great effort, he carries it to the nearby river, but as he strains under the weight of the body, he must leave the clothing and other evidence behind, telling himself that he will return for it in a few moments. "But in his toilsome journey to the water his fears redouble within him," Dupin continues. "The sounds of life encompass his path. A dozen times he hears or fancies he hears the step of an observer. Even the very lights from the city bewilder him. Yet, in time, and by long and frequent pauses of deep agony, he reaches the river's brink, and disposes of his ghastly charge—perhaps through the medium of a boat. But *now* what treasure does the world hold—what threat of vengeance could it hold out—which would have power to urge the return of that lonely murderer over that toilsome and perilous path, to the thicket and its blood-chilling recollections? He returns not, let the consequences be what they may. He *could* not return if he would. His sole thought is immediate escape. He turns his back *forever* upon those dreadful shrubberies, and flees as from the wrath to come."

A gang would not have been prone to the same fears, Dupin insists. "Their numbers would have inspired them with confidence," he says, "if, indeed, confidence is ever wanting in the breast of the errant blackguard." And where one man might quail at the thought of returning to the thicket, the problem would not have arisen with a group of four or more. "They would have left nothing behind them; for their number would have enabled them to carry *all* at once. There would have been no need of *return*." The same logic applies to the cloth hitch said to have been used to drag the corpse to the water. "The device is that of a single individual," Dupin reasons. "To three or four, the limbs of the corpse would have afforded not only a sufficient, but the best possible hold." Similarly Dupin can see no reason why the fence posts along the route to the river should have been taken down. "Would a *number* of men," he wonders, "have put themselves to the superfluous trouble of taking down a fence, for the purpose of dragging through it a corpse which they might have *lifted over* any fence in an instant?"

By this time Dupin appears to have thoroughly reversed himself on the question of whether or not the murder thicket had been the actual scene of the crime. But on the question of a gang, he remains consistent throughout. Marie Rogêt, he maintains, met her death at the hands of a single murderer.

For the identity of this man, Dupin turns to the first and second of the extracts he has culled from the newspapers, which concerned Marie's brief disappearance from the parfumerie more than three years earlier:

> About three years and a half ago, a disturbance very similar to the present was caused by the disappearance of this same Marie Rogêt from the parfumerie of Monsieur Le Blanc, in the Palais Royal. At the end of a week, however, she re-appeared at her customary comptoir, as well as ever, with the exception of a slight paleness not altogether usual. It was given out by Monsieur Le Blanc and her mother that she had merely been on a visit to some friend in the country; and the affair was speedily hushed up. We presume that the present absence is a freak of the same nature, and that, at the expiration of a week or, perhaps, of a month, we shall have her among us again.

> An evening journal of yesterday refers to a former mysterious disappearance of Mademoiselle Rogêt. It is well known that, during the week of her absence from Le Blanc's parfumerie, she was in the company of a young naval officer much noted for his debaucheries. A quarrel, it is supposed, providentially, led to her return home. We have the name of the Lothario in question, who is at present stationed in Paris, but for obvious reasons forbear to make it public.

Dupin expresses contempt for the "extreme remissness" of the police in failing to explore the full ramifications of this earlier disappearance. He insists that "it is mere folly to say that between the first and second disappearance of Marie there is no *supposable* connection." He puts forward the possibility that an intended elopement lay behind the first disappearance, a marriage to which Madame Rogêt would presumably have objected. Before the marriage was to have taken place, Dupin speculates, the two lovers fell to quarrelling and the affair ended with "the return home of the betrayed."

Poe draws a clear parallel between Marie's disappearance from the parfumerie and the equivalent episode from the life of Mary Rogers: her brief, widely reported absence from Anderson's Tobacco Emporium in 1838. In Dupin's formulation, the murder and the earlier disappearance must be viewed as two halves of a single event. He is convinced that the circumstances surrounding Marie's departure from home on the fatal Sunday indicate "a renewal of the betrayer's advances." If so, the man who lured Marie away from home in 1838 and the man she went to meet on the fatal Sunday of 1841 are one and the same.

In linking the two disappearances in this manner, Poe opened up a provocative and original line of thought. Although the earlier disappearance had not been entirely overlooked in the New York investigation, the episode did not draw a great deal of comment in the days following her murder. The fact that Poe knew of it at all must owe something to the time he spent in New York in 1838, just before the disappearance, and also the degree to which he studied the New York newspapers afterward. Poe's ambition in yoking the two events was plain enough: The New York police, he suggested, had missed an opportunity. They had concentrated their energies exclusively on the crime of 1841. Poe's surmises, if correct, gave an equal weight to the disappearance of 1838, and suggested an entirely new means of tracking the murderer. If Poe could identify the man who had squired the young woman away in 1838, instead of focusing his energies on the events of 1841, the murder might be solved.

Dupin gives several reasons for believing that Marie intended to elope at the time of her murder. He recalls that Marie had told St. Eustache, her "accepted suitor," that she was simply going to visit her aunt on the day in question, and that she arranged to meet him at nightfall so that he might escort her safely home. At first glance, Dupin admits, this tends to cut against the suggestion that Marie was planning to run off with another man. And yet, he points out, it is clear that Marie was intentionally deceiving St. Eustache at the time. She did not go to her aunt's home and was never expected there. Instead, according to the testimony of numerous witnesses, she met with a male companion and crossed the river with him, arriving at the Barrière du Roule at three o'clock in the afternoon. Marie must surely have been aware that there would be "surprise and suspicion aroused in the bosom of her affianced suitor, St. Eustache," when she failed to keep their evening rendezvous. It seems probable to Dupin that she did not intend to face the consequences. "She could not have thought of returning to brave this suspicion," Dupin says, "but the suspicion becomes a point of trivial importance to her if we suppose her *not* intending to return."

Seen in this light, Dupin says, the matter becomes plain. Marie left home on the morning of her disappearance with the intention of eloping with her secret lover, never to return, just as she had three years earlier at the start of her week-long disappearance. Dupin is adamant that the second episode must be viewed as a continuation of the first, rather than a second, unrelated entanglement. "We are prepared to regard it as a 'making up' of the old *amour*, rather than as the commencement of a new one," Dupin says. "The chances are ten to one that he who had once eloped with Marie would again propose an elopement, rather than that

she to whom proposals of an elopement had been made by one individual, should have them made to her by another."

Who is the mysterious swain?

> Beyond St. Eustache, and perhaps Beauvais, we find no
> recognized, no open, no honorable suitors of Marie. Of
> none other is there any thing said. Who, then, is the se-
> cret lover, of whom the relatives (at least most of them)
> know nothing, but whom Marie meets upon the morn-
> ing of Sunday, and who is so deeply in her confidence,
> that she hesitates not to remain with him until the shades
> of the evening descend, amid the solitary groves of the
> Barrière du Roule? . . . And what means the singular
> prophecy of Madam Rogêt on the morning of Marie's
> departure?—"I fear that I shall never see Marie again."

For an answer, Dupin turns once again to the second of the extracts he has drawn from the newspapers, concerning the mysterious
"Lothario," "a young naval officer much noted for his debaucheries," who is believed to have been in Marie's company during her first disappearance. The language of this invented extract,
particularly in the use of the word "Lothario," recalls the strangely
ribald "gallant gay Lothario" article from the *Times and Commercial
Intelligencer* of 1838. The core of the information, however, was
plainly culled from a *Herald* article of August 3, 1841:

> This young girl, Mary Rogers, was missing from Ander-
> son's store three years ago for two weeks. It is asserted that
> she was then seduced by an officer of the U.S. Navy, and
> kept at Hoboken for two weeks. His name is well known
> aboard his ship.

These three lines from the *Herald* are of vital importance, as they comprise the only known reference to a "naval officer" being implicated in the affair, as opposed to an enlisted man such as the sailor William Kiekuck. Poe, through the character of Dupin, fastens onto this fleeting mention with a steely determination:

"[L]et me call your attention to the fact," Dupin says, "that the time elapsing between the first ascertained and the second supposed elopement is a few months more than the general period of the cruises of our men-of-war." In other words, the gap of time between Marie's two disappearances corresponds almost exactly with a naval officer's average length of service at sea. "Had the lover been interrupted in his first villainy by the necessity of departure to sea," Dupin asks, "and had he seized the first moment of his return to renew the base designs not yet altogether accomplished—or not yet altogether accomplished by him? Of all these things we know nothing."

Before the reader has a chance to reflect on any possible short-comings in Dupin's reasoning, he moves on to other details of the case. When he returns to the subject later in the narrative, there has been a shift in tone. The hypothesis that Marie met her death at the hands of a naval officer is now presented as established fact:

"Let us sum up now the meagre yet certain fruits of our long analysis. We have attained the idea of a murder perpetrated, in the thicket at the Barrière du Roule, by a lover, or at least by an intimate and secret associate of the deceased. This associate is of swarthy complexion. This complexion, the 'hitch' in the bandage, and the 'sailor's knot' with which the bonnet-ribbon is tied, point to a sea-man. His companionship with the deceased, a gay but not an abject young girl, designates him as above the grade of the common sailor." Dupin adds that the "circumstance of the first elopement" as described in the first of his newspaper extracts has served to "blend the idea of this seaman with that of that 'naval officer' " mentioned in the second extract. It is this shadowy figure, Dupin states, who "is first known to have led the unfortunate into crime."

With these statements Dupin is asking his companion (and, by extension, the reader) to take a great deal on faith. As with his earlier statements about mildew and grass growth, his steady flow of persuasive rhetoric masks several highly dubious claims. His confession of ignorance of the mysterious sailor's intent serves to disarm the reader, inspiring confidence in the deceptively offhand assertions of fact that follow. The implications of the sailor's knot and hitch had been discussed in numerous sources, and had been put forward by the New York police and the New Jersey coroner as evidence of the likelihood of a sailor's involvement in the crime. But Poe's insistence that the sailor must have been an officer is the vital link between the murder and the earlier disappearance, and the arguments here are decidedly less convincing. Dupin describes Marie as "gay but not abject" to suggest that she enjoyed an elevated social status, placing her beyond the reach of common sailors and into the more rarified realm of the officers' table. It is certainly possible that a clerk in a parfumerie—or a cigar store—should have enjoyed the attentions of an officer, but it is too much to say that she should have been outside the sphere of the lower classes. As the daughter of a boardinghouse keeper, Mary Rogers performed a daily round of chores ranging from scrubbing floors to beating rugs. She was hardly upper crust, and had in fact descended in social status from her early years in Connecticut.

Poe employs a similar tactic in his discussion of the "general period" of naval voyages. Although his words have an authoritative ring, several historians have argued that in fact there were no set periods governing the length of a nineteenth-century warship's service. Mary Rogers's own life provided several examples of navy men whose service records contradict Poe's assertion, ranging from the sailors who frequented Anderson's Tobacco Emporium to the young William Kiekuck, whose visits to the boardinghouse occurred at far more regular intervals than three and a half years. Once again, Poe is asking the reader to take a great deal on faith, and employing the language of ironclad certainty to describe what had heretofore been simple conjecture.

Poe's cunning language and persuasive tone serves to obscure a central weakness of his argument. In his judgment, the suitor who trifled with Marie's affections in 1838 must also have swept her away in 1841, with tragic consequences. But Marie Rogêt—like Mary Rogers—was a young woman who had achieved some measure of fame on the strength of her "intense and irresistible" beauty. Indeed, as Dupin had noted earlier in the narrative, Marie's employer Monsieur Le Blanc found that his shop "soon became notorious through the charms of the sprightly *grisette*." Is it truly impossible that a woman of such potent allure might attract two offers of elopement in the space of three years or more? Dupin asks us to believe so. At the same time, Dupin assumes that the impulse to elope, rather than follow a more traditional course of courtship, must have originated with Marie's paramour, rather than with Marie herself. It is plausible, however, that a young woman, upon receiving a marriage proposal, might suggest an elopement as a means of overcoming objections from her mother, or extricating herself from an unwanted betrothal.

Poe's theory also leans heavily on the fifth of his extracts from the newspapers, with its reference to "forcibly written urgent communications" to the press that attempt to place the blame for Marie Rogêt's death on a "band of blackguards." The fact that these communications were "well-written," he suggests, lends credence to the notion of an officer's hand, as common sailors were not noted for literacy. Once again, however, Poe has taken a vague and unsubstantiated surmise from earlier in the narrative—that Marie's murderer *might* have written misleading letters to the press—and reintroduced it later in the story as a proven fact. Of all of Dupin's many speculations and conjectures, this is perhaps the most suspect. In discussing the discovery of the murder thicket, Dupin had put forward the idea that Marie's murderer might have sent these letters with "the view of diverting attention from the real scene of the outrage." Even within Dupin's own framework of the case, however, the notion does not support itself. By the end of his lengthy discourse, Dupin has brushed aside his earlier objections and embraced the murder thicket as the likely scene of the crime. If the assault actually took place in that "umbrageous hall," as Dupin describes it, surely the murderer would not have sent letters, well written or otherwise, directing the authorities to its vicinity.

By this time, Dupin has made several repetitions of his assertion that a naval officer stationed in Paris was "first known to have led the unfortunate" Marie astray. In this case, however, the parallel to the New York investigation is extremely slight—limited to the single passing reference in the *Herald* to the effect that Mary Rogers had been "seduced by an officer of the U.S. Navy, and kept at Hoboken for two weeks." It is worth noting, then, that the statement in the *Herald* appeared in a brief, two-paragraph announcement of Mary Rogers's death, intended to prod the mayors of New York and New Jersey to "do their duties." The article marked the *Herald*'s first mention of the murder, and was printed in the pell-mell torrent of early speculation in the days following the crime, at a time when hastily assembled accounts in the other newspapers were bungling the basic facts of the case, including Mary Rogers's name and address. In these circumstances, the accuracy of Bennett's story is difficult to gauge. A great deal of false and contradictory information appeared in the New York press in the first week of August of 1841, a fact that is clearly reflected in the pages of "The Mystery of Marie Rogêt." Early in the story, Dupin states that the interval between Marie's first and second disappearances lasted "about five months." By the final pages, the period has lengthened to three and a half years.

The crucial assertion of the *Herald* story, that Mary Rogers had been "seduced by an officer in the U.S. Navy," was never confirmed. It did not appear in any of the newspaper accounts at the time of the disappearance in 1838, including those in the *Herald*. Adding to the confusion, the *Herald* story contended that Mary had been "kept at Hoboken for two weeks." This is difficult to reconcile with the accounts of the episode that appeared after Mary's return to the cigar counter, some of which described the period of her absence as amounting to only a few hours.

Much of the weight of Poe's reasoning rests on this fleeting, isolated, and highly questionable reference in the *Herald*. Poe clearly assumed that the paper was correct in describing their suspect as an officer, rather than an enlisted man such as William Kiekuck—who was, in fact, arrested two days after the appearance of the *Herald* article. Having fastened on the notion of a naval officer as the villain, however, Poe allows Dupin to carry it through to a compelling conclusion. Dupin begins by pondering the "continued absence of him of the dark complexion." If Marie's escort on the fatal Sunday had been innocent of any crime, Dupin reasons, he would surely have stepped forward if, as the authorities believe, the assault had been committed by a gang. "But why is this man absent?" Dupin asks. "Was he murdered by the gang? If so, why are there only *traces* of the assassinated *girl*?"

Dupin raises the possibility that the officer might have hesitated to come forward for fear of being charged with the crime. But this, he concludes, is a notion that would only have occurred to him well after the fact, not in the immediate aftermath. "The first impulse of an innocent man would have been to announce the outrage," Dupin insists, "and to aid in identifying the ruffians." Indeed, Dupin suggests, this course would have been far safer than staying silent for fear of prosecution. "He had been seen with the girl. He had crossed the river with her in an open ferry-boat. The denouncing of the assassins would have appeared, even to an idiot, the surest and sole means of relieving himself from suspicion. We cannot suppose him, on the night of the fatal Sunday, both innocent himself and incognizant of an outrage committed. Yet only under such circumstances is it possible to imagine that he would have failed, if alive, in the denouncement of the assassins."

As Dupin lays out the facts, the conclusion appears to him to be obvious. Marie's companion is not dead, or his body would have been discovered. By the same token, he cannot be innocent of the crime or he would have gone to the authorities. He must, therefore, be the murderer himself. All that remains, then, is to discover his identity, a process made far easier by linking the murder to Marie's earlier thwarted elopement. "And what means are ours of attaining the truth?" Dupin asks. "We shall find these means multiplying and gathering distinctness as we proceed. Let us sift to the bottom this affair of the first elopement. Let us know the full history of 'the officer,' with his present circumstances, and his whereabouts at the precise period of the murder." Here Dupin returns to his theory that the murderer himself sent "forcibly written communications" to one of the evening papers, to throw the police off his scent. "Let us carefully compare with each other the various communications sent to the evening paper, in which the object was to inculpate a gang," Dupin advises. "And, all this done, let us again compare these various communications with the known

MSS. of the officer." If the handwriting matches, Dupin reasons, it would go a long way toward establishing the officer's guilt.

If all else fails, Dupin says, there is a final means of tracking the guilty Lothario, one suggested by the sixth and final of the newspaper extracts, concerning the empty boat found floating down the Seine. "Let us now trace *the boat*," says Dupin. According to the notice in the paper, a bargeman discovered the empty boat on the Monday after the murder. He then towed it back to the boatyard, removed its rudder, and pulled it onto shore. The following morning the boat was found to be missing, spirited away without the knowledge of its owner, and in such haste that the rudder was left behind. The notice drawing the matter to Dupin's attention did not appear until Thursday, after the discovery of Marie's body. Since there were no earlier notices concerning the boat, Dupin believes that only a navy man, availing himself of some "personal permanent connection" to the barge office, could have learned so quickly that the boat had been recovered. Realizing that it might incriminate him, the guilty sailor used his private access to remove the boat from the barge office.

"In speaking of the lonely assassin dragging his burden to the shore, I have already suggested the probability of his availing himself of *a boat*," Dupin says. "Now we are to understand that Marie Rogêt *was* precipitated from a boat. This would naturally have been the case. The corpse could not have been trusted to the shallow waters of the shore. The peculiar marks on the back and shoulders of the victim tell of the bottom ribs of a boat." Dupin speculates that the guilty officer pushed off from shore having neglected to bring along a weight with which to sink the body. Unwilling to risk a return to "that accursed shore," he instead throws the corpse overboard in the middle of the river, hoping that it will remain at the bottom long enough to conceal his escape. "Having rid himself of his ghastly charge," Dupin continues, "the murderer would have hastened to the city. There, at some obscure wharf, he would have leaped on land. But the boat—would he have secured it? He would have been in too great haste for such things as securing a boat. Moreover, in fastening it to the wharf, he would have felt as if securing evidence against himself. His natural thought would have been to cast from him, as far as possible, all that had held connection with his crime." That being the case, Dupin reasons, he would have set the boat adrift in the river, hoping in his distress that it would never be found. After an uneasy night in which he imagines the consequences if the boat is discovered, he awakes to find his worst fears realized. "In the morning," Dupin says, "the wretch is stricken with unutterable horror at finding that the boat has been picked up and detained at a locality which he is in the daily habit of frequenting—at a locality, perhaps, which his duty compels him to frequent. The next night, *without daring to ask for the rudder*, he removes it." Here, Dupin proclaims, providence has provided an opportunity. "Now *where* is that rudderless boat?" he asks. "Let it be one of our first purposes to discover. With the first glimpse we obtain of it, the dawn of our success shall begin. This boat shall guide us, with a rapidity which will surprise even ourselves, to him who employed it in the midnight of the fatal Sabbath. Corroboration will rise upon corroboration. *The murderer* will be traced."

Dupin's call for action presumes that each link in his chain of reasoning is sound. It takes for granted that a single Lothario stands behind both of Marie's disappearances, and that this man wrote letters to the press that might serve to incriminate him. It also assumes that this man's identity is widely known, if not a matter of public record. Finally, it presupposes that the villain made his escape in a rowboat, leaving behind some form of incriminating evidence which he subsequently felt compelled to obscure, even at the risk of being discovered in the act of stealing the boat from its mooring. But if some of the individual pieces didn't quite seem to fit, the finished puzzle appeared to come together in a clear and compelling way. Poe had shown extraordinary skill in linking Marie Rogêt's murder to her earlier disappearance, so as to place the blame on the debauched naval officer, and Dupin's technique of approaching the matter from the "outskirts" gave a forceful demonstration of the power of ratiocination. When Dupin boldly pronounced that the murderer would be captured, the reader could not help but feel that a just resolution would not be long in coming.

Unfortunately, Poe had backed himself into a corner. "The Murders in the Rue Morgue" had offered a tidy resolution: Poe had no sooner laid out his conclusions than the murderer arrived with a knock at the door. But "Marie Rogêt" had promised an even more dramatic climax. In the opening paragraphs of the story, and in his letters to prospective publishers, Poe had promised that his rigorous examination of the case would offer a series of exact parallels to the facts and theories of the Mary Rogers drama, and that he would "indicate the assassin in a manner which will give renewed impetus to investigation." Now, within a page of his conclusion, Poe faced a creative impasse. Since the actual Mary Rogers investigation had failed to produce the murderer, Poe's story could not name a villain without deviating significantly from established fact. Although Poe had sketched out a compelling theory, he had not left himself the breathing space needed to create a dramatically satisfying ending. Unlike "The Murders in the Rue Morgue," there could be no climactic confrontation, and no unmasking of the killer.

Poe's solution was ingenious and audacious, but also something of a cheat. Reaching back to *The Narrative of Arthur Gordon Pym*,

Poe fell back on a fabricated "editor's note" to cover a narrative gap while blurring the line between fact and fiction. Thus, Dupin's climactic statement, "*The murderer* will be traced," was followed by an explanatory paragraph attributed to the editor of the *Ladies' Companion*, inserted within editorial brackets: "[For reasons which we shall not specify but which to many readers will appear obvious, we have taken the liberty of here omitting, from the MSS. placed in our hands, such portion as details the *following up* of the apparently slight clew obtained by Dupin. We feel it advisable only to state, in brief, that the result desired was brought to pass; that an individual assassin was convicted, upon his own confession, of the murder of Marie Rogêt, and that the Prefect fulfilled punctually, although with reluctance, the terms of his compact with the Chevalier. Mr. Poe's article concludes with the following words. — *Eds*.]"

Poe's feint leaves the reader to understand that Dupin's conjectures were entirely correct—brilliantly so—and that the villain was, in fact, apprehended along precisely the lines of inquiry he had suggested. However, one must appreciate this marvel of deductive skill from arm's length. Instead of joining in the discovery, the reader is asked to accept that it occurred offstage. Although it is clearly suggested that "Mr. Poe" supplied his answer in his original manuscript, the editor is cast in the role of censor and killjoy, removing the presumably thrilling passages for reasons of unstated propriety. One can only admire Poe's outlandish cunning, but his bait-and-switch leaves the reader with a sense of having missed the final leg of a horse race.

"There is a radical error, I think, in the usual mode of constructing a story," Poe once wrote. "Either history affords a thesis—or one is suggested by an incident of the day—or, at best, the author sets himself to work in the combination of striking events to form merely the basis of his narrative—designing, generally, to fill in with description, dialogue, or authorial comment, whatever crevices of fact, or action, may, from page to page, render themselves apparent."

There were a great many "crevices of fact" in the Mary Rogers case. The manner in which Poe chose to fill them showed extraordinary flashes of inspiration set off by an equal measure of guile. In several important respects, Poe had reason to feel pride in his interpretation of the case. The manner in which he demolished James Gordon Bennett's "gang of ruffians" theory was brilliant, and his linking of the murder to Mary Rogers's earlier disappearance showed a masterful grasp of the complexities of the case. The value of Poe's conclusions, however, ultimately rests with the accuracy of his facts, and especially with the crucial six "extracts" upon which he based his solution. For many years it was assumed that Poe's extracts were near-verbatim transcriptions of New York newspapers. More recent studies have effectively refuted this notion, and demonstrated that most of them were paraphrases and compilations, reflecting varying degrees of faithfulness. In five of the six extracts, however, the original sources are readily apparent. Although Poe occasionally gives greater emphasis to a fact or supposition than can be found in the source, he rarely strayed from the spirit of the original.

The sixth extract, concerning the missing boat, is a different matter. The mock editorial comment at the conclusion of Poe's story made a point of saying that the "slight clew" provided by Dupin had been followed up with stunning success. One presumes this refers to the matter of the missing boat, which Dupin believed would lead to the murderer "with a rapidity which will surprise even ourselves." The extract was supposed to have been taken from the pages of the New York *Standard*, but no trace of the original has ever been found. Although the *Herald* urged the police at one stage to "find out what boats and what crews were over at Weehawken that day," there seems to have been no barge cast adrift in the Hudson, or surreptitiously removed from a boatyard.

In the final paragraphs of his story, Poe appears to acknowledge that he has taken poetic license. He attempts to cover a multitude of sins by referring back to the device of creating "exact coincidences" between real and imagined events. "It will be understood that I speak of coincidences *and no more*," he declares. "And farther: in what I relate it will be seen that between the fate of the unhappy Mary Cecilia Rogers, so far as that fate is known, and the fate of one Marie Rogêt up to a certain epoch in her history, there has existed a parallel in the contemplation of whose wonderful exactitude the reason becomes embarrassed. I say all this will be seen. But let it not for a moment be supposed that, in proceeding with the sad narrative of Marie from the epoch just mentioned, and in tracing to its *denouement* the mystery which enshrouded her, it is my covert design to hint at an extension of the parallel, or even to suggest that the measures adopted in Paris for the discovery of the assassin of a *grisette*, or measures founded in any similar ratiocination would produce any similar result." Poe then retreats into a convoluted discussion of the Calculus of Probabilities, a process he likens to a roll of the dice: "Nothing, for example, is more difficult than to convince the merely general reader that the fact of sixes having been thrown twice in succession by a player at dice, is sufficient cause for betting the largest odds that sixes will not be thrown in the third attempt. . . . It does not appear that the two throws which have been completed, and which lie now absolutely in the Past, can have influence upon the throw which exists only in the Future."

★ ★ ★

THE WORDS WOULD COME BACK to haunt him in the days to come. In effect, "The Mystery of Marie Rogêt" had been a roll of the dice, with Poe placing all of his chips on a mysterious, unnamed naval officer. Had the real-life murder investigation remained at a standstill, Poe's glossy speculations would have achieved their purpose admirably. His bold and provocative new theory would likely have sparked renewed interest in the case, and perhaps even brought calls to reopen the investigation. The shotgun blast in Weehawken, however, had changed everything. From the moment he saw the chilling headline "THE MARY ROGERS MYSTERY EXPLAINED," Poe knew that the stakes had been raised. His story made no mention of the possibility of Mrs. Loss's involvement in the crime, or of a "premature delivery" gone wrong. Dupin, the hero of "The Murders in the Rue Morgue," would be a laughingstock, and his creator would suffer the consequences.

It was too late for Poe to make changes of any kind to the first two installments of the story, but the third and final section was still in the hands of William Snowden at the *Ladies' Companion*. Steeling his nerves, Poe calculated the odds and made a decision. Then he picked up his pen and set to work.

XVIII

At Variance with Truth

POE HAD VERY LITTLE TIME in which to act. As the gravity of the situation became clear, his long experience as a magazine editor came to the fore. With "Politan" and other earlier efforts, he had simply allowed an unsuccessful work to trail off rather than prolong a fruitless effort. Certainly he must have considered canceling the third installment of "Marie Rogêt," so as to spare himself the embarrassment of advocating a solution that now appeared to have been proven wrong. But with his hopes for *The Stylus*, his projected literary magazine, hanging in the balance, he must have realized that he could not afford such a public admission of failure.

A more logical course, then, would have been a hasty revision of the third installment to reflect the new information from Weehawken. Unfortunately, since he could not make any changes to the first two sections, this plan could only succeed to a limited degree. At the conclusion of the second section Dupin had already presented the six crucial newspaper extracts from which he derived his solution, and had even gone so far as to chide the French police for their "extreme remissness" in failing to arrest and question the mysterious naval officer mentioned in the second of the clippings. A total reversal was clearly out of the question; Poe had already established the forward momentum of the narrative, and planted the seeds of his solution. The challenge before him was to revise the final section without unsettling what had already been done, a process similar to trying to replace the bottom tier of a house of cards.

There were only a few days remaining before the January issue of the *Ladies' Companion* went to press. If anything was to be done, Poe and his editor, William Snowden, would have to work quickly. A decision was reached to push back the publication of the third installment until the February issue. This bought Poe a month's breathing space in which to try to rescue the situation.

It is not certain exactly how he proceeded. A widely circulated anecdote describes a drunken foray to New York at this time, during which Poe is said to have stumbled across an old sweetheart named Mary Starr Jennings. The woman had known Poe in Baltimore, but had since married and was living with her husband in Jersey City when Poe unexpectedly appeared at her door. Mrs. Jennings described Poe as having been "on a spree" that left him so disoriented that he had crossed the Hudson several times on the ferry, asking random strangers if they happened to know where she could be found.

Upon finding her by lucky chance, Poe made surly accusations about her recent marriage. "Do you love him truly?" he demanded. "You don't love him. You do love me. You know you do." When Mrs. Jennings brushed aside his questions Poe lapsed into moody silence, chopping at some radishes with a table knife. At length he took his leave, only to be found a few days later "in the woods on the outskirts of Jersey City, wandering about like a crazy man," in a scene reminiscent of the final hours of Daniel Payne.

It is tempting to seize on this anecdote as evidence of Poe's distress over "Marie Rogêt." It places him in the vicinity of the Nick Moore House, suggesting that he might have attempted a firsthand investigation of the alleged scene of Mary Rogers's death. It also gives evidence of the extreme agitation and recourse to drink that one might have expected under these stressful circumstances. But it is impossible to say for certain that he traveled to New York to investigate the Mary Rogers saga. Although he is known to have made a trip to New York in 1842, the exact dates are uncertain. Mrs. Jennings's reminiscence of the event was published in 1889, long after Poe's death. She placed the incident in the spring of 1842, whereas the death of Mrs. Loss and the subsequent revelations did not transpire until November of that year. While it is possible that Mrs. Jennings, looking back over more than forty-five years, could have been mistaken as to the precise month, or even the year, there are many details about her story that invite skepticism. Not the least of these is Poe's apparent ardor for another woman at a time when all contemporary accounts show him to be assiduously attentive to his wife and her illness.

If Poe had troubled to visit Weehawken personally, it is difficult to say what effect it might have had on the final portion of "Marie Rogêt." Poe had been at pains to establish that Dupin would solve the crime without stirring from his armchair, and by means readily available to the casual observer. In contrast to "The Murders in the Rue Morgue," the fact that Dupin did not visit the crime scene was presented as an important component of his method. Poe, too, placed great value in this sense of distance, underscoring the notion that he was pitting his own cunning against that of the reader, just as he had done with his popular cryptography articles. Poe never wavered from this position. In later years he would claim that the story had been "composed at a distance from the scene of the atrocity," with only the newspapers as a guide. Earlier, when writing about the chess-playing automaton, Poe stated unequivocally that his conclusions had been based on "frequent visits to the exhibition." Although the credibility of his solution to the Mary Rogers mystery might have benefited from a statement that he had visited the crime scene personally, Poe never claimed to have done so. "Thus," he would later write, "much escaped the writer of which he could have availed himself had he been upon the spot and visited the localities."

In the absence of Poe's manuscript, and lacking any of his correspondence with Snowden, it is impossible to say exactly what changes were made to the story to allow for the revelations at Weehawken. Seen in the light of the new information, however, some of the more muddled passages of the story come into sharper focus. At one or two points Poe seems to have attemped to insert hasty and perhaps ill-considered revisions that only serve to contradict the earlier portions of the story. His strange vacillation over the murder thicket would seem to be the foremost of these inconsistencies. Through the first two-thirds of the story Poe appeared resolute in his determination to disprove that the crime had taken place in the thicket. The entire rationale behind the mysterious naval officer's "forcibly written communications" to the press had been, Dupin claimed, to divert attention "from the real scene of the outrage." Having insisted so adamantly on this point, however, the third portion of the story found Dupin retreating into uncertainty on the matter, and finally changing his opinion entirely: "You will not have apprehended me rightly, however, if you suppose it is my design to *deny* this thicket as the scene of the outrage. . . . I *admit* the thicket as the scene . . ." This abrupt change of direction may be more clearly understood if one imagines the Weehawken revelations arriving in the pause between the second and third portions of the story.

Other aspects of the story show no signs of alteration, even where they appear to contradict the new interpretation of the crime. Madame Deluc (Poe's stand-in for Mrs. Loss) is described in the third portion of the narrative as an "honest and scrupulous old lady" whose only crime is that she may have misjudged the time of day at which certain events occurred. Dupin remarks on the manner in which she spoke "lingeringly and lamentingly" about some cakes and ale stolen by members of a gang, and speculates that she "might still have entertained a faint hope of compensation." Not even the most suspicious of the readers of the *Ladies' Companion* would have cast a sinister interpretation on this behavior.

By contrast, Poe's meandering discussion of the Calculus of Probabilities at the end of the story shows signs of being a late addition to the narrative. At the beginning of the story Poe had referred to this calculus as a means of applying the most "rigidly exact" aspects of science to the intangible "shadow and spirituality" of speculation. By the end, he has retreated from this confident position, saying that "it should be considered that the most trifling variation in the facts of the two cases might give rise to the most important miscalculations, by diverting thoroughly the two courses of events; very much as, in arithmetic, an error which, in its own individuality, may be inappreciable, produces, at length, by dint of multiplication at all points of the process, a result enormously at variance with truth." In other words, two raindrops will not follow the same path down a windowpane—the slightest speck of grit will cause them to diverge. This passage, though undeniably true, hints strongly of an attempt to cover all contingencies.

In spite of the limitations imposed on him by the urgent deadline and the previous publication of the earlier sections of the story, Poe managed to do just enough to salvage "The Mystery of Marie Rogêt." He successfully backed away from his earlier insistence that the murder thicket and its environs could not have been the scene of the outrage, and he found additional breathing space in his concluding remarks about the notoriously problematic nature of scientific speculation. More importantly, Poe's cunningly deceptive editorial note gave the impression that Dupin had emeged triumphant, but it scrupulously avoided giving any detail. The passage revealed only that "the result desired was brought to pass," but gave no information as to the identity of the villain or the exact nature of what had transpired. In effect, Poe claimed to hold a winning hand without actually showing his cards.

The third and final installment of "The Mystery of Marie Rogêt" appeared in February of 1843, with no explanation offered for the delay of one month. The story made a startling and original impression on its early readers, for whom the details of the Mary Rogers case were still very much a matter of concern. In an early review, the critic Thomas Dunn English noted:

> "The Mystery of Marie Rogêt" has a local, independent of any other, interest. Everyone at all familiar with the internal history of New York for the last few years will remember the murder of Mary Rogers, the segar-girl. The deed baffled all attempts of the police to discover the time and mode of its commission, and the identity of the offenders. To this day, with the exception of the light afforded by the tale of Mr. Poe, in which the faculty of analysis is applied to the facts, the whole matter is shrouded in complete mystery. We think he has proven, very conclusively, that which he attempts. At all events, he has dissipated in our mind all belief that the murder was perpetrated by more than one.

Although Poe had made no specific reference to Mary Rogers's presumed death at the hands of an abortionist, his skillful dissection of the gang theory of the murder did a great deal to align his story with the dramatic shift in the public's perception of the case. The previous year, when it was thought that the cigar girl had fallen victim to a gang of blacklegs and ruffians, the newspapers had united in calling for a more efficient police force. Now, in the wake of Mrs. Loss's death and the drama at Weehawken, the editorial pages turned their energies to the outlawing of abortion. As Mrs. Loss had now passed beyond the reach of the law, much of the public outrage came to focus on the notorious Madame Restell, who continued to provide her powders and "still and lost" treatments—as opposed to "live and found" treatments, in which the patient would carry the pregnancy to term in a "lying in" house and then give the child up for adoption. "The exposures which we have recently made of this base woman's practices have excited the profound attention of the community," wrote the *Police Gazette*, "and moved by the deep necessity of providing a punishment adequate to her horrid and unnatural crimes, an association is already in the process of formation, whose intention it is to petition the legislature to make abortion a State Prison offense."

George Dixon, the editor of the weekly New York *Polynathos*, saw the fate of Mary Rogers as a threat to the very notion of female virtue. If women could so easily rid themselves of the evidence of sexual congress, he believed, the "coin of maidenhood" would be forever debased. "Madame Restell's Preventative Powders have counterfeited the handwriting of nature," Dixon insisted. "You have not a medal, fresh from the mint, of sure metal; but a base, lacquered counterfeit, that has undergone the sweaty contamination of a hundred palms."

The *Police Gazette*, meanwhile, demanded to know "if a community professing to be civilized will any longer tolerate this wholesale murder under their very eyes? Will a city possessing courts and a police wink at such an atrocious violation of the laws, and if it will, and the demon murderess Restell be too rich to be within the power of the law, will the community, in the last resort, suffer her to go on unrebuked by some sudden application of popular vengeance?" In raising the specter of "popular vengeance," a reference to public lynching, the paper gave a fair measure of the depth of public feeling against Restell. "We are not now demanding justice upon the perpetratress of a single crime, but upon one who might be drowned in the blood of her victims, did each but yield a drop, whose epitaph should be a curse, and whose tomb a pyramid of skulls."

POE, EVER ALERT to the tide of popular opinion, would seize on this groundswell of sentiment to great effect in the months to come. For the moment, he was obliged to turn his attention to more pressing concerns. In February of 1843, as the final section of "The Mystery of Marie Rogêt" helped to stir indignation in New York, Poe issued a prospectus for *The Stylus*, a last-ditch effort at collecting enough subscription money to allow him to proceed. In contrast to the frivolous tone of the other magazines of the day, Poe declared that *The Stylus* would be "more vigorous, more pungent, more original, more individual and more independent." Thomas Clarke, his partner in the enterprise, published the prospectus in his journal the *Saturday Museum*, along with a lengthy biographical sketch that praised Poe as a Byronic hero, describing heroic (though fictitious) exploits in Greece and St. Petersburg. Of greater merit were the lengthy extracts from his work, demonstrating that Poe, at thirty-four, had become one of the most distinctive literary voices in America. Although the sketch itself was immensely flattering, the woodcut portrait of Poe that accompanied it was not. "I am ugly enough, God knows," he complained, "but not quite so bad as that."

Having averted a ruinous misstep with "Marie Rogêt," it now appeared that Poe's dream of running his own magazine would at last be realized. Within three months, however, Thomas Clarke had withdrawn his backing, having apparently become discouraged by Poe's continued bouts of drunkenness. In a letter to James Russell Lowell, Poe wrote that the "magazine scheme has exploded, or, at least, I have been deprived, through the imbecility, or rather through the idiocy of my partner, of all means of prosecuting it for the present."

With his hopes dashed, Poe once again considered abandoning literature, and briefly explored a career in law. Predictably, this inspiration did not bear fruit. Finding himself with a great deal of unused material that he had intended for *The Stylus*, Poe set his sights on a new arena. Although he had disparaged "the present absurd rage for lecturing" when writing about Dickens, Poe launched his own career as a lecturer in November of 1843 with a speech at the William Wirt Literary Institute in Philadelphia on "The Poetry of America." The timing was auspicious. A few months earlier, in June, Poe had published "The Gold-Bug," a story in which the unusual markings of a dung beetle hold the key to a pirate treasure. Coming only a few months after the final installment of "Marie Rogêt," the story marked a continuation of Poe's tales of ratiocination, with the Dupin-like figure of William Legrand using his "unusual powers of mind" to solve a baffling cipher. The story appeared in Philadelphia's *Dollar Newspaper* as the winning entry of a fiction contest, and would become the most popular and widely read of the stories Poe published in his lifetime. The success of "The Gold-Bug" helped to attract notice to the first of his Philadelphia lectures, with the result that hundreds of people were turned away at the door. Poe proved to be an engaging orator, alternating his passionate and melodic readings of poetry with the sharp literary insights that had made his reputation as a critic. The newspapers responded with enthusiasm, describing the lecture as "second to none" and praising Poe's "command of language and strength of voice." The evening brought Poe a payment of nearly one hundred dollars, and led to repeat performances in Wilmington and New York.

Poe used his new public forum to settle a grudge against Rufus Griswold, the man who had succeeded him as an editor at *Graham's*. The previous year, Griswold had compiled an anthology entitled *The Poets and Poetry of America* (which included Poe), in which he attempted to set forth a rigid critical ranking of the country's poets. Although Poe initially praised the work as "the best collection of the American Poets that has yet been made," his prospectus for *The Stylus* made it clear that he thought little of the work and intended to do a better job himself. In his lectures, Poe railed against Griswold's "miserable want of judgment" and accused him of devoting an "extravagant proportion of space" to his cronies while giving short shrift to poets of "superior merit." Although he did not say so, Poe undoubtedly resented that only three of his own poems had been included, as opposed to forty-five by the now-forgotten Charles Fenno Hoffman. George Graham would recall that Poe "gave Mr. Griswold some raps over the knuckles of force sufficient to be remembered." Griswold would prove to have a very long and unforgiving memory.

By the following year, the success of Poe's lectures and "The Gold-Bug" had faded. As the family fell back into a state of destitution, Poe decided that Philadelphia held no more promise for him.

In April of 1844, with barely five dollars to his name, Poe decided to return to New York—"where I intend living for the future"—to make a final stab at literary success.

The moment of his greatest fame was at hand, but first he would have to write the final chapter in the saga of the beautiful cigar girl.

PART FOUR

The Lady Sleeps

*". . . a corpse had just been towed ashore by some fishermen,
who had found it floating in the river."*
Illustration of "The Mystery of Marie Rogêt,"
from an 1852 edition of Poe's stories.

—⧃⧃⧃—

The lady sleeps: oh! may her sleep
As it is lasting so be deep—
No icy worms about her creep.
I pray to God that she may lie
Forever with as calm an eye,
That chamber chang'd for one more holy—
That bed for one more melancholy.
                    —Edgar Allan Poe, "Irene"

—⧃⧃⧃—

XIX

⚯⚯⚯

It May Not Be Improper to Record

·

ON APRIL 13, 1844, barely a week after Edgar Allan Poe's return to New York, a dramatic story broke in the pages of the New York *Sun.* "Astounding Intelligence By Private Express From Charleston Via Norfolk!" announced a special stop-press broadside. "Atlantic Ocean Crossed in Three Days!" The "gripping exclusive" went on to inform readers that a group of "valiant and greatly daring men of science" had contrived to cross from Dover, England, to Sullivan's Island, South Carolina, in a hot-air balloon. Given the fact that the previous distance record for a hot-air balloon was some twelve miles, the news of a transatlantic crossing, with its "breathless drama and constant peril above the icy waves," caused a major sensation. A large crowd gathered at the offices of the *Sun,* eager for further news. The newspaper promised that additional details would be available shortly.

It soon emerged that the story was an elaborate hoax orchestrated by Poe, in the tradition of Richard Adams Locke's "Great Moon Hoax," published in the *Sun* nine years earlier. Initially, Poe was gratified by the strong response to the story: "I never witnessed more intense excitement to get possession of a newspaper," he declared. "As soon as the first few copies made their way into the streets, they were bought up, at almost any price, from the news-boys, who made a profitable speculation beyond doubt. I saw a half-dollar given, in one instance, for a single paper, and a shilling was a frequent price. I tried in vain during the whole day to get possession of a copy."

After two days, when sales of the special edition had exceeded fifty thousand copies, the *Sun* felt obliged to print a retraction. The editors offered a winking declaration that they were "inclined to believe that the intelligence is erroneous," but added that they "by no means think such a project impossible." For Poe, the article proved to be a mistake. He had hoped that the success of the hoax would help him to find his footing in New York, but the episode ultimately had the opposite effect, reinforcing the notion among editors that he was not trustworthy.

In spite of this misstep, Poe was determined to put the best possible face on his return to New York. While Aunt Maria remained behind to wind up the family's affairs in Philadelphia, Poe and Virginia found comfortable rooms in a boardinghouse at 130 Greenwich Street. Poe sent an ecstatic letter to his mother-in-law, describing the bounty of its table: "Last night, for supper, we had the nicest tea you ever drank, strong & hot—wheat bread & rye bread—cheese—tea cakes (elegant) a great dish (2 dishes) of elegant ham, and 2 of cold veal, piled up like a mountain and large slices—3 dishes of the cakes, and everything in the greatest profusion." He added: "No fear of starving here."

Poe seemed equally effusive in presenting New York as a restorative for Virginia's health, as well as his own. "[W]e are both in excellent spirits," he wrote. "She has coughed hardly any and had no night sweat. She is now busy mending my pants which I tore against a nail. . . . I feel in excellent spirits & haven't drank a drop—so that I hope to get out of trouble."

For all of Poe's optimism, within weeks the familiar pattern of itinerant poverty resumed. As Mrs. Clemm joined them in New

York, the household progressed through a series of more humble lodgings, ranging from an isolated house at Eighty-fourth Street and Broadway—then at the center of two hundred acres of farmland—to a modest set of rooms near Washington Square. Although Poe continued his lectures with some success, he was frequently reduced to seeking loans from his shrinking circle of friends.

One month after his arrival in New York, Poe took a position at the New York *Evening Mirror* as an assistant editor and "mechanical paragraphist," or writer of anonymous filler material. The editor, Nathaniel Willis, would later describe his duties in fairly bleak terms: "It was his business to sit at a desk, in a corner of the editorial room, ready to be called upon for any of the miscellaneous work of the moment—announcing news, condensing statements, answering correspondents, noticing amusements—everything but the writing of a 'leader,' or constructing any article upon which his peculiar idiosyncrasy of mind could be impressed." This was quite a step down from Poe's work at *Graham's* and *Burton's*, and a far cry from his dream of editing his own journal. Even so, Poe felt grateful to Willis for his fifteen dollars a week. He would later praise the editor as someone who "has made a good deal of noise in the world—at least for an American."

As it happened, the offices of the *Mirror* stood at the corner of Nassau and Ann streets, a few steps from the site of the Rogers boardinghouse. By this time Phoebe Rogers had long since closed her doors, finding herself unable to run the boardinghouse without her daughter's help. She now lived with one of her sisters, and the house on Nassau Street had stood empty for several months. Many in the neighborhood believed it to be haunted, and tales were told of a dark-eyed apparition peering out from the upper windows.

As Poe settled into the routine of the neighborhood, the memory of Mary Rogers made itself felt in his work. In a series of letters published in a Pennsylvania newspaper called the *Columbia Spy*, he offered a despairing comment on the unsolved case. "It is difficult to conceive anything more preposterous than the whole conduct . . . of the Mary Rogers affair," he wrote. "The police seemed blown about, in all directions, by every varying puff of the most unconsidered newspaper opinion. The *truth*, as an end, appeared to be lost sight of altogether. The magistracy suffered the murderer to escape, while they amused themselves with playing court, and chopping the technicalities of jurisprudence." Although he avoided any mention of his own attempt to illuminate the mystery, Poe suggested a line of inquiry that clearly recalled "The Mystery of Marie Rogêt." "Not the least usual error, in such investigations, is the limiting of inquiry to the immediate, with total disregard of the collateral, or circumstantial events," he declared. "It is malpractice to confine evidence and discussion too vigorously within the limits of the seemingly relevant. Experience has shown, and Philosophy will always show, that a vast portion, perhaps the larger portion of truth, arises from the apparently irrelevant. It is through the spirit of this principle that modern science has resolved to *calculate upon the unforeseen.*"

Poe's interest in the case may have been rekindled by the success of a new potboiler novel entitled *The Beautiful Cigar Girl: or the Mysteries of Broadway*. The author, J. H. Ingraham, was a prolific writer whose work frequently appeared in Snowden's *Ladies' Companion*, where he may have seen and drawn inspiration from "The Mystery of Marie Rogêt." Ingraham's novel traced the misfortunes of a "modest, sensible and industrious" young woman named Mary Cecilia, who finds employment in a New York cigar store. "The reputation of her charms," Ingraham wrote, "of her modesty, and of her exceeding grace in conversation, for she was alike affable to all, spread throughout the city, and the Beautiful

Cigar-Girl became the theme of every young man's conversation in the city. Hundreds visited there only to see her, and those who never smoked cigars, now lounged in there to purchase them, that they might behold her, who had turned the heads of half the young men in town. Her beauty impressed not only the gentlemen; for the ladies as they passed *en promenade*, would linger to glance in at the beautiful Cigar-Girl."

As related by Ingraham, the young woman's life is nothing if not eventful; she endures not one but three kidnappings, culminating in headlines that report a "HORRIBLE SUSPICION OF MURDER!" In case any of his readers might have failed to recognize the inspiration of the tale, Ingraham paused to give a helpful reminder of the real-life drama and the "fruitless issue of the investigations that followed her disappearance, and the deep mystery which to this hour, envelopes, like the pall of the tomb, the whole of this painful and most extraordinary affair." Unlike Poe, Ingraham made no further effort to parallel the progress of the actual crime; instead, he offered a contrived if happy ending in which Mary Cecilia was found to be alive and well in England, having captured the heart of a British aristocrat.

Poe himself made a further reference to the saga in "The Purloined Letter," which appeared in December of that year. The story marked the third appearance of C. Auguste Dupin and his unnamed companion, who are found at the beginning of the narrative in yet another period of "profound silence," mulling over their past experiences: "I mean the affair of the Rue Morgue," says the narrator, "and the mystery attending the murder of Marie Rogêt." Soon enough their reverie is interrupted by the arrival of Monsieur G——, the prefect of the Paris police, who seeks Dupin's assistance in recovering a highly incriminating letter that has been stolen from the royal apartments. Dupin agrees, after negotiating a generous fee.

The problem of the missing letter proves highly unusual in that the identity of the villain is known at the outset. He is Minister D——, a man of extraordinary cunning, who plans to use the document to gain political advantage. Hoping to avoid a scandal, the author of the letter, "a personage of most exalted station," is relying on the ingenuity and discretion of the prefect. ("Than whom," Dupin comments archly, "no more sagacious agent could, I suppose, be desired, or even imagined.") As Dupin considers the dilemma, he notes that the prefect has erred in "the supposition that the Minister is a fool, because he has acquired renown as a poet. All fools are poets; this the Prefect *feels*; and he is merely guilty of a *non distributio medii* in thence inferring that all poets are fools." Dupin, himself a poet, makes no such mistake. He reexamines the problem from the minister's perspective, attempting to mimic his adversary's likely chain of thought, and concludes that the missing letter has been hidden in plain sight. By substituting a facsimile for the genuine article, Dupin is able to recover the letter and save the reputation of his exalted client.

"The Purloined Letter" demonstrates that Poe's enthusiasm for Dupin remained strong after the travails of "Marie Rogêt." For several years he had been attempting to persuade a publisher to issue a revised edition of his short stories. Now, in a letter to James Russell Lowell, he described "The Purloined Letter" as "perhaps the best of my tales of ratiocination." He had reason to hope the appearance of the story in *The Gift*, a popular Christmas annual, might bring about this new collection, featuring all three Dupin tales.

He would not have long to wait. In January of 1845, Poe happened to run across a friend, the poet William Ross Wallace, on the street. Poe had been in the habit of reading his "not yet published poetical work" to Wallace, and on that particular day he seemed more than usually eager to share his latest creation.

"Wallace," he said, "I have just written the greatest poem that ever was written."

"Have you?" said Wallace. "That is a fine achievement."

"Would you like to hear it?" asked Poe.

"Most certainly," Wallace answered.

Poe then read out the verses in "an impressive and captivating way," and when he finished, he turned to hear Wallace's opinion. "Poe," said his friend, "they are fine; uncommonly fine."

"Fine?" snapped Poe. "Is that all you can say for this poem? I tell you it's the greatest poem that was ever written."

Wallace's response is not recorded, but other critics of the new poem, "The Raven," would respond in terms that were nearly as rhapsodic as Poe's. The poem appeared on January 29, 1845, in the *Evening Mirror*, where Poe was doing his humble service as a mechanical paragraphist. An instant sensation, "The Raven" soon became the most popular American poem yet published. It went through dozens of reprints over the course of the year, culminating in *The Raven and Other Poems*, a collection of Poe's verse published in November of 1845 by Wiley & Putnam. In his essay "The Philosophy of Composition," Poe gave a deceptively simple outline of the action of the poem:

A raven, having learned by rote the single word, "Nevermore," and having escaped from the custody of its owner, is driven, at midnight, through the violence of a storm, to seek admission at a window from which a light still gleams—the chamber-window of a student, occupied half in poring over a volume, half in dreaming of a beloved mistress deceased. The casement being thrown open at the fluttering of the bird's wings, the bird itself perches on the most convenient seat out of the immediate reach of the student, who, amused by the incident and the oddity of the visiter's demeanor, demands of it, in jest and without looking for a reply, its name. The raven addressed, answers with its customary word, "Nevermore"—a word which finds immediate echo in the melancholy heart of the student.

Poe went on to offer an illuminating account of how he found his inspiration for the poem. Having decided to offer a meditation on the subject of beauty, he recalled, "my next question referred to the *tone* of its highest manifestation—and all experience has shown that this tone is one of *sadness*. Beauty of whatever kind, in its supreme development, invariably excites the sensitive soul to tears. Melancholy is thus the most legitimate of all the poetical tones." Having reached this conclusion, Poe had laid the groundwork for one of his most famous dictums. "I asked myself—'Of all melancholy topics, what, according to the *universal* understanding of mankind, is the *most* melancholy?' Death—was the obvious reply. 'And when,' I said, 'is this most melancholy of topics most poetical?' From what I have already explained at some length, the answer, here also, is obvious—'When it most closely allies itself to *Beauty*: the death, then, of a beautiful woman is, unquestionably, the most poetical topic in the world—and equally is it beyond doubt that the lips best suited for such topic are those of a bereaved lover.' "

This elegant formulation played well on the lecture circuit, but privately Poe would admit that he composed the poem with his eye on commercial success. " 'The Raven' has had a great 'run,' " he told his friend Frederick Thomas, "but I wrote it for the express purpose of running—just as I did the 'Gold-Bug,' you know. The bird beat the bug, though, all hollow."

For all the bluster, Poe's success had yet to earn him any real money. Despite the endless reprintings of "The Raven," the poem earned him only nine dollars, while "The Gold-Bug," which sold well over a quarter of a million copies, brought him only one hundred dollars. Still, Poe believed that fortune would come. Only a month previously he had been a literary pariah, grateful for the journalistic hackwork offered by Nathaniel Willis. Now, with the success of "The Raven," he became a sought-after figure in New York's literary salons, where his verses were received with worshipful respect. The talents he had developed on the lecture platform now came into full flower. To heighten the effect of his readings, he would "turn down the lamps till the room was almost dark," one listener reported, "then standing in the center of the apartment he would recite those wonderful lines in the most melodious of voices . . . So marvelous was his power as a reader that the auditors would be afraid to draw breath lest the enchanted spell be broken."

With his black suit and haunted air, Poe appears to have cut a romantic figure. "His remarkable personal beauty," an acquaintance would write, "the fascination of his manners and conversation, and his chivalrous deference and devotion to women, gave him a dangerous power over the sex." Poe began to form a series of intense, if platonic, attachments with the women of his new literary circle, echoing the passion of his youth in Richmond for the unattainable Jane Stanard (who had died in 1824). In March of 1845 Poe became enamored of a Massachusetts poet named Frances Sargent Osgood, known to her friends as "Fanny." Like Mrs. Stanard, Fanny Osgood was a beautiful woman in fragile health, a combination that conformed to Poe's poetical ideal. Separated from her husband, she was free to respond to Poe's attentions, and he came to think of her as the only friend who truly understood him. She offered him numerous poetic tributes—"And all should cry, Beware! Beware! / His flashing eyes, his floating hair!"—and he returned the favor with "A Valentine," a puzzle poem in which her name was encoded in the first letter of the first line, the second letter of the second line, and so on. Virginia Poe was not only aware of the friendship but actually condoned it. Mrs. Osgood would later claim that Virginia "imagined that my influence over him had a restraining and beneficial effect." As fate would have it, Mrs. Osgood later drew the attentions of Rufus Griswold, the man Poe had roundly criticized in his public lectures, adding a new and deeply personal shading to the rivalry between the two men.

As Poe's renown spread, a new forum became available to him. In January of 1845, just as "The Raven" was being readied for publication, Poe accepted a position as assistant editor of a new magazine called the *Broadway Journal*. The following month he received a promotion to coeditor, with the additional responsibility of contributing a full page of original material to each issue. In return, Poe was to receive one-third of the magazine's revenues. After his experiences at the *Southern Literary Messenger*, *Burton's*, and *Graham's*, Poe was gratified to have a chance to share in the profits of his labors. Not surprisingly, however, his tenure at the *Broadway Journal* was marked by controversy. In March of 1845 he accused Henry Wadsworth Longfellow, who was fast becoming the most distinguished poet in the country, of gross plagiarism, launching a protracted episode that came to be known as the "Longfellow War." Although Poe had cultivated a friendly correspondence with Longfellow over the years, and praised him in print as "unquestionably the best poet in America," he now felt moved to charge Longfellow with the theft—"too palpable to be mistaken"—of a poem by Tennyson. The dispute brought no esteem upon Poe, who was in turn roundly attacked by Longfellow's many advocates.

Longfellow himself would not be drawn into the fray. Unlike other writers with whom Poe quarreled, Longfellow would later offer a magnanimous reflection: "The harshness of his criticisms I have never attributed to anything but the irritation of a sensitive nature, chafed by some indefinite sense of wrong."

In June of 1845, seeking to capitalize on the success of "The Raven," Wiley & Putnam published a collection of twelve of Poe's short stories under the title of *Tales*. The stories were selected by Poe's editor, Evert Duyckinck, a man Poe described as having an "almost Quixotic fidelity to his friends." Duyckinck's story selection was also quixotic. Of the more than seventy stories Poe had published at that stage, Duyckinck omitted several of his best— including "The Tell-Tale Heart" and "The Masque of the Red Death"—in favor of some notably inferior efforts such as "Lionizing," a rather pallid literary satire. Poe appears to have had no influence on the choices.

Significantly, Duyckinck saw fit to include "The Mystery of Marie Rogêt." The decision is not difficult to understand; the editor had also selected "The Murders in the Rue Morgue" and "The Purloined Letter," two stories of undisputed merit that had enjoyed previous success. Together with "Marie Rogêt" they formed a natural grouping of all three of the Dupin tales. "Marie Rogêt" would also have retained some of its topical appeal, bolstered by the success of J. H. Ingraham's novel the previous year.

Only five months elapsed between the appearance of "The Raven" and the publication of *Tales*, suggesting that Poe had to work quickly to prepare his stories for publication. He was in the habit of revising and improving his work over the course of his career, and had already made alterations to some of the stories in hopes of publication elsewhere. With "Marie Rogêt," however, he faced a unique challenge. His initial revision of the story for the

Ladies' Companion had been carried out with untoward haste, and Poe had been severely limited by the fact that the first two sections of the story had already passed out of his hands. For the new revision, he would be able to make changes to the entire manuscript. By the same token, in his earlier effort he had been content simply to soften some of his earlier conclusions about the case, such as his insistence that the murder thicket had not been the scene of the crime. Although there had been no subsequent revelations to confirm or contradict the suspicions surrounding Mrs. Loss and the goings-on in her tavern, the general public had now come to believe that Mary Rogers had died during a bungled abortion. In revising his story for the second time, Poe faced the challenge of further refining his earlier efforts, so as to reflect what had now become the prevailing view of the case.

In order to mold the story into a true depiction of the Mary Rogers saga, however, Poe would have been obliged to rewrite a major portion of his text. Given the time constraints of readying his stories for the *Tales* collection, he could not undertake a wholesale revision. Poe may also have feared that making changes on a large scale would be taken as an admission that his initial theory had been wrong. In order to preserve the impression that his story had anticipated and even influenced the New York investigation, Poe's changes would have to be almost invisible.

Seen in that light, Poe's second revision of "Marie Rogêt" proved to be an audacious piece of editorial manipulation. By means of a series of small but cunning alterations to the manuscript, Poe managed to scale back his earlier emphasis on the swarthy naval officer while allowing for the possibility of Marie's death at the hands of an abortionist. Unfortunately, as with his first set of revisions, many of these changes only served to add a layer of confusion. Poe's discussion of whether or not the "murder thicket" had been the actual scene of the crime, for example, was now all but submerged in a tide of qualifiers and evasions. At almost every mention of the thicket he added an extra line—such as "if the thicket it was," or "whether from the thicket or elsewhere"—designed to back away from committing himself one way or the other. This wavering reached its height when a definitive statement—"That it was the scene, I believe . . ."—was changed to its opposite: "That it was the scene, I may or I may not believe . . ." At the same time, Dupin's earlier declaration that "I admit the thicket as the scene of the outrage" was omitted altogether.

Poe also worked his editorial wiles on his portrait of Mme. Deluc, the stand-in for Mrs. Loss, who was no longer presented as the "honest and scrupulous old lady" she had been in the previous version. Her testimony to the police, which had previously been described only as "somewhat tardy," was now found to be "somewhat tardy and very suspicious." Readers were also told that there "might have been . . . an accident at Madame Deluc's." Although he could not make a more definitive accusation without unsettling the other elements of the theory, Dupin's summing up the "meager yet certain fruits" of his analysis was modified to include the notion of "a fatal accident under the roof of Madame Deluc."

Even Marie's private thoughts, as imagined by Dupin, were tailored accordingly. Previously, Dupin had said, "We may imagine her thinking thus—'I am to meet a certain person for the purpose of elopement.'" Now, an alternative was appended: "or for certain other purposes known only to myself." Similarly, where Dupin declared that Marie had left the boardinghouse "never to return," he now added a counterbalance: "—or not for some weeks—or not until certain concealments are effected—"

Perhaps the most blatant manipulation surrounded Dupin's earlier insistence that only one villain, the swarthy naval officer, had been responsible for the crime. Previously, Dupin had reached a dramatic crescendo with these words: "The horrors of this dark deed are known only to *one* living human being, and to God." With a stroke of Poe's pen, these horrors became "known only to *one*, or two, living human beings, and to God." Poe's modifications even extended to the clumsy editorial passage originally attributed to the editor of the *Ladies' Companion*. There, Poe had written "that an individual assassin was convicted, upon his own confession, of the murder of Marie Rogêt." For the republication in *Tales*, this line was struck out.

Even more audaciously, Poe added a scattering of footnotes in which he stepped out from behind the mask of Dupin and commented directly on the actual investigation in New York, using the names of the people and places associated with the case. As with "The Great Balloon Hoax" and *The Narrative of Arthur Gordon Pym*, the inclusion of concrete and recognizable details appeared to bolster the credibility of the enterprise, and allowed Poe to maintain the illusion that his deductions had been correct from the beginning.

In the first of Poe's footnotes, he offered a calculated summary of the story's inspiration, aimed at convincing his readers of the truth of what followed:

> Upon the original publication of "Marie Rogêt," the foot-notes now appended were considered unnecessary; but the lapse of several years since the tragedy upon which the tale is based, renders it expedient to give them, and also to say a few words in explanation of the general design. A young girl, *Mary Cecilia Rogers*, was murdered in the vicinity of New York; and although her

death occasioned an intense and long-enduring excitement, the mystery attending it had remained unsolved at
the period when the present paper was written and
published (November, 1842). Herein, under pretence of
relating the fate of a Parisian *grisette*, the author has
followed, in minute detail, the essential, while merely
paralleling the inessential, facts of the real murder of
Mary Rogers. Thus all argument founded upon the
fiction is applicable to the truth: and the investigation of
the truth was the object.

This was an astonishing display of bravado. Poe's unequivocal
claim that "all argument founded upon the fiction is applicable to
the truth" clearly invites the reader to believe that every word of
the story is drawn from fact. This marks a strange contrast to his
equally forceful statement in the concluding passages of the story
that "I speak of coincidence *and no more* . . . let it not for a moment be supposed that . . . it is my covert design to hint at an extension of the parallel, or even to suggest that the measures
adopted in Paris . . . or measures founded in any similar ratiocination, would produce any similar result."

But Poe wasn't finished. His introductory footnote continued:

The "Mystery of Marie Rogêt" was composed at a distance from the scene of the atrocity, and with no other
means of investigation than the newspapers afforded.
Thus much escaped the writer of which he could have
availed himself had he been upon the spot and visited
the localities. It may not be improper to record, nevertheless, that the confessions of *two* persons (one of them

the Madame Deluc of the narrative), made, at different periods, long subsequent to the publication, confirmed, in full, not only the general conclusion, but absolutely *all* the chief hypothetical details by which that conclusion was attained.

This, to most readers, would have been a bombshell. Although his tone appeared self-effacing, he now stated unambiguously that he had been right all along, and had a pair of confessions to back up his theory.

Poe was bluffing with a very weak hand. In making specific reference to the confession of "Madame Deluc in the narrative," Poe would have stirred the memories of his contemporary readers with regard to the rumored confession of Mrs. Loss—a widely circulated story that was never officially confirmed. The reference to Mrs. Loss would have lent some measure of credence to his assertion that there had been a second, corroborating confession. If there was a second confession, however, it has been lost to posterity. But Poe presents both confessions as a *fait accompli*, creating the impression that the facts of the New York investigation eventually caught up with and confirmed the innovative theory advanced by Dupin. Poe's concluding statement that "*all* the chief hypothetical details" were confirmed is calculated to hammer the point home, leaving no doubt in the reader's mind.

Yet it is clear that not all of Dupin's speculations could have been verified, since not all of them were based on actual fact. In the later stages of the story, Dupin spent much of his time contemplating the problem of the barge found drifting in the Seine—as described in the sixth of his crucial newspaper extracts—and had confidently asserted that the "boat shall guide us, with a rapidity which will surprise even ourselves, to him who employed it in the midnight of the fatal Sabbath." Since this detail had been fabricated for the occasion of the story, it is unlikely that this "chief hypothetical detail" could have found confirmation in New York.

As a noted Poe scholar would later remark, the extraordinary latticework of revisions and shortcuts through which he achieved his effect "deserves some measure of admiration—even if grudgingly given—for its nonchalant audacity." For the moment, Poe's bold assertions about the case would pass unchallenged, and the *Tales* collection sold well on publication in the summer of 1845. Poe would claim that sales climbed to some 1,500 copies, at fifty cents apiece, bringing him a royalty of about $120. The reviews were generally kind. Even Rufus Griswold, who had been the target of Poe's criticism from the lecture platform, gave it a glowing notice, ranking Poe among "the first class of tale writers who have appeared since the marvel-loving Arabian first attempted fabulous history." Many of the critics made special mention of "Marie Rogêt," with the London *Spectator* praising Poe's "great analytical skill in seizing upon the points of circumstantial evidence and connecting them together."

Poe must have felt considerable satisfaction. He had managed to stave off a disaster, absorbing the late-breaking news and theories about the Mary Rogers case into his own fictional design, and transforming the potentially ruinous Weehawken findings into an artistic success. At the same time, the ambiguities and outright deceptions of "Marie Rogêt" illustrated the degree to which Poe felt free to indulge himself, unapologetically, in poetic exaggeration. It is perhaps significant that in the interval between the two revisions of "Marie Rogêt," Poe published a mock scientific treatise entitled "Diddling Considered as One of the Exact Sciences." "A crow thieves; a fox cheats; a weasel outwits; a man diddles," Poe observed. "To diddle is his destiny . . . Diddling, rightly considered, is a compound, of which the ingredients are minuteness, interest, perseverance, ingenu-ity, audacity, nonchalance, originality, impertinence, and grin."

Others, like the poet James Russell Lowell, had a different word for it. After a falling-out with Poe, Lowell offered a cutting portrait in "A Fable for Critics," a poem that lampooned many of the writers of the day:

> *There comes Poe, with his raven, like Barnaby Rudge;*
> *Three-fifths of him genius and two-fifths sheer fudge.*

XX

The Imp of the Perverse

BY THE CLOSE OF 1845, Poe's moment in the sun was fading. With the peculiar instinct for self-destruction that had continually stunted his career, Poe now sabotaged the opportunities presented by the success of "The Raven."

In a story published that year titled "The Imp of the Perverse," Poe commented at length on this seemingly preordained impulse toward self-immolation. "With certain minds, under certain conditions, it becomes absolutely irresistible," he wrote. "I am not more certain that I breathe, than that the assurance of the wrong or error of any action is often the one unconquerable force which impels us, and alone impels us to its prosecution. Nor will this overwhelming tendency to do wrong for the wrong's sake, admit of analysis, or resolution into ulterior elements. It is a radical, a primitive impulse—elementary."

Perched behind his desk at the *Broadway Journal*, Poe once again descended into the cycle of alcohol and argumentation that had soured his chances of success at the *Southern Literary Messenger, Burton's,* and *Graham's*. Soon his health began to suffer, and his work habits became erratic. He grew fixated on the subject of plagiarism and hurled accusations at writers and critics who might otherwise have become his allies. "It is too absurd for belief," wrote Charles

Briggs, his coeditor, "but he really thinks that Longfellow owes his fame mainly to ideas which he borrowed from Poe's writings in the *Southern Literary Messenger*." Later, Briggs would add a perceptive assessment of his colleague's temperament: "One of the strange parts of his strange nature was to entertain a spirit of revenge towards all who did him service."

By June of 1845, only six months after signing on with the *Broadway Journal*, Poe had reached a crisis. Briggs wrote to James Russell Lowell that Poe "has latterly got into his old habits and I fear he will injure himself irretrievably." Aware that he was about to be fired, Poe sought help from Evert Duyckinck, his editor at Wiley & Putnam. Pleading ill health, Poe asked Duyckinck to buy out his share of the magazine. "I am still dreadfully unwell and fear that I shall be very seriously ill," he wrote. "I have resolved to give up the *B. Journal* and retire to the country for six months, or perhaps a year, as the sole means of recruiting my health and spirits."

Matters took an unexpected turn when Briggs attempted to force Poe out by buying up control of the magazine. Finding the price too high, Briggs was forced to withdraw at the last minute. By this time the magazine was barely solvent, and publication temporarily ceased. Unwilling to risk further losses, the publisher, John Bisco, decided to sell the journal outright to Poe for the sum of fifty dollars. This was a bargain price and an extraordinary opportunity, but Poe had trouble raising the money. Desperate, he even sought a loan from Rufus Griswold, whom he had regularly mocked in print and from the lecture platform. "Lend me $50 and you shall never have cause to regret it," Poe wrote, adding that the magazine "will be a fortune to me if I can hold it—which I can easily do with a very trifling aid from my friends. May I count you as one?" Griswold, along with numerous others, felt unable to comply. Finally Poe secured the funds through a note endorsed by Horace Greeley. At the end of October, Poe found that he had suddenly and unexpectedly achieved his lifelong ambition of owning a magazine. He was determined to make a success of it, but soon found that he needed additional money to fund the operation. He resumed his pleadings to his friends, claiming that his very existence was bound up in the fate of the journal. "I will make a fortune of it yet," he wrote. "If I live until next month I shall be beyond the need of aid."

Amid these struggles, Poe received an invitation to travel to Boston to read an original poem at the celebrated Lyceum. It was understood that a great honor had been bestowed on him, signaling Poe's acceptance among the Boston literary elite. Once again, however, Poe's contrary nature got the better of his self-interest. Instead of reading a new poem, Poe dusted off a copy of "Al Aaraaf," a lengthy and singularly off-putting early effort, in what seems to have been a deliberate attempt to provoke his audience and alienate his hosts. Poe had barely hit his stride when the bulk of the audience, already wearied by a local politician's two-hour speech, rose and began filing out of the hall. When the ordeal finally ended, Poe compounded the insult by taunting his hosts over dinner, claiming to have deliberately fobbed off on them a poem written when he was ten years old. "There lives no man who at some period has not been tormented, for example, by an earnest desire to tantalize a listener by circumlocution," he wrote in "The Imp of the Perverse," published three months earlier. "The speaker is aware that he displeases; he has every intention to please, he is usually curt, precise, and clear, the most laconic and luminous language is struggling for utterance upon his tongue, it is only with difficulty that he restrains himself from giving it flow; he dreads and deprecates the anger of him whom he addresses; yet, the thought strikes him, that by certain involutions and parentheses this anger may be engendered. That single thought is enough."

Back in New York, Poe promptly ran the *Broadway Journal* into the ground, writing increasingly desperate letters to friends for the money needed to keep it afloat. The strain began to tell, inspiring further drinking binges that left him unable to perform his editorial duties. When the money he needed could not be found, Poe detected the hands of his enemies trying to thwart him. "On the part of one or two persons who are much imbittered against me," he told the poet Fitz-Greene Halleck, "there is a deliberate attempt now being made to involve me in ruin, by destroying *The Broadway Journal.*"

"I really believe that I have been mad," Poe told Duyckinck in yet another plea for a loan, "but indeed I have had abundant reason to be so." At least one of these abundant reasons had to do with the strain of his concern over Virginia's health. In December of 1845 he published a story called "The Facts in the Case of M. Valdemar," in which his fears for his wife, now four years into her illness, can be plainly read. The story concerns a man dying of "confirmed phthisis," a term used to describe the wasting effects associated with tuberculosis and other diseases. Poe is unsparing in his details of the manner in which the unfortunate patient literally putrefies before his eyes, employing language that suggests a morbid study of medical texts: "The left lung had been for eighteen months in a semi-osseous or cartilaginous state, and was, of course, entirely useless for all purposes of vitality. The right, in its upper portion, was also partially, if not thoroughly, ossified, while the lower region was merely a mass of purulent tubercles, running one into another. Several extensive perforations existed; and, at one point, permanent adhesion to the ribs had taken place." Where he departs from the clinical texts, Poe's imaginative powers produce an even more chilling effect. He describes the patient's voice as striking the ear much as "gelatinous or glutinous matters impress the sense of touch," and captures the final agonies in horrifying detail: "[H]is whole frame at once—within the space of a single minute, or even less, shrunk—crumbled—absolutely rotted away beneath my hands. Upon the bed, before that whole company, there lay a nearly liquid mass of loathsome—of detestable putridity."

By the end of December of 1845, the *Broadway Journal* had lost both its readership and its financial backing. The magazine had been all but bankrupt when he took the helm, and no amount of borrowing from friends could save it. At length, Poe resigned himself to the fact that nothing more could be done. In a note published in the final issue, he tried to strike a conciliatory tone: "Unexpected engagements demanding my whole attention, and the objects being fulfilled, so far as regards myself personally, for which the *Broadway Journal* was established, I now, as its Editor, bid farewell—as cordially to foes as to friends."

It was the last editorial position he would ever hold. Cut loose from the moorings of steady employment, Poe sank deeper into his destructive habits. His drinking bouts became more pronounced, and his quarrels with former friends began to have more serious consequences. Rumors circulated that he had gone insane and been confined to an asylum. At one stage he came to blows with his former friend Thomas Dunn English. "Poe was drunk and getting the worst of it," wrote a witness, "and was finally forced partly under the sofa, only his face being out. English was punching Poe's face, and at every blow a seal ring on his finger cut Poe." Even now, Poe managed to put up a brave front. When friends moved forward to intervene, he shouted: "Leave him alone, I've got him just where I want him!"

English's antipathy would spill over into the pages of a satirical novel in which he portrayed Poe as a singularly unpleasant character named Marmaduke Hammerhead: "The bloated face—blood-shotten eyes—trembling figure and attenuated frame, showed how rapidly he was sinking into a drunkard's grave; and the driveling smile, and meaningless nonsense he constantly uttered, showed the approaching wreck of his fine abilities."

In May of 1846 Poe removed his household to the quiet village of Fordham, fourteen miles north, in what is now the Bronx, New York City. Poe hoped that the more sedate setting might have a beneficial effect on his health, but he lost none of his combativeness. In a series of essays called "The Literati of New York City," published in *Godey's Lady's Book*, Poe took shots at many of his former friends and colleagues. Foremost of these was Thomas Dunn English, with whom Poe continued to trade insults in the press, culminating in a libel suit filed by Poe. English fled the city rather than defend himself in court, with the result that Poe was awarded some $325 in damages and costs. Poe celebrated the victory with the purchase of a new black suit.

The triumphant mood was short-lived. By the end of the year, Poe's circumstances had reached a desperate state, and grave concerns were expressed about his health. In November, a group of well-meaning friends drew attention to his plight with a notice in the *Morning Express*:

ILLNESS OF EDGAR A. POE — We regret to learn that this gentleman and his wife are both dangerously ill with the consumption, and that the hand of misfortune lies heavily upon their temporal affairs. We are sorry to mention the fact that they are so far reduced as to be barely able to obtain the necessaries of life. That is, indeed, a hard lot, and we do hope that the friends and admirers of Mr. Poe will come promptly to his assistance in his bitterest hour of need.

A second notice, in the pages of the *Saturday Evening Post*, was even more pitiable: "It is said that Edgar A. Poe is lying dangerously ill with brain fever, and that his wife is in the last stages of consumption—they are without money and without friends."

Poe appreciated the concern that had motivated these actions, and felt gratitude for the donations they brought, but it wounded his pride to be presented to the public as a charity case. The following month, he sent a letter to his friend Nathaniel Willis of the *Mirror*, putting a brave face on his distress. "That, as the inevitable consequence of so long an illness, I have been in want of money, it would be folly in me to deny," he said. Nevertheless, he insisted, the notion that "I am 'without friends' is a gross calumny . . . which a thousand noble-hearted men would have good right never to forgive me for permitting to pass unnoticed and undenied." As to his declining health, he offered a brave assessment: "The truth is, I have a great deal to do; and I have made up my mind not to die till it is done."

Unfortunately, the same could not be said of Virginia. Her health had been in a steady decline through the winter months, and in the absence of warm blankets, she lay shivering in the thick overcoat Poe had worn in the army. In her final hours, she pleaded with her mother to take care of Poe when she was gone. She died—"suffering much pain"—on January 30, 1847, at the age of twenty-four.

For Poe, the loss was incalculable. In June of 1846, still smarting from the loss of the *Broadway Journal*, Poe had sent a heartfelt letter to his wife. "Keep up your heart in all hopefulness, and trust yet a little longer," he wrote. "In my last great disappointment, I should have lost my courage *but for you*—my little darling wife you are my *greatest and only* stimulus now to battle with this uncongenial, unsatisfactory and ungrateful life."

It now became clear that Virginia's long illness had taken its toll. A year later, Poe described his torment during her long decline. "I became insane," he wrote. "I drank—God only knows how often or how much. As a matter of course, my enemies referred the insanity to the drink, rather than the drink to the insanity. I had, indeed, nearly abandoned all hope of a permanent cure, when I found one in the *death* of my wife. This I can and do endure as becomes a man. It was the horrible, never-ending oscillation between hope and despair which I could *not* longer have endured, without total loss of reason. In the death of what was my life, then, I received a new but—Oh God!—how melancholy existence."

This new existence offered few advances over the old one. Poe's habits remained dissolute, and his fortunes gave no sign of improvement. He threw himself into work on a book called *Eureka: An Essay on the Material and Spiritual Universe*, a work of metaphysical abstraction that he judged to be of earthshaking significance. The publisher George Putnam would recall a meeting in which Poe literally shook with excitement as he described the "profound importance" of the work. Putnam recalled Poe as saying that "No other scientific event in the history of the world approached in importance the original developments of this book." When it finally appeared in March of 1848, the book and the lectures Poe gave to support it were dismissed as "hyperbolic nonsense." Even the usually supportive Evert Duyckinck described the enterprise as a "mountainous piece of absurdity."

Poe's relationship with the poet Fanny Osgood had come to an end by the time of Virginia's death, but in his loneliness he sought renewed companionship through a series of earnest, even frantic courtships. Many of the women he pursued were married or otherwise unattainable, which had the effect of increasing Poe's ardor. At times his romantic overtures were thrown out in several directions at once, with predictably unhappy results. Some of the women to whom he turned were uncomplicated and good-hearted in the mold of Virginia and even Mrs. Clemm (with whom he still lived), offering domestic stability if not intellectual companionship. Marie Shew, a family friend who had nursed Virginia in her final days, became the first of his new obsessions, followed soon afterward by Annie Richmond, whom he described in a story as "the perfection of natural, in contradistinction from artificial grace." By contrast, Sarah Helen Whitman, an ethereal young widow, was an aspiring poet who engaged Poe's creative instincts and flattered his intellect. The urgent and scattershot nature of Poe's many courtships suggests that his motives were complicated and perhaps contradictory. In time his love life grew so chaotic that upon the publication of "Annabel Lee," one of his greatest poems, no fewer than four of the women in his life believed themselves to be its inspiration.

Poe's health remained fragile after Virginia's death. Marie Shew, a doctor's daughter, noted that Poe had an irregular heartbeat and arrived at a dramatic diagnosis: "I decided that in his best health he had lesion of one side of the brain, and as he could not bear stimulants or tonics, without producing insanity, I did not feel much hope that he could be raised up from brain fever brought on by extreme suffering of mind and body." Brain lesion or no, his behavior made an erratic downward spiral. In November of 1848, distraught over the rebuff of his attentions to Sarah Helen Whitman, he took an extreme measure. In a scene that recalled Daniel Payne's final hours, Poe wrote to remind Annie Richmond of a "holy promise" to attend him on his deathbed and then swallowed an ounce of laudanum. It is difficult to say whether Poe actually intended to kill himself or merely hoped that the dramatic gesture would inspire sympathy and compassion from Helen. He reported to Annie Richmond that "the laudanum was rejected from the stomach," but Poe nevertheless suffered a lengthy period of "awful horrors." A daguerreotype made four days later shows the ravages of the episode in his deeply lined face, drooping eyelids, and haunted expression.

No sooner had he recovered than he threw himself into another round of drinking. In June of 1849, on his way to lecture in Richmond, Poe stopped in Philadelphia to fortify himself. Arrested for public drunkenness, he was thrown into the Moyamensing prison, where he suffered a terrifying bout of delirium tremens. In his distress he suffered hallucinations that would not have been out of place in "The Pit and the Pendulum." In one horrifying vision he imagined Maria Clemm, the person dearest to him in all the world, being made to suffer unspeakable agonies: "As a means to torture me and wring my heart," Poe recalled, unseen tormentors brought his helpless aunt forward and sought to "blast my sight by seeing them first saw off her feet at the ankles, then her legs to the knees, her thighs at the hips, and so on."

Not surprisingly, Poe appeared careworn and bedraggled by the time he finally reached Richmond in July of 1849. To his delight, he was greeted warmly as a returning native son and his lecture drew a rapturous crowd. "I *never* was received with so much enthusiasm," he told his aunt. "The papers have done nothing but praise me before the lecture & since." Many of the friends of his youth turned out to see him, and it pleased him to be reminded of happier times. Soon enough, Poe renewed his acquaintance with Elmira Royster, now Mrs. Alexander Shelton, to whom he had been secretly engaged when he left Richmond for the University of Virginia. Now a wealthy widow with two children, Mrs. Shelton had never entirely forgotten the romance of her youth, and had followed Poe's career with fond longing. In his marriageable frame of mind, Poe's youthful passion was soon rekindled. Within days he proposed that they renew their decades-old engagement. Mrs. Shelton hesitated, knowing something of Poe's history and his weakness for drink. Her uncertainty had the usual effect of increasing Poe's ardor; he promised to reform, and even joined the Richmond chapter of the Sons of Temperance. Apparently Mrs. Shelton gave Poe reason to hope that she would soon consent. In September, he made plans to return to New York and settle his affairs, so as to return to Richmond permanently—with his Aunt Maria in tow. "I hope," he wrote to Mrs. Clemm on the eve of his departure, "that our troubles are nearly over."

Stopping in Baltimore on September 27 on his way back to New York, Poe ran into some old friends who suggested that they celebrate their reunion with a glass of whiskey. Poe, who had been sober for three months, seems to have offered no resistance. What followed has long been a blank page in Poe's time line, though it has invited a great deal of speculation. Poe's cousin Neilson, who was living in Baltimore at the time, would later say that "where he spent the time he was here, or under what circumstances, I have been unable to ascertain."

Six days later, on Wednesday, October 3, Poe was found collapsed in a gutter outside an Irish tavern. A local election was under way, and the tavern was serving as a polling place, leading to speculation that Poe had been encouraged to cast a ballot in exchange for a drink. The fact that he was wearing clothes that were evidently not his own suggests that he may have done it more than once, having changed his appearance to avoid recognition at the polls.

A short time later, Joseph Evans Snodgrass, Poe's old Baltimore friend, who was a doctor as well as an editor, received an urgent note. Snodgrass, the man to whom Poe had originally offered "Marie Rogêt" seven years earlier, learned that Poe was "rather worse for wear" and "in need of immediate assistance." Hurrying to the tavern, Snodgrass found Poe in a ragged and desperate state, muttering incoherently. Snodgrass called for a carriage to take him to a hospital. When the carriage arrived, Snodgrass recalled, "we tried to get the object of our care upon his feet, so that he might the more easily be taken to it. But he was past locomotion. We therefore carried him to the coach as if he were a corpse, and lifted him into it in the same manner. While we were doing this, what was left of one of the most remarkable embodiments of genius the world has produced in all the centuries of its history—the author of a single poem, which alone has been adjudged by more than one critic as entitling its producer to a lasting and enviable fame—was so utterly voiceless as to be capable of only muttering some scarcely intelligible oaths, and other forms of imprecation, upon those who were trying to rescue him from destitution and disgrace."

At the nearby Washington College Hospital, resident physician John Moran locked Poe up in the drunk ward. For several hours Poe appeared to be unaware of his condition or his surroundings. Soon he lapsed into a hallucinatory state. Moran recorded that Poe began a "vacant converse with spectral and imaginary objects on the walls. His face was pale and his whole person was drenched in perspiration."

After two days the hallucinations dissipated, but Poe remained confused and agitated. When Moran tried to calm him, Poe insisted that the best thing to do "would be to blow out his brains with a pistol." By the end of the day, Moran noted, Poe had entered "a violent delirium, resisting the efforts of two nurses to keep him in bed."

In the early hours of the following morning, Moran reported, "a very decided change began to affect him. Having become enfeebled from exertion, he became quiet and seemed to rest for a short time, then gently moving his head he said, '*Lord help my poor Soul,*' and expired." The doctor recorded the time as five A.M. on Sunday, October 7, 1849. Poe was forty years old.

POE'S FUNERAL, held the following day at the cemetery of the Westminster Presbyterian Church in Baltimore, was austere even by a pauper's standards. Virginia Poe's cousin, Reverend William Clemm, presided over a ceremony that lasted all of three minutes, and Poe was laid to rest in a shoddy coffin that lacked handles, a nameplate, or even a pillow for his head. "A grave had been dug among the crumbling mementos of mortality," recorded Joseph Snodgrass. "Into this the plainly-coffined body was speedily lowered, and then the earth was shoveled directly upon the coffin-lid. This was so unusual even in the burials of the poor, that I could not help noticing the absence of not only the customary box, as an inclosure for the coffin itself, but of even the commonest boards to prevent the direct contact of the decomposing wet earth with it. I shall never forget the emotion of disappointment, mingled with disgust and something akin to resentment, that thrilled through my whole being as I heard the clods and stones resound from the coffin-lid."

Within hours, Poe's enemies were lining up to heap further indignities on the corpse. On the day after the funeral, an obituary appeared in Horace Greeley's *Tribune*. "Edgar Allan Poe is dead," the article began. "He died in Baltimore on the day before yesterday. This announcement will startle many, but few will be grieved by it. The poet was known, personally or by reputation, in all this country; had readers in England and in several of the states of Continental Europe, but he had few or no friends; and the regrets for his death will be suggested principally by the consideration that in him literary art has lost one of its most brilliant but erratic stars." The obituary went on to describe Poe variously as a lunatic with a diseased imagination and a crass beggar prone to "vulgar fancies" and "ignoble passions." The notice concluded with a passage lifted from a novel by Edward Bulwer-Lytton: "He had, to a morbid excess, that desire to rise which is vulgarly called ambition, but no wish for the esteem or the love of his species; only the hard wish to succeed—not shine, not serve—succeed, that he might have the right to despise a world which galled his self-conceit."

Signed by the name of "Ludwig," the damning article was actually the work of Rufus Griswold, who had lost no time in exacting revenge on Poe, who was not only his literary foe but also his rival for the affections of Fanny Osgood. Although several of Poe's former friends, including George Graham and Nathaniel Willis, rushed to defend Poe's memory, Poe himself had already insured that Griswold's opinions would hold sway in years to come. With his uncanny instinct for self-destruction, Poe had appointed Griswold his literary executor. This afforded his enemy the chance to expand on the hostile obituary in a thirty-five-page "Memoir of the Author," appended to a posthumous two-volume edition of Poe's work. Eager to present Poe as morally debased, Griswold put forward a lengthy catalog of sins and offenses, many of them fabricated for the occasion. Griswold accused Poe of having been expelled from the University of Virginia, of deserting the army, of drug addiction, of attempts to seduce his foster father's second wife, and of making drunken advances on Sarah Helen Whitman that "made necessary a summons of the police." He concluded that Poe had been a man who exhibited "scarcely any virtue in either his life or his writings. . . . Irascible, envious—bad enough, but not the worst, for these salient angles were all varnished over with a cold repellent cynicism, his passions vented themselves in sneers." Privately, Griswold would carry his attacks to even greater extremes, even spreading a rumor that Poe had developed a sexual relationship with his aunt Maria.

Griswold's damning "memoir" of Poe was occasionally leavened by grudging praise for the author's prose and poetry. Griswold had a notably high opinion of "The Mystery of Marie Rogêt," which he presented as an example of Poe's great cunning. Griswold even voiced approval of the deceptive footnotes that Poe had appended to the 1845 revision in *Tales*, praising the manner in which they brought clarity and "verisimilitude" to the story.

Griswold's praise for Poe as an artist, however, was all but overwhelmed by his venom for Poe as a man. This astonishing display of character assassination, presented under the guise of official biography, would throw a dark cloud over Poe's reputation for years to come. Not content to slander his dead rival, Griswold also dealt roughly with his rightful heir. Although Griswold's edition of Poe's work sold well and went through seventeen editions, he denied any proceeds to Maria Clemm, who finished her days in a charity home in Baltimore. More than once she railed against Griswold for dragging her "poor poor Eddie's" faults before the public. "Did you ever feel as if you wished *to die*?" she asked. *"It is thus I feel."*

It was an impulse Poe himself would have well understood. Four years earlier, as the fame of "The Raven" slipped away at the end of 1845, he had provided himself with a far more fitting, if mournful, epitaph: "I have perserveringly struggled, against a thousand difficulties, and have succeeded, although not in making money, still in attaining a position in the world of Letters, of which, under the circumstances, I have no reason to be ashamed."

EPILOGUE

One Last Wild Cry

And so, all the night-tide, I lie down by the side
Of my darling—my darling—my life and my bride,
In the sepulchre there by the sea,
In her tomb by the sounding sea.
—"Annabel Lee" by Edgar Allan Poe
A daguerreotype of Poe taken on November 9, 1848,
shortly after an attempted suicide with laudanum.

Oh! Shield me from that fearful sight—
That crime of darkest, blackest night,
    Appalling even the brave.
Wild shriek on shriek, and pray'r on pray'r
And deepest curses mingle there—
    Oh God! In pity save.

Who heeds thy shrieks, poor helpless maid?
There is no arm with strength to aid—
    No heart that has the will.
One last wild cry that reaches heaven,
One bitter pray'r for mercy given—
    Tis past!—and all is still . . .

Alas! The scene is passing fair,
Yet foul pollution revels there,
    And crime too black for name.
Far, far from all whose arm might save,
Welcome the cold, and bloody grave,
    That hides a wretch's shame.

—"Lines on the Death of Mary Rogers,"
Anonymous (1841)

AT THE TIME OF POE'S DEATH, the Mary Rogers saga had entered its final act. Poe had survived Mary Rogers by only eight years, but while his reputation now fell into a sad if temporary eclipse, the fame and influence of the cigar girl continued to grow. Her place in the public imagination had undergone a strange transformation in the wake of "The Mystery of Marie Rogêt." Where previously she had been viewed as a victim of gang violence, and a symbol of a failed and corrupt police force, Mary Rogers now became an emblem of the city's moral decay. Her name was frequently invoked on the pulpits of New York churches as a sorrowful reminder of the wages of sin.

Although Poe's story had helped to dispel the notion that Mary Rogers fell prey to a gang, the initial furor over "blacklegs and ruffians" had touched a nerve with the public, and would serve as a catalyst for a series of sweeping reforms. James Gordon Bennett had declared, in the weeks following that murder, that New York had been "disgraced and dishonored in the eyes of the Christian and civilized world." The subsequent revelations about the case did nothing to derail Bennett's campaign for "a truly great moral movement" to revitalize the city's law enforcement. The forces set in motion at the Committee of Safety meeting in August of 1841 would result, the following year, in a blistering city council report on the sad state of the New York police, complete with an unmistakable reference to the death of Mary Rogers: "The property of the citizen is pilfered, almost before his eyes," the document stated. "Dwellings and warehouses are entered with ease and apparent coolness and carelessness of detection which shows that none are safe. Thronged as our city is, men are robbed in the street. Thousands that are arrested go unpunished and the defenseless and the beautiful are ravished and murdered in the day time, and no trace of the criminal is found."

It would take three more years and two changes of city administration before concrete action was taken, but in May of 1845, the New York state legislature finally passed a Police Reform Act, abolishing the old network of night watchmen and marshals, and creating a full-time, salaried police force. The Police Reform Act emphasized the need for crime prevention, as opposed to the detection of crimes already committed, and finally did away with the untenable system of rewards for the return of stolen goods and other police services. "Rigid rules were made for the appointment of policemen," wrote the Reverend Matthew Hale Smith. "A vigorous and efficient body of men became guardians of the city . . . and the dignity of her keepers was restored." For Bennett, there was an added, personal satisfaction in the fact that the upheavals at City Hall also brought about an end to the judicial career of his rival Mordecai Noah, who retreated from the bench into a successful tenure as president of the Hebrew Benevolent Society.

Several of the proposed additions to New York's revised criminal code of 1845 clearly showed the influence of the Mary Rogers murder. A series of laws were proposed to govern acts of adultery and "other forms of seduction," with particularly harsh punishments mandated in cases of "abduction for immoral purposes."

Easily the most significant addition was an 1845 statute known as "The Abortion Law," which strengthened the city's existing statutes to a degree that effectively outlawed the "still and lost" treatments practiced in the city's many commercial abortion parlors. As it happened, the passage of the Abortion Law received a strong push from a New York attorney by the name of Frederick Mather, who was serving a term in the state senate at the time. Mather, who kept an office on Nassau Street not far from the Rogers boardinghouse, was a cousin of Mary's through a Hartford branch of the Mather clan—the family of Phoebe Rogers's first husband.

The new abortion law was pressed into immediate service as a tool against Madame Restell, whose abortion empire continued to flourish in spite of unrelenting attacks in the city's editorial pages. Although the police never found evidence to link Restell to the death of Mary Rogers, several newspapers took the abortionist's guilt to be a matter of established fact. "The wretched girl was last seen in the direction of Madame Restell's house," reported the *Police Gazette* in February of 1846. "The dreadfully lacerated body at Weehawken Bluff bore the marks of no ordinary violation. . . . These are strange but strong facts. . . . Such are these abortionists! Such their deeds, and such their dens of crime!" The *Gazette* went on to list a number of other, better-established accusations against Restell, followed by a characteristic call for "some sudden application of popular vengeance."

The article produced an immediate and dramatic result. On Monday, February 23, 1846, two days after the *Police Gazette* published its inflammatory statements, an angry mob formed outside Madame Restell's Greenwich Street residence. The *Morning News* reported that "not a few apparently came with the intention of being actors in some scene of violence and popular outbreak." The crowd was no ordinary band of troublemakers and hooligans, the paper observed. "There were very many of our most respectable citizens noticed among the mass—a result unlooked for, and certainly ominous of a deep and abiding feeling of abhorrence and detestation among the better classes for the practices of this miserable female."

As the crowd pressed against the gates of Restell's mansion, a shout was raised of "Hanging is too good for the monster!" The angry mood deepened as the size of the mob swelled. "Curses loud and deep upon Restell and her coadjutors were rife amid the crowd," reported the *Morning News*, along with cries of "Haul her out!" "Where's the thousand children murdered in this house?" and "Who murdered Mary Rogers?" Soon the mob had pushed through the gates and was pounding at the doors of the mansion. As the crisis mounted, it became clear that "the strong feeling of popular indignation was about to be manifested in an outbreak of serious character, and that the unhappy object of their dislike was about to realize that there is in this land a power above all law, whose mandates would—when the arm of justice became paralyzed and insufficient, was daringly sneered at by those who depend upon their ill-earned wealth and *certain peculiar influences* for immunity from the just reward of crime—be suddenly executed in violence and confusion."

Just when it seemed inevitable that Madame Restell would be dragged from her home and subjected to mob vengeance, her "*peculiar influences*" made themselves felt. George Matsell, New York's chief of police, arrived on the scene at the head of a squad of able-bodied officers, who immediately plunged into the heart of the mob. After arresting several of the "most active spirits," Matsell's forces were able to subdue and dispel the remaining agitators. Madame Restell, it emerged, was not actually present at the time, having received advance notice of the threatened disturbance. Her many years of generous payoffs to the police and other officials had done their work.

Edgar Allan Poe was still living in New York at this time, and it is possible that he was even doing some scattered service as a "mechanical paragraphist" at the *Police Gazette*. "There is a standing Gazette tradition that Poe, sometime between 1846 and 1849, the year of his death, had been temporarily on the staff of this journal," wrote Edward Van Every in *Sins of New York*, a compendium of *Gazette* writings published in 1930. "How much actual foundation there is to this tradition remains a question. . . . If such was the case, Poe never attached his name to any scrivening that he may have been driven to do." It is certainly tempting to speculate that Poe had a hand in the *Gazette*'s inflammatory article about Madame Restell. Poe's tenure at the *Broadway Journal* had ended in failure just one month before the appearance of the article, leaving him at loose ends and desperate for work. His final revision of "The Mystery of Marie Rogêt" had appeared in *Tales* the previous year, so the details of the case, and especially the late revelations, would have been fresh in his mind. The anonymity of the *Police Gazette* would have given him greater freedom to speculate on Mary Rogers's final fate, and perhaps even to make use of information or theories circulating among his coworkers. The incident at the Restell mansion, however, coincides with one of the more chaotic periods of Poe's life, giving rise to rumors of drunken binges and confinement in lunatic asylums, and eventually culminating in his removal to the relative tranquillity of the farmhouse in Fordham. It is impossible to say with any certainty whether Poe ever set foot in the offices of the *Police Gazette*, much less attach his name to a particular piece of "scrivening."

In any event, the episode had little effect on Madame Restell. In spite of the new laws and several other outbreaks of public indignation, the "most wicked woman in New York" continued to run her empire for another three decades. Every so often she would be subjected to a public arrest and trial, but in each case she managed to escape without serious or lasting consequences. On the occasion of one arrest she posted bail in the amount of $10,000, which she paid in cash, adding an additional thousand to demonstrate her continued goodwill. "The law has swept every rival from her path, and she remains mistress paramount in the scheme of practical destruction," wrote the *Police Gazette*. "We are not led to these remarks with the view of spurring the authorities to bring this woman to justice. That hope is past."

At last, in 1878, the many decades at the helm of the "bloody empire" took their toll. Facing renewed criticism from the press and mounting suspicion over the mysterious death of her husband, Madame Restell was placed under arrest following a confrontation with Anthony Comstock, the celebrated antivice crusader. After a brief stint in the Tombs, she once again posted bail and returned home to her mansion on Fifth Avenue. Making her way upstairs, Madame Restell calmly settled back into a warm bath and slit her own throat.

The *New York Times* responded with satisfaction to "a fit ending to an odious career." Even in death, however, Madame Restell cast a long shadow over the city. James Gordon Bennett, Jr., who had taken control of the *Herald* upon his father's retirement in 1867, announced that he planned to publish Restell's client list for the public's edification. Shock waves spread through the city's smoking parlors and fashionable clubs. Before the incriminating lists could come to light, however, they disappeared from police custody.

Thirty-seven years had now elapsed since the death of Mary Rogers, but Madame Restell's death occasioned yet another surge of interest in the fate of the cigar girl, not least because of the flood of sensational literature that had linked the crime to the notorious abortionist. In life, Mary Rogers had inspired a great deal of leaden poetry; in death, she called forth an entire shelf of badly written novels, beginning with J. H. Ingraham's *The Beautiful Cigar Girl* in 1844, the tone of which may be judged by the exclamation of young Herman de Ruyter at learning that his sister Maria has taken employment in a cigar store: "But consider, mother, this young, pure girl! Consider Maria is guileless, so beautiful, placed in a situation surrounded with such great dangers. Consider the peril to her reputation! Were she fair as the lily, the breath of slander would blast her fair fame forever! Oh, Maria! Would to God you had reflected ere you had taken this step!"

The breath of slander also blew hot in *Mysteries and Miseries of New York*, a novel published in 1848 by Ned Buntline, the pen name of the prolific journalist Edward Zane Carroll Judson. A central episode of the book concerns a young woman named Mary Sheffield, also known as "The Beautiful Cigar Girl," whose lifeless and battered body is discovered floating in the Hudson River. An account of the crime in the New York *Herald* attributes the misfortune to "ill treatment and murder by a gang of rowdies at Hoboken," but it soon develops that the marks of violence on the corpse were inflicted "not by a gang of rowdies," but by an infamous abortionist known as Caroline Sitstill—"a hag, a she devil, an abortion of her own sex, one whom it would be blasphemy to call a woman." In lieu of a happy ending, Buntline tacked an appendix onto his novel that included the entire text of the 1845 Police Reform Act.

In 1851, a cheaply produced pamphlet appeared entitled *Confession of the Awful and Bloody Transactions of Charles Wallace*. The cover identified Wallace as "the fiend-like murderer of Miss Mary

Rogers, the beautiful cigar girl of Broadway, New York, whose fate has for several years been wrapt in the most profound mystery." An obvious hoax, the phony confession fit into a tradition of lurid and sensational pamphlets of the time, describing the murder in terms calculated to shock its readers:

> I kept tightening the cord until her cheeks assumed a purple hue. The blood began to ooze from her nostrils and ears, and at last she fell back on the grass, her hands tightly grasped around my left arm. Hell was swelling in my bosom, and revenge seemed sweeter at that instant than life itself. I felt even if she were to live, she would hate me for this still more than previously. With this thought running in my head, I grew frantic, and kept gradually drawing the ends of the string, and when I came to my senses, I found she was dead. I unwound the fatal rope with a *smile* upon my countenance.

The drama was presented in an even more graphic light in Andrew Jackson Davis's *Tale of a Physician: or the Fruits and Seeds of Crime*, published in 1869. A popular novelist, Davis was also known as the "Poughkeepsie seer" for his interest in spiritualism—a growing belief in the possibility of communication with the dead—and he claimed to have brought psychic knowledge to his interpretation of the cigar girl's fate. Davis's retelling centers on a "celebrated beauty" named Molly Ruciel who is a "selling clerk in a popular down-town store." Having left her home on a Sunday morning, after leaving word that she intends to spend the day with her aunt, Molly goes instead to a "foeticidal" establishment run by a Madame La Stelle. There, as she prepares to receive treatment from a physician, she pens a heartfelt letter to her mother: "I cannot tell you in language how deeply I have been wronged . . . Oh! Do not ask who has deceived me. I believed him sincere in all his promises. I relied upon his word. I drank until my senses were lost; then my fears and all my resolutions left me forever!" Sensing that she will not survive the ministrations of her doctor, the subtly named Doctor Morte, Molly adds a poignant conclusion. "I am glad that death is so near," she insists. "My pride and my hope, my self-respect and ambition, are all gone, dearest mother; and I do not want to outlive the fruit of my temptation and transgression . . . farewell! Forever farewell!"

Moments later, as the beautiful patient lies dead before him, Dr. Morte offers a callous epitaph. "Damn bad luck, this hitch!" he declares. "Fact is, the girl was in a devilish bad temper."

Whatever the merits of Davis's claim to psychic insight, he signaled his debt to Poe by quoting from the poem "The Conqueror Worm" at the start of the fatal chapter:

> Out, out are the lights—out all!
> And over her quivering form
> The curtain, a funeral pall,
> Comes down with the rush of a storm.

Davis's novel appeared at a time when Poe's reputation was on the brink of rehabilitation. Poe's friends had eloquently defended his work and character in the years following Poe's death, but the effects of Rufus Griswold's bitter attack continued to stain his reputation. "His heart was as rotten as his conduct was infamous," wrote one critic in 1854. "Poe was a habitual drunkard, licentious, false, treacherous, and capable of everything that was mean, base, and malignant." But in Europe, a robust revival had already begun, with the French poet and critic Charles Baudelaire taking a leading role. Baudelaire's lyrical translations would have a profound influence on French literature and helped to inspire the symbolist movement. Where other critics attacked Poe's "debased" lifestyle, Baudelaire embraced "*le pauvre Eddie*" as a thumb in the eye of America's repressive and overly moralistic society. In Germany, Nietzsche and Rilke would find their way to Poe in their turn, joining in the celebration of an artistic martyr, as would Kafka in Prague. "Poe was ill," wrote Kafka. "He was a poor drunk devil who had no defenses against the world. So he fled into drunkenness. Imagination only served him as a crutch. . . . Imagination has fewer pitfalls than reality has."

In Britain, Poe's admirers included Tennyson, Charles Dickens, and Elizabeth Barrett Browning. Oscar Wilde praised him as "this marvelous lord of rhythmic expression," while Swinburne wrote of his "strong and delicate genius, so sure of aim and faultless of touch in all the better and finer part of work he has left us." America's literary establishment, meanwhile, remained slow to give ground. Although Hawthorne praised the "force and originality" of Poe's work, Emerson would dismiss the poet as a "jingle man."

John Henry Ingram produced the first significant study of Poe's life and work in English in 1874, which he expanded to two volumes in 1880. An enthusiastic defender of Poe's reputation, Ingram also edited a four-volume edition of Poe's work and corresponded with numerous people who had known the author. Ingram's work opened the door to further efforts at rehabilitation. The critic George Woodberry published an impressive two-volume biography in 1885, which attempted to give a balanced portrait of Poe while erasing many of Rufus Griswold's fabrications.

By the end of the nineteenth century, numerous editions of Poe's work had appeared on both sides of the Atlantic, with almost all of them reprinting "The Mystery of Marie Rogêt" alongside

"The Murders in the Rue Morgue" and "The Purloined Letter." These three "tales of ratiocination," often grouped together with "The Gold-Bug," would serve as both the inspiration and the template for the new and wildly popular field of detective fiction. In "The Purloined Letter," Dupin had exercised his ingenuity to recover an incriminating letter on behalf of a royal personage. It was no accident that "A Scandal in Bohemia," one of the first stories featuring an "amateur reasoner" named Sherlock Holmes, centered on the recovery of an incriminating letter on behalf of a royal personage. Over the span of some forty years, Poe's influence would be felt over and over again in the sitting room of Baker Street. In "Rue Morgue," Dupin had offered a telling comment on the manner in which the police had discarded a theory that seemed to be impossible: "It is not our part, as reasoners, to reject it on account of apparent impossibilities. It is only left for us to prove that these apparent 'impossibilities' are, in reality, not such." Sherlock Holmes would offer numerous variations on this theme over the course of his career. "How often have I said to you," he tells Watson in *The Sign of the Four*, "that when you have eliminated the impossible, whatever remains, *however improbable*, must be the truth."

"Poe is the master of all," wrote Holmes's creator, Arthur Conan Doyle. "Poe is, to my mind, the supreme original short story writer of all time. His brain was like a seed-pod full of seeds which flew carelessly around, and from which have sprung nearly all our modern types of story. Just think of what he did in his offhand, prodigal fashion, seldom troubling to repeat a success, but pushing on to some new achievement. To him must be ascribed the monstrous progeny of writers on the detection of crime. . . . If every man who receives a cheque for a story which owes its springs to Poe were to pay a tithe to a monument for the master, he would have a pyramid as big as that of Cheops."

Within the "monstrous progeny" of crime writers, "The Mystery of Marie Rogêt" exerted a singular fascination. Conan Doyle was just one of many authors who took a special interest in the interplay between crime fiction and factual crimes, even going so far as to apply his fictional detective's "science of deduction" to a pair of real-life crimes. In *The Story of Mr. George Edalji*, Conan Doyle offered an eloquent defense of a young lawyer accused in a series of gruesome cattle mutilations, and with *The Case of Oscar Slater* the author was instrumental in winning the release of a man wrongly imprisoned for murder. Over the years countless other writers would find inspiration in true crime stories to create works of fiction, poetry, or creative nonfiction, ranging from Browning, Hawthorne, and Melville to Dreiser, Capote, and Mailer.

Mary Rogers, meanwhile, had been all but forgotten. As Poe's reputation and influence flowered, the details of the cigar girl saga slowly faded from public memory. Though she remained lodged in the lore of New York City, and her name was often mentioned alongside other prominent murder victims such as Helen Jewett and Stanford White, the particulars of the crime grew hazy with the passage of years. Over time, as "The Mystery of Marie Rogêt" became detached from the saga of the cigar girl, Poe's interpretation of the murder came to be the accepted view. Anchored between the twin monuments of "The Murders in the Rue Morgue" and "The Purloined Letter," the story made an unlikely progress from the *Ladies' Companion* to literary immortality. Although Poe's facts had been gleaned from incomplete newspaper accounts, and hastily tweaked to accommodate late-breaking developments, the story rose above the chaos that had attended its composition and took on the mantle of established fact. Later critics would marvel over the manner in which Poe had not only solved a crime that baffled the police but also demonstrated the power of ratiocination. As early as 1874, John Ingram felt obliged to remind his readers that Mary Rogers had, in fact, been a real person: "Latterly it has been the fashion (especially by foreigners) to disbelieve that Marie Rogêt's mystery had any real existence, and that the whole recital was the coinage of the poet's brain."

Poe himself had done a great deal to blur the line between Mary Rogers and Marie Rogêt. In the years following the publication of *Tales*, he had received inquiries about the case from interested readers. In January of 1848, Poe answered a letter from George Eveleth, an admirer from Maine, in which he responded to a published criticism of the story. "Nothing was omitted in 'Marie Rogêt' but what I omitted myself," Poe declared. "The 'naval officer' who committed the murder (or rather the accidental death arising from an attempt at abortion) *confessed* it; and the whole matter is now well understood—but, for the sake of relatives, this is a topic on which I must not speak further." This extraordinary and audacious statement, suggesting once again that Poe knew more than he could tell, added a strange and baffling coda to the affair.

Given the stresses and heavy drinking of the final years of Poe's life, it is difficult to know how much weight to give to this deceptively offhand remark. The tone echoes the self-congratulatory assertion in "Marie Rogêt" that "*all* the chief hypothetical details" had been confirmed, and that the identity of Mary Rogers's killer was an open secret among the New York cognoscenti. Beneath this bland and confident air, however, a number of significant new details struggle to the surface, marking a considerable change of emphasis from the story's initial publication. Poe's statement that nothing had been omitted from the story apart from what he omitted himself may well refer to the clumsy editorial intervention at the conclusion of the story—"we have taken the liberty of here omitting, from the MSS. placed in our hands . . ."—which invited the reader to believe that Poe had initially named the killer, but that cooler heads had moved to suppress the information. If so, it is a clear admission that Poe never intended to name the killer, but for purposes of storytelling naturally wished to make it appear that Dupin had done so.

More significantly, in his letter to George Eveleth, Poe referred to the swarthy naval officer, whose occupation he had so painstakingly deduced, in quotation marks, as if to qualify or disavow the designation. Possibly Poe meant to suggest that circumstances had forced him to employ this vague title in place of a more specific description, which might have more readily identified the killer. The quotation marks have the effect, however, of implying that the naval officer was perhaps not a naval officer at all. After all of his previous mental gymnastics in establishing the point—the companionship with a "gay but not an abject" young woman; the "well-written and urgent communications" to the newspapers—Poe's apparent hedging on this point must be seen as a major reversal.

More remarkable still is his reference to an "accidental death arising from an attempt at abortion." This is the first and only time that Poe is known to have used that term in connection with the case. Previously he had employed vague euphemisms such as "certain concealments" or "a fatal accident." The fact that he now mentions the procedure directly suggests that he had come to accept it as the likely cause of death. Even now, however, he preserves his characteristic ambiguity. The offhand manner in which he raises the possibility of an "attempt at abortion," in a set of parentheses, allows him to vacillate between an "accidental death" and outright murder. But an accidental death while under the care of an inept abortionist is a very different thing from strangulation at the hands of an enraged lover. In "Marie Rogêt," Poe devoted considerable attention to the aftermath of the murder: "He is alone with the ghost of the departed. He is appalled by what lies motionless before him. The fury of his passion is over, and there is abundant room in his heart for the natural awe of the deed." This is not a scene that would have attended a botched medical procedure, no matter how tragic.

All of these reversals pale next to Poe's unambiguous assertion that the villain, naval officer or otherwise, had confessed to the crime, only to have the matter hushed up in deference to a presumably influential family. The statement echoes Poe's claim in "Marie Rogêt" that a second person had admitted guilt, in addition to the confession attributed to Mrs. Loss. Poe's repeated insistence on this confession, one of the few points on which he remained consistent, is extremely provocative. While it is entirely possible that his dogged persistence is simply another example of poetic license, akin to the embellishments of the "Balloon Hoax," one is forced to consider the possibility that at some stage he may have gained inside knowledge of the case. On his return to New York in 1844, Poe's work at the *Evening Mirror* placed him almost literally on the doorstep of the Rogers boardinghouse. In his work at the *Mirror*, the *Broadway Journal*, and elsewhere, he would have come into close contact with newsmen who had covered the case and been instrumental in the investigation. (Although it is not known whether he ever worked at the *Police Gazette*, he could easily have come into contact with the paper's reporters.) Poe came to know Horace Greeley of the *Tribune* well enough to ask him for a fifty-dollar loan. Justice Mordecai Noah, who had recently returned to the world of journalism as the editor of the *Sunday Times and Messenger*, was one of the three witnesses who spoke in Poe's defense during his libel suit against Thomas Dunn English. It is natural that these men, upon meeting the author of "The

Mystery of Marie Rogêt," should have spoken of their involvement with the Mary Rogers case. If there was gossip about the case, or some form of open secret concerning a hushed-up confession, it is natural that Poe should have learned about it. Possibly the promise of immunity offered by Governor Seward had brought forth information that remained protected under the terms of confidentiality. At the very least, Poe would have been party to a great deal of speculation as to what had actually occurred. Poe would naturally have tried to assimilate whatever knowledge or insight he gained into his previous view of the affair.

John Ingram, Poe's early biographer, would add to the confusion about the mysterious naval officer. Writing of "The Mystery of Marie Rogêt" in 1874, Ingram insisted that "the narrative *was* founded on fact, although the incidents of the tragedy differed widely from those recounted in the tale. The naval officer implicated was named Spencer." Ingram offered no elaboration and gave no source for this identification, though it may have been suggested to him in a letter from Sarah Helen Whitman, the young widow who had enjoyed Poe's attentions in his last years. Subsequent scholars would track this fleeting reference to a prominent seagoing family headed by a Captain William Spencer. At first glance, Captain Spencer appeared to be a promising suspect. He was known to have been in New York both in 1838 and 1841, and his family was sufficiently influential to hush up even the gravest of scandals—his brother, John Canfield Spencer, was President Tyler's secretary of war. On closer examination, however, the fact that Captain Spencer would have been forty-eight years old at the time of the murder tends to cut against Poe's portrait of a "young Lothario."

Captain Spencer's nephew, a young midshipman named Philip Spencer, also makes an intriguing suspect. In 1842, the year after

Mary Rogers's murder, the younger Spencer was hanged at sea after attempting to stage a mutiny, in an incident that helped to inspire Herman Melville's *Billy Budd*. But Poe's "swarthy naval officer" theory relied upon the villain's complicity in Mary Rogers's earlier disappearance in 1838, three years prior to the murder. At that time, Philip Spencer was a fifteen-year-old schoolboy at an academy in Schenectady. It is unlikely that he could have courted and seduced a young woman who lived in New York City, some one hundred and fifty miles away.

Whatever the merits of the two Spencers as suspects in the crime, it is possible that the subsequent nationwide attention surrounding the Philip Spencer drama sparked Poe's imagination and caused him to fasten onto the name. In regaling Sarah Helen Whitman with the story of Marie Rogêt's inspiration, Poe may have indulged his poetic fancies. A mention of the notorious young Spencer—who, like Poe's naval officer, was noted for his debaucheries—would have offered a tidy and sensational resolution.

In the absence of more concrete evidence against the Spencer family, one is tempted to seek the guilty party closer to home. In the decades following Mary Rogers's death, even as the notion of her death in an abortion parlor gained acceptance, there remained an insistent thread of speculation over the exact chain of events that had led to the tragedy. If, indeed, Mary Rogers died during a failed abortion, many questions remained unanswered. The body had been found covered with bruises and scrapes. Her arms were tied together at the wrists by a heavy rope. The signs of manual strangulation (fingermark bruises) were plainly seen on her throat, along with a lace garrote buried deep in her flesh. Clearly this had been no ordinary medical mishap. In all the many attempts to understand the cigar girl's fate, these troubling inconsistencies remained. How and why had this violence occurred and, above all, who was responsible?

Over the years, speculation on this point has taken a great many interesting twists and turns. As with the Jack the Ripper drama at the end of the nineteenth century, the energetic climate of speculation around the death of Mary Rogers has produced a seemingly endless line of suspects, often with little regard for evidence or plausibility. One pair of researchers has carried this theorizing to a fantastic conclusion, pointing the finger of suspicion at none other than Poe himself. Although it has never been demonstrated that Poe ever actually laid eyes on Mary Rogers, this intriguing speculation posits that he not only consorted with the beautiful cigar girl, but also did away with her in a fit of "alcoholic insanity."

It is a twist that would undoubtedly have appealed to Poe's narrative instincts, if not his passion for logical reasoning. "It was not, and could not have been, arrived at by any inductive reasoning," he wrote in "Maelzel's Chess-Player," while discarding a line of faulty assumptions. "To show that certain things *might* possibly be effected in a certain way is very far from showing that they *are* actually so effected." Though Poe himself did not always observe this distinction, he fully grasped its importance.

A more compelling theory places the blame on the shoulders of Daniel Payne, whose death at Weehawken and the anguished note left behind certainly point to a guilty conscience. In this scenario, Payne discovers that Mary is pregnant and helps to arrange an abortion at the Loss tavern. In gratitude, Mary agrees to marry him and forsake other men, but after the successful procedure she changes her mind and breaks off the engagement. Enraged, Payne lashes out and strangles her, perhaps inadvertently, later telling Mrs. Rogers that she has died at the hands of the abortionist. Unable to live with his conscience, Payne takes his own life two months later.

The theory is persuasive for a number of reasons, not the least of which being that it accounts for both the evidence of an abortion and the obvious signs of death by strangulation. The difficulty is that Payne had an alibi, not only on the fatal Sunday but also the day following, when he was seen to be making a search for Mary at the homes of her relatives. One writer has speculated that the murder did not take place until late Tuesday—two days after Mary's disappearance—when Payne's actions are less well documented. According to this hypothesis, Payne could have murdered Mary over the broken engagement, then placed a false ad in the *Sun* ("it is supposed some accident has befallen her") in order to cover his tracks. This hypothesis, however ingenious, fails to account for the fact that the ad in the *Sun* appeared on Tuesday, July 27, and would therefore have to have been placed before Payne's crime of passion is supposed to have occurred.

Another intriguing player in the drama is Alfred Crommelin, the jilted suitor who identified the body at Elysian Fields. Mary Rogers is known to have called at his office twice in the days before her death. Although it is entirely plausible that she came seeking money to pay for an abortion, the rose placed in Crommelin's keyhole invites further speculation. Crommelin may have dared to hope that his romantic feelings were now to be reciprocated. Possibly Mary came in hopes of extricating herself from her betrothal to Payne. Crommelin's refusal to answer her messages can only have complicated her predicament. In the absence of money from Crommelin, Mary may have been forced to forgo the services of Madame Restell and make recourse to the less expensive and presumably far riskier facilities of Mrs. Loss. If Crommelin knew of her intentions, it might explain how he happened to be on the scene when the body came ashore in Hoboken: He would have been on his way to the Nick Moore House.

Neither Payne nor Crommelin makes an entirely satisfactory suspect. Both had alibis for the fatal Sunday, and neither had sufficient influence to conceal an involvement with the crime if the authorities or press had known of it. The fact that the papers found on Payne's body at the time of his death were not put forward as evidence of his guilt argues strongly in favor of his innocence, and the fact that Crommelin made such a nuisance of himself to the police and Gilbert Merritt suggests that he had little to hide. At the same time, if we accept—or at least consider—Poe's formulation that the murder was somehow linked to the brief disappearance in 1838, it must be noted that Payne and Crommelin probably did not know Mary Rogers in that year, as the boardinghouse had not yet opened.

One man who did know Mary Rogers at the time of her disappearance from Anderson's Tobacco Emporium was John Anderson himself. Even the most casual observer of the case would be forced to admit that Anderson's interest in Mary Rogers appears to have exceeded that of a typical employer. Mary and her mother lived in his home for a time before they purchased their boardinghouse, and when Mary quit her job at the cigar store, Anderson is said to have literally pleaded on his knees to win her return. Then as now, there was no shortage of attractive women in New York; if Mary Rogers had been simply a decorative employee, she could easily have been replaced.

Anderson's business grew steadily in the years following Mary Rogers's death. He branched out into real estate and eventually became one of the wealthiest men in the city. For all of his success, however, Anderson never entirely escaped a taint of suspicion that he had somehow been culpable in the death of the famous cigar girl. Rumors circulated that he had been having an affair with his young employee, leading, perhaps, to an unwanted pregnancy and the disastrous consequence that followed. He had managed to suppress the information that he had been interrogated at police headquarters in connection with the crime, but nevertheless rumors circulated among the city's leading citizens, creating an impression of the tobacconist as a man with a skeleton in his closet. James Gordon Bennett was among those who knew the details of Anderson's police interview, and one senses a certain animus toward Anderson in the *Herald*'s tone at the time of the murder. For all of Anderson's wealth and political promise, Bennett dismisses him imperiously as "the cigar man" and records that Mary Rogers had "not been at Anderson's hole for nearly three years."

Anderson's political ambitions soon foundered. At one stage Fernando Wood, the legendary political power broker, tried to persuade Anderson to make a run for the office of mayor, but Anderson declined, fearing that the publicity would churn up even more speculation about the Mary Rogers case. Anderson grew bitter in later life, and frequently blamed Mary Rogers for thwarting his political fortunes. His business partner Felix McCloskey recalled that on one occasion, passing the building that had once been the Rogers boardinghouse, Anderson cursed the murdered girl's memory as "the cause of driving him out of politics and belittling him in New York." On another occasion, McCloskey quoted him as saying "I want people to believe that I had no hand in her taking off," and he went on to offer an assurance "that he *hadn't* anything *directly, himself,* to do with it." Like Poe's remark about the mysterious second confession, the statement labors under the weight of what has been left unsaid, and invites closer attention.

As an old man Anderson fell under the thrall of spiritualism, the belief in communication with dead souls, and confided to several friends that he was now in regular communication with Mary's spirit. He once claimed that he received particularly sound business advice from the dead girl. Abner Mattoon, a New York state senator, recalled Anderson as saying that Mary Rogers "appeared to him in the spirit from time to time." Anderson went on to say that "I have had a great deal of trouble about Mary Rogers, but everything is settled now. I take great pleasure in communicating with her face to face."

An attorney who looked into Anderson's business affairs in later years insisted that the murder made "an impression which he was in after years never able to shake off and which, when his faculties began to fail and old age to creep upon him, lent a controlling force which undermined his intellectual powers." Late in life, Anderson withdrew into a mansion in Tarrytown, where he installed steel-lined shutters to ward off some vaguely defined threat. He came to believe that his children were trying to poison him, and that his cook was plotting to kill him by "putting pins in his roast beef."

Anderson died in Paris in November of 1881 at age sixty-nine, having outlived Mary Rogers by forty years. At the time of his death, he was widely believed to have been insane. As a result, his heirs would contest his final will and testament in various legal challenges that stretched over more than a decade. In May of 1887, the *New York Times* would report on a suit brought by Anderson's daughter. Under the headline of "An Old Tragedy Recalled," the testimony in an otherwise mundane property suit contains a stunning disclosure, delivered in an offhand, matter-of-fact manner. Andrew Wheeler, a former associate of Anderson's, was recalling a discussion with Anderson concerning Poe and "Marie Rogêt" when he was interrupted by one of the legal advisors in the case, a former judge by the name of Curtis. As the *Times* reported it: "Ex-Judge Curtis asked him if he did not know that John Anderson gave Poe $5,000 to write the story of Marie Rogêt in order to draw people's attention from himself, who, many believed, was her murderer." Wheeler, according to the *Times* reporter, answered that "now was the first time he had ever heard of such a thing," and no more was said on the matter.

The notion that John Anderson commissioned Poe to write "Marie Rogêt" as a means of covering his own tracks appears at first blush to be fanciful. Most commentators on the case have dismissed it, although it does give an index of the degree to which the Rogers case dogged Anderson's later years. It should be remembered, however, that Poe, as the author of the ill-fated *Conchologist's First Book*, would have been known to Anderson as a man willing to undertake almost any sort of hackwork. Thomas Ollive Mabbott, the editor of a definitive scholarly edition of Poe's works, has noted that Poe must have been on good terms with Anderson as late as 1845, even after the revision of "Marie Rogêt" in *Tales*, with its hints of a fatal abortion. Two weeks after Poe took the helm of the *Broadway Journal*, advertisements for Anderson's Tobacco Emporium began to run in the magazine. At a time when Poe desperately needed money to save the struggling magazine, Anderson paid in advance for three months of notices. Needless to say, the fact that the two men had business dealings, while suggestive, does not establish that Anderson commissioned "Marie Rogêt" as a smoke screen. If nothing else, one must regard the figure of $5,000 with great suspicion. For Poe, who earned only nine dollars for "The Raven," this would have been a life-altering bounty. Thomas Mabbott, perhaps the most careful of Poe scholars, takes pains to note that the story of Anderson's involvement with the writing of "Marie Rogêt" is nothing more than a tradition, but he adds, "I have come to regard it with respect."

The legal proceedings over John Anderson's will would stretch out over several years, and in that time the matter of Mary Rogers would be raised several times. On one occasion, during testimony by Felix McCloskey, Anderson's former partner, the judge attempted to quash the topic—declaring that he "could not see what relevancy the witness's memory of a tragedy that happened 45 years ago could have to a controversy respecting the soundness of mind of the millionaire tobacconist." In spite of the judge's reservations, McCloskey soon returned to the subject. In the spring of 1891, McCloskey stated in open court that Anderson once told him that "an abortion had been committed on the girl—the year before her murder took place, or a year and a half—something of that kind—and that he got into some trouble about it—and outside of *that* there was no grounds on earth for anybody to suppose he had anything to do with the murder."

Although McCloskey's memory of dates may have grown vague with the passage of fifty years, his statement strongly suggests that Mary Rogers's disappearance from the cigar store in 1838 came as a consequence of an abortion. Whether Anderson was actually responsible for the pregnancy or merely paid for its termination is unclear, but the recollection that he "got into some trouble about it" goes a long way toward explaining his extreme sensitivity over the murder in later years. Even if Anderson had nothing at all to do with the events of 1841, which remains an open question, he would have placed himself in an extremely delicate position if he provided money for an earlier abortion—especially if Mary Rogers died while undergoing a second procedure three years later. Even if, as he later protested, he had "no hand in her taking off," his complicity in the earlier abortion, to whatever degree, would have branded him as a villain who helped to set her down the path to destruction. Given the level of public outrage, one can only imagine Anderson's thoughts as he attended the meeting of the Committee of Safety in August of 1841, and pledged fifty dollars toward "the arrest of any or all of those concerned in the late murder."

If Mary Rogers truly perished while undergoing a second abortion in 1841—and if the notorious "Swarthy Man" was in fact the abortionist himself—it does not explain how she came to be found with a battered face and a lace cord tied around her neck, and the marks of a man's fingers visible upon her neck. Although the abortion scenario came to be widely accepted after the death of Mrs. Loss, it did not allow for the obvious signs of strangulation.

A possible explanation is suggested in the pages of *Tale of a Physician: or the Fruits and Seeds of Crime*, the 1869 novel by Andrew Jackson Davis. When the heroine, Molly Ruciel, presents herself at the "foeticidal" establishment of Madame La Stelle, it emerges that she had been there three years previously: "Oho! The pretty store-girl come again, eh? About three and a half years ago, I'm thinking, you disappeared from this hospital with your life, and in fair health, didn't you, Miss Molly Ruciel?" When the frightened young woman expresses misgivings, the hopelessness of her situation becomes apparent. "Don't trouble yourself, Miss Molly," she is told. "Your wealthy lover, the gallant Jack Blake, has been here. It's all fixed. The handsome villain paid all fees and left full instructions. He says that you're a candidate for 'still and lost' treatment, and he footed the bill accordingly." When the unfortunate store clerk perishes during the procedure, the physician is wildly alarmed. "Everybody in New-York knows that girl!" cries his assistant. "We've got a hell of a job on hand, I'll bet." Loading the corpse into a cab, they hatch a plan to cover the traces of the deed: "This passenger will put all New-York in a thundering quiver of excitement. . . . She must be found floating with every imaginable evidence of violence committed by several men." Having reached this conclusion, the guilty men set about to inflict "sufficient marks of cruelty" on the corpse, while dispatching assistants to dispose of her tattered clothing in Weehawken. The battered corpse is then dumped into the Hudson, and four days later "the great city of New-York is convulsed with a profound and intense excitement."

Poe might have admired the ingenuity, if not the prose. It is worth mentioning that Andrew Jackson Davis met Poe on at least one occasion, and that his activities as the "Poughkeepsie seer" may well have overlapped with those of John Anderson, the eager adherent of spiritualism. Unfortunately, as Poe would have acknowledged, the value of such coincidences is open to debate, and even the revelations of the John Anderson court case, coming fifty years after the death of Mary Rogers, must be treated with caution. Whatever value one might place in Poe's Calculus of Probabilities, it must be admitted that by the time of Anderson's death the secrets of Mary Rogers had passed beyond mere ratiocination.

In time, Poe himself might have come to appreciate this. "There are some secrets which do not permit themselves to be told," he wrote in "The Man of the Crowd." "Men die nightly in their beds, wringing the hands of ghostly confessors, and looking them piteously in the eyes—die with despair of heart and convulsion of throat, on account of the hideousness of mysteries which will not suffer themselves to be revealed. Now and then, alas, the conscience of man takes up a burden so heavy in horror that it can be thrown down only into the grave. And thus the essence of all crime is undivulged."

ACKNOWLEDGMENTS

The case of Mary Rogers presents many challenges to the modern researcher, not the least being the scarcity of contemporary records. "As there was never any trial," observed the writer Edmund Pearson in 1930, "the facts must be sought in the files of the New York newspapers of the late summer of 1841—when this sensational murder, discussed by everyone, was mentioned perhaps not more than thrice a week, usually in a paragraph of small type, tucked away on the editorial page. The sight of me, hunting for the news would be enough to make my optician beam with honest pleasure."

My optician, too, has had cause for satisfaction over my interest in the fate of the beautiful cigar girl. Unlike Edmund Pearson, however, I have also had the benefit of a rich vein of more recent scholarship concerning the case and its aftermath. I would like to express my gratitude and admiration for the work of Amy Gilman Srebnick, John Evangelist Walsh, Raymond Paul, William K. Wimsatt, and Samuel Worthen. At the same time, I am indebted to the work of many distinguished Poe scholars, including Thomas Ollive Mabbott, John Ward Ostrom, Kenneth Silverman, and Jeffrey Meyers.

I would also like to acknowledge the generous assistance of the following people and institutions: The New York Public Library,

The New-York Historical Society, The Municiple Archives of New York City, The Museum of the City of New York, Thomas Mann and the staff of The Library of Congress, Jackie Donovan and The American Antiquarian Society, The Poe Museum of Richmond, The Edgar Allan Poe Society of Baltimore, The Edgar Allan Poe House and Museum of Baltimore, The Edgar Allan Poe National Historic Site of Philaldelphia, The Edgar Allan Poe Cottage of New York, the gentlemen of Squatting Toad and especially Allen Appel and Larry Kahaner, Sean Tinslay of The Antique Bookshop of Australia, Ben Robinson, Jon Lellenberg, Lloyd Rose, Mitch Hoffman of Dutton, Erika Kahn, Donald Maass of the Donald Maass Literary Agency, David Stashower, and Sonny Wareham.

SELECTED BIBLIOGRAPHY

Allen, Hervey. *Israfel: The Life and Times of Edgar Allan Poe.* New York: Farrar & Rinehart, 1934.

Anbinder, Tyler. *Five Points: The 19th-Century New York City Neighborhood That Invented Tap Dance, Stole Elections, and Became the World's Most Notorious Slum.* New York: Plume, 2002.

Anonymous. *Madame Restell, An Account of Her Life and Horrible Practices, Together with Prostitution in New York, Its Extent, Causes, and Effects upon Society.* New York: Privately published, 1847.

Anonymous. *Tragic Almanack 1843.* New York: C. P. Huestis, 1843.

Asbury, Herbert. *All Around the Town.* New York: Thunder's Mouth Press, 2003.

————. *The Gangs of New York.* Garden City: Garden City Publishing Co., 1927.

Belden, Ezekiel Porter. *New York, Past, Present, and Future: Comprising a History of the City of New York.* New York: G. P. Putnam, 1849.

Borowitz, Albert. *Blood & Ink: An International Guide to Fact-Based Crime Literature.* Kent, Ohio: The Kent State University Press, 2002.

Botkin, B. A. (Ed.). *New York City Folklore.* New York: Random House, 1956.

Burdett, Charles. *Lilla Hart: A Tale of New York*. New York: Baker & Scribner, 1846.

————. *Never Too Late*. New York: D. Appleton & Co., 1845.

————. *Chances and Changes, or, Life As It Is*. New York: D. Appleton & Co., 1863.

Burrows, Edwin G. and Mike Wallace. *Gotham: A History of New York City to 1898*. New York and Oxford: Oxford University Press, 1999.

Byrnes, Thomas. *1886 Professional Criminals of America*. New York: The Lyons Press, 2000.

Cohen, Patricia Cline. *The Murder of Helen Jewett: The Life and Death of a Prostitute in Nineteenth-Century New York*. New York: Alfred A. Knopf, 1998.

Crockett, Albert Stevens. *When James Gordon Bennett Was Caliph of Bagdad*. New York: Funk & Wagnalls, 1926.

Crouse, Russel. *Murder Won't Out*. New York: Doubleday, Doran & Co., 1932.

Crouthamel, James L. *Bennett's New York Herald and the Rise of the Popular Press*. New York: Syracuse University Press, 1989.

Davis, Andrew Jackson. *The Present Age and Inner Life*. Rochester: Austin Publishing Co., 1910.

————. *Tale of a Physician, or, the Seeds and Fruit of Crime*. Boston: William White & Co., 1869.

Dickens, Charles. *American Notes*. New York: Penguin Classics, 2000.

Foster, George G. *New York By Gas-Light and Other Urban Sketches*. Berkeley: University of California Press, 1990.

Geary, Rick. *The Mystery of Mary Rogers*. New York: NBM/Comics Lit., 2001.

Harrison, James A. *Life of Edgar Allan Poe*. New York: Haskell House, 1970.

Homberger, Eric. *The Historical Atlas of New York City*. New York: Henry Holt & Co., 1994.

Hone, Philip. *The Diary of Philip Hone, 1828–1851*. (2 vols.) Ed. Alan Nevins. New York: Dodd Mead & Co., 1927.

Ingraham, J. H. *The Beautiful Cigar Girl, or, the Mysteries of Broadway*. New York: Robert M. De Witt, 1844.

Ingram, John H. *Edgar Allan Poe: His Life, Letters and Opinions*. (2 vols.) London: John Hogg, 1880.

Irving, Washington. *The Works of Washington Irving, Volume 5: Salmagundi, Voyages and Discoveries of the Companions of Columbus*. New York: The Co-operative Publication Society, 1920.

Jackson, Kenneth T. (Ed.). *The Encyclopedia of New York City*. New Haven: Yale University Press, 1995.

Jacobs, Robert D. *Poe: Journalist & Critic*. Baton Rouge: Louisiana State University Press, 1969.

Judson, Edward Zane Carroll [Ned Buntline]. *Mysteries and Miseries of New York: A Story of Real Life*. New York: Berford & Co., 1848.

———. *Three Years After: A Sequel to Mysteries and Miseries of New York*. New York: Berford & Co., 1849.

Keller, Allan. *Scandalous Lady: The Life and Times of Madame Restell, New York's Most Notorious Abortionist*. New York: Atheneum, 1981.

Kennedy, J. Gerald (Ed.). *A Historical Guide to Edgar Allan Poe*. Oxford: Oxford University Press, 2001.

Kluger, Richard. *The Paper: The Life and Death of the New York Herald Tribune*. New York: Alfred A. Knopf, 1986.

Lardner, James and Thomas Reppetto. *NYPD: A City and Its Police*. New York: Henry Holt & Co., 2000.

Lauvrière, Emile. *The Strange Life and Strange Loves of Edgar Allan Poe*. Philadelphia: J. B. Lippincott Co., 1935.

Link, S. A. (Ed.). *Edgar Allan Poe: Biography and Selected Letters.* Dansville: F. A. Owen Publishing Co., 1910.

Lippard, George. *New York: Its Upper Ten and Lower Million.* Cincinnati: E. Mendenhall, 1854.

Mabbott, Thomas Ollive (Ed.). *Edgar Allan Poe: Complete Poems.* Urbana: University of Illinois Press, 2000.

————. *Edgar Allan Poe: Complete Tales & Sketches.* (2 vols.) Urbana: University of Illinois Press, 2000.

McCullough, Esther Morgan (Ed.). *As I Pass, O Manhattan: An Anthology of Life in New York.* North Bennington: Coley Taylor, 1956.

Meyers, Jeffrey. *Edgar Allan Poe: His Life & Legacy.* New York: Charles Scribner's Sons, 1992.

O'Connor, Richard. *The Scandalous Mr. Bennett.* New York: Doubleday & Company, 1962.

Ostrom, John Ward (Ed.). *The Letters of Edgar Allan Poe.* Cambridge: Harvard University Press, 1948.

Paul, Raymond. *Who Murdered Mary Rogers?* New Jersey: Prentice-Hall, 1971.

Pearce, Charles E. *Unsolved Murder Mysteries.* London: Stanley Paul & Co., 1924.

Pearson, Edmund. *Instigation of the Devil.* New York: Charles Scribner's Sons, 1930.

Phillips, Mary E. *Edgar Allan Poe: The Man.* (2 vols.) Chicago: John C. Winston Co., 1926.

Porges, Irwin. *Edgar Allan Poe.* Philadelphia: Chilton Books, 1963.

Pray, Isaac. *Memoirs of James Gordon Bennett and His Times.* New York: Stringer & Townsend, 1855.

Quinn, Arthur Hobson. *Edgar Allan Poe: A Critical Biography.* Baltimore: The Johns Hopkins University Press, 1998.

Rosenheim, Shawn and Stephen Rachman (Eds.). *The American Face of Edgar Allan Poe.* Baltimore: The Johns Hopkins University Press, 1995.

Sante, Luc. *Low Life: Lures and Snares of Old New York.* New York: Vintage Books, 1992.

Silverman, Kenneth. *Edgar A. Poe: Mournful and Never-ending Remembrance.* New York: HarperCollins Publishers, 1991.

Smith, Matthew Hale. *Sunshine and Shadow in New York.* Hartford: J. B. Burr & Co., 1869.

Sova, Dawn B. *Edgar Allan Poe A to Z.* New York: Checkmark Books, 2001.

Srebnick, Amy Gilman. *The Mysterious Death of Mary Rogers: Sex and Culture in Nineteenth-Century New York.* New York and Oxford: Oxford University Press, 1995.

Stanard, Mary Newton. *The Dreamer: A Romantic Rendering of the Life Story of Edgar Allan Poe.* Philadelphia: J. B. Lippincott Co., 1925.

Symons, Julian. *The Tell-Tale Heart: The Life and Work of Edgar Allan Poe.* New York: Harper & Row, 1978.

Thomas, Dwight and David K. Jackson. *The Poe Log: A Documentary Life of Edgar Allan Poe, 1809–1849.* New York: G. K. Hall, 1987.

Van Every, Edward. *Sins of New York as "Exposed" by the Police Gazette.* New York: Frederick A. Stokes, 1930.

Wallace, Charles. *A Confession of the Awful and Bloody Transactions in the Life of Charles Wallace.* New Orleans: E. E. Barclay & Co., 1851.

Wallace, Irving. *The Fabulous Originals.* New York: Alfred A. Knopf, 1956.

Walling, George W. *Recollections of a New York Chief of Police.* New Jersey: Patterson Smith Reprint Series, 1972.

Walsh, John Evangelist. *Midnight Dreary: The Mysterious Death of Edgar Allan Poe*. New Brunswick: Rutgers University Press, 1998.

———. *Poe the Detective: The Curious Circumstances Behind The Mystery of Marie Roget*. New Brunswick: Rutgers University Press, 1968.

Wimsatt, William K., Jr. *Poe and the Mystery of Mary Rogers*. New York: Modern Language Association of America, 1941.

Winwar, Frances. *The Haunted Palace: A Life of Edgar Allan Poe*. New York: Harper & Row, 1959.

Woodberry, George E. *The Life of Edgar Allan Poe: Personal and Literary with his Chief Correspondence with Men of Letters*. (2 vols.) New York: Biblio & Tannen, 1965.

Worthen, Samuel Copp. "A Strange Aftermath of the Mystery of Marie Roget." *Proceedings of the New Jersey Historical Society* 60 (1942): 116–123.

———. "Poe and the Beautiful Cigar Girl." *American Literature* 20 (1948): 305–312.

Journals, Magazines, and Newspapers Consulted

American Literature, The Broadway Journal, Brother Jonathan, Collier's, The Commercial Advertiser, Detective Magazine, Era Magazine, Harper's New Monthly Magazine, The Ladies' Companion, Littell's Living Age, The Morning Courier, The National Police Gazette, The New Yorker, The New York Enquirer, The New York Evening Post, The New York Herald, The New York Journal of Commerce, The New York Sun, The New York Times, The New York Tribune, The Proceedings of the New Jersey Historical Society, The Sunday Morning Atlas, The Tattler

INDEX

Note: Page numbers in *italics* refer to illustrations.

ABOUT THE AUTHOR

Daniel Stashower is the author of the highly acclaimed biography of Arthur Conan Doyle *Teller of Tales* (1999), which won the Edgar Award for Best Biographical Work. A winner of the Raymond Chandler Fulbright Fellowship in Detective and Crime Fiction writing, Stashower is also the author of several mystery novels. He lives with his family in Bethesda, Maryland.

Visit the author's website at www.stashower.com.